COMMUNISM
AND EASTERN EUROPE

COMMUNISM
AND EASTERN EUROPE

A COLLECTION OF ESSAYS
EDITED BY FRANTISEK SILNITSKY, LARISA SILNITSKY, KARL REYMAN

THE HARVESTER PRESS

This edition first published in Great Britain in 1979 by
THE HARVESTER PRESS LIMITED
Publisher: John Spiers
17 Ship Street, Brighton, Sussex

ISBN 0-85527-288-0

Copyright © 1979 by Karz Publishers.
All rights reserved under International and
Pan-American Copyright Conventions.
Printed in the United States of America

Grateful acknowledgment is made to the following for permission to publish articles in this collection:

INDEX for Antonin Liehm, "From Culture to Politics," in *Sbornik Systemove Zmeny* (Koln, 1972), pp. 159–182.
Rinascita for Milan Hubl, "The Legacy of 1968" No. 3 (January 1978).
Svedectvi for excerpts from Jan Starek, "Emigration and Opposition" 50 (1975): 207–225.
EDITIONS DU SEUIL for excerpts from Adam Michnik, *The Church and the Left: A Dialogue* (Paris, 1977).
Kortars for Gyorgy Markus, "Debates and Trends in Marxist Philosophy" 12 (July 1968): 1109–1128.
EDITIONS DU SEUIL for excerpts from *Marx in the Fourth Decade* (Bence & Kis, Endreffy, Bauer, and Haraszti) published in *0.1 Percent* (Paris).
VERLAG EUROPAISCHE IDEEN for Robert Havemann, "The Socialism of Tomorrow," in *Berliner Schriften* (Berlin, 1977).
EUROPAISCHE VERLAGSANSTALT for Rudolf Bahro, "Zur Kritik des real existierenden Sozialismus—Sechs Vortrage uber das Buch 'Die Alternative,'" in *Eine Dokumentation* (Koln, 1977), pp. 9–55. Permission for the Fernbach-Fowkes translation from the *New Left Review*.
New York Times for excerpts from BDKD, "Das Manifest der ersten organisierten opposition in der DDR," *Der Spiegel*, 2 and 9 January 1978.

INTRODUCTION
FRANTISEK SILNITSKY

> What would I have done differently in 1968? Everything, had I known then what I know now about the USSR.
> A. J. Liehm

> "We tell the Russians we love them," he says. "But then we also tell them we are Communists," he snorts with laughter.
> Hungarian intellectual to an American journalist.

The countries included in this collection—Poland, Hungary, the GDR, and Czechoslovakia—all have in common the fact that they belong to the Soviet sphere of influence; in all these countries, the Communist parties declare themselves the vehicles of historical necessity and embrace a scientific Weltanschauung—Marxism-Leninism. The works in our symposium show, however, that Eastern European countries are not characterized only by what they have in common.

Despite the unified character of so-called "actual socialism,"* these countries, peoples, and states have each, during a certain period, found the strength to demonstrate their attitude to conditions imposed from outside. In all these countries people came out against their dehumanization and manipulation by the powers that be. In 1953 a part of the German working class, or so-called "social foundation," came out against the Communist government. In 1956, Poland forced personnel changes at the top, winning a certain degree of freedom for itself and preventing Soviet military intervention at the same time. In the same year, Hungary liquidated the

---

*"Actual socialism" was coined in response to the many accusations challenging the socialist authenticity of Soviet Communism. It implies that the existing socialism is real socialism—i.e., that it is the result of putting Marxist theories into practice.

INTRODUCTION

Communist terror (Rakosi's, Farkasa's, and Gero's) and, led by Imre Nagy, worked out a revolutionary program of political freedoms. Crushed by the Soviet army, it still succeeded in achieving some sort of balance and the maximum maneuvering room possible in the Soviet sphere—later this became known as "Kadarization."

In 1948, Czechoslovakia, without the assistance of the Soviet army, replaced a pluralistic political system with the Communist party's monopolistic power.

Frequently characterized since by foreign observers as the citadel of orthodox Stalinism, in reality, Czechoslovakia underwent a long, intensive process of cultural and political reform. In the process of critically reevaluating the politico-economic and spiritual system, the moral principles of Western civilization and Czechoslovakia's national tradition were revived. And the result was the reform of 1968—the shift from totalitarianism to civil liberties and political pluralism, including economic reform.

In Czechoslovakia in 1968, the reform of a Communist government elapsed without bloodshed. And for the first time in history the Soviet army (with symbolic Warsaw Pact participation) attacked a loyal ally, and one which did not in any way pose a military threat to the USSR. Czechoslovakia raised the question of whether national sovereignty could be reconciled with Communism, or whether the national sovereignty of a small country could be preserved in a Soviet dominated sphere; the question of whether the terroristic character of a Soviet-type society can be erased or whether it is, in fact, inherent in all Communist governments. Czechoslovakia raised the question of the Communist party's power, whether democratic competition was compatible with this power, and whether civil liberties and rights could be maintained. In response to all these questions the Soviet side answered with its army.

In Eastern Europe, as for that matter in Western Europe and other regions of the world, discussions about Marxism, socialism, democracy, and Communism were conducted in a completely new way after the 1968 occupation.

* * *

The term Eastern Europe came into use after World War II. It is a political and not a geographical term. It applies to that part of Europe with Communist governments in the sphere of the USSR's political, military, economic, and ideological influence. Characteristic of Eastern Europe is the forming of a political, economic, and spiritual system based on the Soviet model, and which takes place within the context of integrating Eastern Europe with the Soviet Union, manifested in a military alliance, the Warsaw Pact Organization. This military organization of Communist states has external tasks with respect to the Western countries (NATO), but along with these the Warsaw Pact Organization also participates in the internal arena of the member states. Its armies are used to suppress those social movements that transcend the norms of the Soviet model.

Comecon (Council for Mutual Economic Assistance) is an instrument of economic integration. And the ruling Eastern European Communist parties are the means of political integration. So-called proletarian internationalism forms the basis of the ideological integration.

Three standard aspects of integration should be stressed when discussing Eastern Europe and the Soviet Union—the military, economic, and ideological. With the collapse of the Russian empire following the 1917 Revolution, independent states were formed. As Lenin said, only Great Russia was left of former Russia. But as the Bolsheviks believed that socialism demands as large a state as possible, immediately after the empire's collapse the Bolsheviks began to effect its reconstruction. Their policy was crowned with success, and by the end of 1922 the independent Soviet republics were integrated into one state. This integration was facilitated by: the Red Army and a military-political alliance signed in 1919 between the republics; the economic alliance between republics, which preceded the formation of the USSR in 1922; and the ideological union between republics, which was an exceptionally disciplined one. It was insured from the very start by the fact that the Communist party (or the Russian Communist Party [Bolshevik], as it was then called) was centrally organized with its leadership in Moscow; that is, there were Communist parties in the various national republics, but they were centered in Russia. Adding to this Lenin's instructions on November 29, 1918 to the Red Army Command, the analogy with the methods and tactical techniques employed by Moscow in the occupation of Czechoslovakia in August of 1968 becomes still more striking. The instructions were as follows:

> As our troops push on westward and into the Ukraine, provisional regional Soviet governments are being formed to back up the Soviets in the

localities. This has the advantage of depriving the Ukrainian, Lithuanian, Latvian and Estonian chauvinists of a chance to regard our troop movements as an occupation and of creating a favorable situation for further advance. Otherwise our troops would have been in an impossible situation on occupied territory, and the local population would not have met them as liberators.

V.I. Lenin, *Collected Works,* vol. 28, p. 225.

Military intervention in Eastern Europe, either actual or threatened, is one of the unchanging conditions of life for the peoples of Eastern Europe. And it backs up the political, economic, and ideological pressures.

* * *

The Communist parties ruling in the Eastern European countries are ideological parties that consider Marxism-Leninism their political, economic, and ideological doctrine. And it is within these limits, to a large extent, that any discussion of party thought and action takes place. But even Marxism in these societies is accepted only in accordance with how the leadership of the Communist Party of the Soviet Union has laid it out. This Soviet variety of Marxism is enforced by the repressive machinery of the state as the only possible way of thought. And hence any questioning of the doctrine becomes a political act fraught with very risky personal consequences. More importantly, deviation in thought is inhibited by the fact that the longer a Communist party stays in power, the more remote becomes the cultural heritage and knowledge accumulated through many centuries. Moreover, in spite of the unprecedented development of the communications media in the twentieth century and the resulting reduction of distances, the Eastern European countries do not share in this. Exchange of unofficial opinions cannot take place even within the confines of the commonwealth of Eastern European states.

In essence, it is not "Marxism-Leninism" that is the dominant ideology in Eastern European countries but Stalinism. In Eastern Europe the foundations of the politico-economic and cultural system were laid under the guidance of Stalin.

Since Khrushchev's speeches on Stalin's crimes (the Twentieth Party Congress) there has been a tendency among Marxists in the Eastern European countries to revise certain tenets of the official doctrine. But the conditions for theoretical discussions on problems of Marxism were very unfavorable—the Communist parties of these countries are not constructed on the basis of a definite political doctrine and ideology, but are above all, ruling organizations embracing all spheres of public life. As such they do not refrain from employing any and every means to preserve their power. So there arises a tension between the ideology and the practice of the political regime. With time this tension overflows into public activity and criticism.

The level of critical and independent political thought is becoming a key question in various Eastern European countries. Independent critical thinking compromises the power monopoly and its raison d'être as the "bearer" of the will of history, the last word of history.

Independent critical analysis is directed against the Soviet Union insofar as the Eastern European system is based on it. This analysis is accompanied by comparison with the everyday lives of non-Communist neighbors which reinforces a sense of national distinction or identity. But the most important impact concerns the comparison of economic standards, scientific and technological progress, living standards, the food supply, and the guarantee of housing. (Constant complications in the supply of food stuffs and the endless housing crises are more significant factors in the domestic political life of Eastern Europe than of the USSR.)

For centuries Eastern Europe was the battleground for the national question. During the course of any one century the question of the interrelationship between the ruling and ruled peoples of Eastern Europe was decided more than once. It is owing to this historical experience that there developed an understanding in Eastern Europe of nations as a cultural and spiritual community of people. The prolonged battle for national freedom is, in Eastern European terms, the battle for the right of nations to an independent government that reflects the national being. An independent national state, by definition, represents its citizens.

At present, nationalism has assumed a certain character in Eastern Europe—opposition to the political system, a system imposed from the outside by the Soviet Union.

Being subject to regional conflicts in its past, Eastern Europe has shared the xenophobia typical of many other nations. But the multinationality of the Eastern European countries has also meant that they never possessed a tendency toward expansionist nationalism, aspiring to hegemony. The nationalism of Eastern Europe was rather a defensive nationalism. And if regional conflicts grew into conflicts of greater significance, it was only because the Great Powers, with their conflicting interests, intervened.*

Expansionist nationalism always suffers a defeat in the conflict with defensive nationalism, in the conflict with the will of nations to govern their own national affairs. And it was postwar Soviet policy in Eastern Europe that called forth defensive nationalism, but on a completely new basis. The nationalism of Eastern European countries is essentially a politico-economic question, which becomes a question of defensive nationalism because it is the Russians, representing the principal nation of the Soviet Union, who have introduced this politico-economic system.

Eastern European nations have no illusions about their situation, nor should one conclude from this that they are ready to sacrifice themselves to save mankind. *The idea of national self-determination, widely supported throughout the world, is the central motive and driving force of political movements in Eastern European countries.*

Eastern European nationalism does not signify isolation from other countries. Its meaning is positive, national freedom, the aspiration to make contact with the world on an equal footing, and not indirectly, through its Soviet guardian. The demand for national freedom—as opposed to the demand for national autonomy—involves the complex of political, economic, cultural, and spiritual questions that constitutes the identity of a nation. This is the alpha and omega of present-day and future Eastern Europe.

Eastern Europe is the test for the applicability or validity of Soviet-type Communism. And that is why all reform efforts in Eastern Europe were a direct challenge to Russian Communism.†

---

*Serbia in 1914 could not embark on a war for world supremacy, as Czechoslovakia in 1938 did not pose a threat to Germany, etc.

†Certain differences—like the different forms of private property in Poland, the GDR and Hungary, the situation of the church in Poland etc.—exist not because the Communist parties of these countries profess a political doctrine different from that of the Communist Party of the Soviet Union, but because the correlation of sociopolitical forces in these countries is different at this stage. These occurrences, nonetheless, go beyond the bounds of doctrine and are perceived as dangerous by the authorities.

Thus it could be said that in Eastern European countries, reform efforts were accompanied by criticism of the Soviet model on a level never carried out in the USSR itself.*

One more political factor is at work in Eastern Europe: perceived by the nations in this area as a colonial power ruling the empire by military means, the dominating people in this empire, the Russians, are on an inferior economic and cultural level to that of the peoples they rule. The result is a policy of the imperial nation that leads to the stagnation and degradation of the peoples of Eastern Europe.†
All criticism of the political and economic system, all efforts to effect reforms or changes in Eastern European countries, may be regarded as efforts to end this stagnation and degradation. Popular support rallies even behind the Communist governments of these states when they act more independently of the USSR and represent national interest. Yugoslavia's people supported Tito after the break with the USSR in 1948; nor did Enver Hoxha lose power in Albania when he fell out with the Soviet Union; it is well known that the Rumanian people support Ceausescu's foreign policy; the Hungarian people supported Nagy, and one can say of Kadar that he has found a *modus vivendi* with the Hungarian people since he won recognition of some degree of autonomy for his country; in Poland Gomulka lost favor due not only to economic complications, but because he lost the aura of national representative of the nation. The policy of Czechoslovakian Communist-reformists was supported by the predominant majority of the population because it returned Czechoslovakia to its national traditions, to national freedom.

The history of the East European countries and, in particular, the occupation of Czechoslovakia had a great influence on leftist move-

---

*Khrushchev launched criticism against Stalin, against the terror, but he did not touch upon the essence of the politico-economic and spiritual system to the extent it was touched upon in Hungary or Czechoslovakia. And it is still difficult even to compare the "dissident movement" in the Soviet Union with the significance of the dissident movement in Poland or Czechoslovakia. If, according to information first received, Charter 77 was signed by 800 people in occupied Czechoslovakia, then in the Soviet Union, according to the same relative proportion of the population, an unofficial document should have been signed by 14,000 people.

†A. Amalrik speaks of this psychological point in his interview with George Urban, *Euro-Communism, Its Roots and Future in Italy and Elsewhere* (London, 1978), pp. 239–240.

ments in democratic countries. The leftists began to question whether the terroristic methods of Communist governments could be separated from Marxism; whether one can select from Marxist teaching or whether it is necessary to approach it as a whole, fixed, doctrinal system; and to what degree does Russian tradition find expression in contemporary Marxism. At first, after World War II, it may have seemed that Communist political slogans in Eastern Europe would be realized and that "there will be as many Marxisms as there are nations." But up against Soviet militarism, Eastern Europe sustained a defeat, and critical elements began to appear in the leftists' attitude toward the USSR.

The tendency of an empire to grab anything unguarded, to be heedless of consequences, and to widen its borders has brought it about that for the first time in history, Russia, through her successor, the Soviet Union, has become a part of Europe. The Russian army had appeared in Europe in the past, but had always returned home. Practically speaking, Russia was separated from Europe and guarded itself against Europeanization. But after 1945, under the banner of Communist ideology, the leaders of the multinational Soviet Union, in accordance with the ideas of Russian messianism, embarked on the path of Sovietizing a considerable part of Europe, oblivious of the consequences. First, the Sovietization of Eastern Europe caused a permanent threat of confrontation. Any suppression of political reforms and national consciousness in Eastern Europe can create national conflicts. Yet otherwise the peoples of Eastern Europe will continue to draw away from the Soviet Union, in spite of their Soviet allied rulers.

It is difficult to understand the relations between the Eastern European countries, the relations between Eastern Europe and the Soviet Union, and the political thinking in these countries without recognizing the central importance of Russian chauvinism. The "Soviet" approach to the process of integration not only does not mitigate tension inside its "Socialist camp," but aggravates it, since in the last 200 years, of all the various social attachments, national consciousness has shown itself the most actively. It is hard to predict at present what the influence of this process will be on the nations of the Soviet Union.

translated by Liza Tucker

CONTENTS

INTRODUCTION   v
   Frantisek Silnitsky

CZECHOSLOVAKIA
   Preface   3
   From Culture to Politics   8
      Antonín Liehm
   The Legacy of 1968
      Milan Hubl   25
   The Nationality Problem   33
      Frantisek Silnitsky
   Opposition   44
      Jan Starek

POLAND
   The Church and the Left: A Dialogue   51
      Adam Michnik

HUNGARY
   Preface   99
   Debates and Trends in Marxist Philosophy   104
      György Márkus
   After the Break   133
      György Bence and János Kis
   What is My Position on Marxism Today   141
      Zoltán Endreffy
   The Science of Economics and the East European
   Systems   144
      Tamás Bauer
   What is Marxism?   148
      Miklós Haraszti

EAST GERMANY
   Preface   159
   The Socialism of Tomorrow   173
      Robert Havemann
   Introductory Lecture to *The Alternative*   186
      Rudolf Bahro
   Manifesto   233
      BDKD

ABOUT THE EDITORS

Frantisek Silnitsky was a Research Fellow and Senior Lecturer at the Higher Party School in Prague before emigrating with his wife (Larisa Silnitsky) to the West following the Soviet invasion of Czechoslovakia in 1968. He presently works as a free lance script writer on the nationality question and political systems for Radio Free Europe/Radio Liberty (RFE/RL) in New York, and his book, *The Nationalities Policy of the Communist Party of the USSR (1917-22),* has recently been published in Russian.

Larisa Silnitsky is a free lance script writer for the show, "For Your Freedom and Ours," which she broadcasts for RFE/RL.

Karl Reyman is Program Advisor for the RFE/RL New York Program Center.

CZECHOSLOVAKIA

PREFACE

In the history of the international Communist system, Czechoslovakia is most distinctly characterized by four stages of development. The first stage was the period 1945–48. During these years in Czechoslovakia, a state with democratic and pluralistic political traditions existed, within whose framework the political tactics developed by Lenin for the Communist party's "peaceable" rise to power were used. These tactics consisted of a combination of "pressure from above" (that of Communists in the government) and "pressure from below" (mass action with Communist slogans and demands). A component of these tactics was the promise of a special, national path to socialism, based on national traditions and corresponding to national conditions, a path without violence and without the Soviet brand of "dictatorship of the proletariat." The violation of this promise was criticized in 1968.

The second stage was the transformation of Czechoslovakia's socio-economic structure in accord with the Soviet model, and it included mass political terror.

This policy also included anti-Semitism. However, unlike the other so-called "People's Democracies," Czechoslovakia was industrially developed and had a democratic past. Such a policy of anti-Semitism was a clear violation of these Czechoslovakian traditions and would result in condemnation of the inhumanity in 1968.

The third stage in Czechoslovakia's postwar history was the reform of the existing politico-economic system, the 1968 period.

For two decades Czechoslovakia was considered an orthodox country, unconditionally loyal to the USSR. The fall of the Novotny regime came as a surprise for many, both within the country and abroad. Throughout the 1968 period, spontaneity, as opposed to premeditation, was the predominant force. Reforms of the political and economic system, only partially realized, led to the military occupation of Czechoslovakia by the armies of the USSR and other Warsaw Pact countries—Bulgaria, GDR, Hungary, and Poland.

Beginning in August 1968, Czechoslovakia entered its fourth stage of postwar development within the framework of the Communist system. Czechoslovakia became the country of Communist counter-reformation, the country of restored Soviet "actual socialism."

PREFACE

In Soviet-type societies (i.e., so-called actual socialism) all intermediate links in the socio-economic and political life of the society are eliminated. Means of production and distribution of goods are nationalized; even spiritual activity is designated and regulated by the political authorities, which is a main source of antagonism between citizen and party. Thus, every disagreement, however minor and insignificant, automatically becomes a protest on behalf of a private citizen against the party and the government. And since the authorities believe that the smallest concession to the citizen jeopardizes their very existence, they preventatively maintain a repressive machinery. Consequently that "law" of socialism typical of every Communist country, namely "Marxism as both an ideology and political doctrine," winds up being but an enormous police apparatus of oppression and subjugation. In 1968, Czechoslovakia subjected this system, of which it had been a part, to philosophical and practical criticism. But since the reformist movement was short-lived, the Czechs were unable to form that system of intermediary links which would have localized the tension between the various social groups and focused at least some issues in the constant conflict between the citizen and the authorities. From this fact numerous arguments concluded that "socialism with a human face" would only have degenerated back into a Soviet-type society, even if the Soviet army had not invaded Czechoslovakia; or else the country would have been led to the restoration of capitalism. This, however, is mere speculation. In reality, the development of the 1968 reforms was interrupted by the Soviet military intervention, after which the restoration of the Soviet-type society and destruction of "socialism with a human face"* were directly supervised by the Communist Party of the Soviet Union and its occupational forces.

Those who scold Czechoslovakia for the lack of armed resistance to the occupational forces often overlook the fact that the Czechoslovakian army, at the time, was not an integral and independent whole. And if the small oppositionist groups had begun waging a partisan war, it would have only resulted in civilian casualties. The

---

*Current in 1968, "socialism with a human face" symbolizes the Czechoslovakians' need to denounce the inhuman methods of the past. The term is by no means a scientific definition and represents no philosophy.
   Throughout 1968, Czechoslovakia witnessed no political violence and proved itself to be disciplined, rational, and faithful to the traditions of democracy and Masaryk's humanism.

Soviet response would have been a counter-revolution similar to their suppression of the Hungarian revolt in 1956. With the major Western democracies assuming the role of observers and the US leaders totally preoccupied with their tense political climate (the student demonstrations and the war in Indo-China), Czechoslovakia found itself practically isolated, which was exactly what the Soviet Union had expected.

But though it did not offer armed resistance, Czechoslovakia successfully offered peaceful resistance, compelling the Soviet Union to change its military personnel stationed in Czechoslovakia. Soviet political goals were also foiled. They were unable to form a Workers' and Peasants' Government and failed to set up revolutionary courts—unlike other Soviet armed occupations, there were no mass executions or mass deportations. Only after the so-called "second occupation," "at the end of March 1969 after the Czechoslovak ice hockey victories over the Russians in Stockholm . . . which led to massive popular demonstrations in many cities and to violent actions . . . Soviet Deputy Foreign Minister Semenov and Marshall Grechko suddenly arrived in Prague reportedly to present a Soviet Ultimatum demanding drastic political changes . . ."*

Thus, only April 1969 marks the beginning of the end of the Czechoslovakian reforms, and their fate was determined primarily by two factors: first of all, discovery by the Soviets that Husak and his followers were willing to demoralize and destroy the reformist movement from inside; and second, the complete exhaustion of the population, which, isolated by the occupation from the outside world, became passive and concerned with "self-preservation." Massive emigration by tens of thousands of the Czechoslovakian citizens also affected the outcome. Yet, despite all that, the country survived politically: in the fall 1975, Alan Levy wrote: "Czechoslovakia is the only country in Eastern Europe where a real opposition exists. The surviving leaders of the Prague Spring and the half-million members expelled from the Communist Party comprise a shadow Cabinet and a shadow Party with more support and experience than those who hold the cards and the titles today."†

---

*Adam Bromke and Teresa Rakowska-Harmstone, eds., *The Communist States in Disarray 1965–1971* (Minneapolis: University of Minnesota Press, 1972), p. 67.
†Alan Levy, *Index of Censorship* (Autumn 1976), cited in Maius Bergman, "Dissent in Czechoslovakia," *The New Republic* 26 (1977):12.

PREFACE

In 1977, Czechoslovakia produced a document which was acclaimed by Milovan Djilas as the most comprehensive political program written in Eastern Europe since World War II—Charter 77. Charter 77 is a political document that attests to the fact that even suppression of the most basic human rights in today's Czechoslovakia cannot baffle the political activity of its citizens.

* * *

One of the most important aspects of the internal political situation in Czechoslovakia is the binational nature of the country and how this is dealt with by the authorities. The only reform preserved intact after the occupation was the one which transformed the state into a federation of two nations. In regard to the relations between the two nationalities of Czechs and Slovaks, even though the 1968 establishment of a federation was preserved—in fact, the only 1968 reform that was—Czechs soon grew resentful of their neighbors. Twice at critical times in the country's recent history, the Slovaks, or rather their political representatives, easily allied themselves with the oppressors of the Czechs: first in 1939, when the Slovaks collaborated with the Germans and formed an independent Slovak state; and again in 1968, when Husak and other Slovakian leaders came to terms with the Kremlin.*†

There is no doubt that today the relations between Czechs and Slovaks are highly strained. The main problem is that the leading Slovakian politicians have acquired a reputation of being conductors of Soviet-inspired policy.

When the federation was first established, it guaranteed equal rights to both nationalities. Very soon, however, the Czechoslovakian federation began to function much like its Soviet counter-

---

*There is a possibility that today we are witness to the coming of a new era in history in regard to relations between Czechs and Slovaks. Initially, the idea of one federal state turned out to be unacceptable to the Slovaks. The day does not seem far off when the Czechs would find such a state undesirable as well.

†Gustav Husak, first secretary of the Central Committee of the Czechoslovakian Communist Party and president of Czechoslovakia after the 1968 occupation, had been a chairman of the Board of Commissioners of Slovakia and a leader of Slovakian nationalism while a member of the Central Committee of the Czechoslovakian Communist Party. Charged with "bourgeois nationalism" he was expelled from the Communist Party in February 1951, and in 1954 he was sentenced to life imprisonment. Husak was released in 1960, and in 1963 he was rehabilitated and restored to the party. Gustav Husak returned to political life thanks to the support of a group of Czech communist-reformists.

part. In 1970, the process of centralization was resumed and Husak, who had heretofore been something like a symbol of Slovakian national consciousness, began advocating the principle of oneness of the two nationalities.

Later, some reforms were passed which aimed at centralizing the unified Czechoslovakian economy by strengthening the controlling functions of the Central Apparatus.

Some institutions that maintained a more or less indigenous image were abolished, jurisdiction of the local Czech and Slovakian governments was curtailed. And today, the opinion shared by many Czechs is that the Slovaks have instituted a federation that is unfavorable to the Czech part of the population.

The problem of the nationalities is further compounded by an official investment policy that clearly favors Slovakia, supplying it with modern technology and leaving it up to the Czechs to provide their own modernization capital from goods produced on their obsolete machinery.

Indeed, even the purges conducted after the Soviet occupation were less severe in Slovakia than in the Czech lands. It was reflected in the fact that Slovakia preserved its educational system virtually intact. Its economic and political apparatus suffered significantly less. As for the cultural life, in comparison to the "Biafran spirit" in the Czech provinces, conditions in Slovakia have been noticeably better. Thus Slovakia today is emerging as a more affluent and more stable state than its partner in the federation. As a result, it can be stated that ten years after the occupation the two peoples of Czechoslovakia are drifting further and further apart.

* * *

The following selection of essays depicts the irrepressible impulse toward reform, leading up to 1968, in culture (Liehm), politics (Hubl), and national consciousness (Silnitsky), and the consequences in post-1968 Czechoslovakia of forestalling this fundamental instinct for self-expression (Starck). The simultaneous and independent development in each area points to the comprehensive and inexorable nature of this need.

František Silnitsky
translated by Bayer Alexei

FROM CULTURE TO POLITICS

ANTONIN LIEHM

In Czechoslovakia, the new stage of "socialist construction" was begun in a country with an impressive cultural tradition of service by the intellectuals to the national cause—a tradition unique in Europe.

Following the Thirty Years War, triggered by the Bohemian insurrection, the Protestant kingdom of Bohemia lost not only its independence but practically the entire class that constituted the backbone of its statehood, the national nobility. Its elite was either executed or forced into exile. What little was left fell victim to a ruthless re-Catholization and Germanization lasting two centuries. The Husite fifteenth century and the humanistic sixteenth century were of great importance for Central Europe and Europe as a whole. But the class representing these traditions in the kingdom was now gone. Such were the conditions that gave birth to plebeianism, a sort of folksiness that created so much good as well as bad. But they also paved the way for representatives of culture and science to take the place still held by the nobility elsewhere in Europe at the time when enlightenment and romanticism were pushing national languages, traditions, and culture into the forefront of European interests.

This was the reason why at the end of the eighteenth and the beginning of the nineteenth centuries the intelligentsia acquired a privileged position in the Czech lands and became their political spokesman. This situation survived until the twentieth century. Its modern representative was T. G. Masaryk, the founder of the Czechoslovak Republic. Paradoxically, it was in a way resuscitated in the sixties.

Antonín Liehm was one of the intellectual leaders of the 1968 Czechoslovak reform movement and an editor of *Literarni Listy*. He is now Professor of Comparative Literature at the University of Pennsylvania.

The identification of culture with national policy had another aspect. Literature, fine arts, theater, and even music were politicized: they had to become part of the struggle for national identity. Their values were gauged according to the utility they contributed to the reconstitution of the nation and its full national independence. The traditional identification with politics and the concept of culture as a servant of politics were the reasons why, in 1948, a large segment of Czech and Slovak cultural representatives backed the new regime and only few chose to emigrate (this was also true of 1968, when the consciousness of a common national responsibility and cohesiveness was even stronger). The canons of so-called socialist realism seemed to many to correspond to national traditions. But soon the first tragic events occurred. In the fifties Czechoslovak poets were exposed to the reality of Stalinist darkness by being imprisoned for works that were pervaded by another ideology. Ideological adversaries were liquidated physically, even for, mostly unpublished, verses. Then came the turn of those who for decades had sided with socialism and had spontaneously welcomed the Soviet armed forces as liberators not only from Nazism but from the old order as well. Essentially, the mere quality of their works condemned them to silence and an internal emigration after the Communist party established its rule in 1948. They began to resurface only in the sixties.

Perhaps, precisely because there was such a close link between culture and politics in Czechoslovakia, it was also a country with a high rate of suicide among its great personalities of culture, both literally as well as metaphorically speaking. Behind each day's obituary pages were gun shots in the night, falls from windows, and the smell of gas; and the national pantheon was filling prematurely with the remains of men whose work was still far from finished, men who, sincerely believing in what they had striven for, could not face the contradiction between dream and reality, between the ideals and the practice of a revolution. But there was something that only became clear sometime later. These sensitive seismographs were first to register that the price to be paid was in going backward, not forward.

Czech culture had its victims even in the infamous trials of the fifties, victims who continued to pay for their opposition to Stalinism twenty years later when it was no more in power in Czechoslovakia. The most bitter suicides were in the art world. With all the dynamic of his unique personality and captivating temperament, E. F. Burian, the founder of modern Czech theater and of avant-garde theater in general in the thirties, repudiated his achievements and turned to a primitive, naturalistic realism of the nineteenth century with its even more naive texts. Two of the greatest Czech writers of the forties, Václav Řezáč and Jan Drda, voluntarily sacrificed their exceptional talents, deeply convinced this was the right thing. These are just examples. The premature deaths of Burian and Řezáč were the result of inner destruction and of having sacrificed their work at a time when their mistake and a possibility of making it good were slowly emerging.

These and other examples were the first contribution of Czech culture to the understanding of Stalinism in Czechoslovakia. The sensitive antennae of talented persons transmitted signals of the catastrophic consequences of regression in the intellectual and cultural development. Artists and their work did not survive the crudity of interference. At the time, these signals were not clearly understood even though they did create concern. They were, of course, not uniquely Czechoslovak. Their study should become an important contribution to understanding the potential dangers of interference in social, economic, and intellectual affairs.

The structure of Czechoslovak cultural life was quickly constructed on the Soviet model in the early fifties. However, it soon became clear that conditions, traditions, and the spiritual climate were very different from those of the Soviet Union. What may have become an integral part of the Stalinist pyramid in the USSR, could, under certain other circumstances, become the seed of its destruction.

The Stalinist social pyramid is based on a very simple, unoriginal principle. At its top is a small group (an individual finally and inevitably), surrounded by a political, security, and military apparatus. The apparatus assures that orders from the top are transmitted down unaltered via a system of the so-called "transmission belts" or "social" organizations. These are run by members of the apparatus and function as a link between the ruling elite and the masses, between the apparatus and the population, between the party and the nonparty members. The transmission belts are therefore well supplied with funds. An important task of the pyramid, and the apparatus in particular, is to see to it that instructions from above are carried out without any change. Next in importance is to report the reactions received from below.

The apparatus functions in a situation in which there is no free press, mass media, or a democratic form of life, where practically all citizens are state employees. The existence of the apparatus members does not depend on economic considerations or on the function of one or another social sector. Their only responsibility is to the pyramid itself. Consequently, the reactions received from below are adjusted to match and confirm the original idea. Since orders from above are based on reports from below, which in turn are adjusted to conform to the aims implicit in the orders, the result is a situation of continuous repetition. It is a feedback mechanism that becomes self-serving and shelters itself against even the least bit of reality that could endanger the existence of the mechanism as a whole.

But parallel with the smoothly operating and order-reproducing pyramid a real territory exists with real problems and even autonomous economic and social structures—illegal, but all the more real. Dependent on this territory for its own survival, the pyramid must tolerate them yet also ensure that their autonomous existence remains on a local level and that their individual units remain unconnected. The degree of tolerance of the pyramid vis-a-vis the living, autonomous fiber of society under neo-Stalinism (where the dualism is recognized at least *de facto,* in contrast to the less pragmatic and more religious, ideological Stalinism) becomes the main and most hazardous problem of the power apparatus. Yielding to the pressure of real structures would endanger the very existence of the pyramid. The result is a contradictory approach to economic and political reforms and in regard to a cultural policy, as well as a contradictory attitude toward personal freedom, freedom of travel, and even foreign policy problems.

Transmission belts in the official pyramid exist not only for every social stratum but even for each special-interest group, regardless of its importance. For instance, crossword-puzzle or rabbit-breeders' clubs have essentially the same structure as any other transmission belt and are expected to carry out practically the same tasks "in their sector," which, understandably, they never do. Automatically, they begin to live a real existence, parallel to its official one within the pyramid. They begin to fulfill tasks according to social needs as opposed to the requirements of the pyramid. This situation was very much in evidence in Czechoslovakia in sports and cultural organizations. The Stalinist pyramid was an artificial graft, without any roots in the preceding system, and these organizations are the key to understanding a number of the political and economic phenomena of the sixties.

It is as a matter of principle that the transmission belts are organized identically, and in their sector exercise a monopoly comparable to the organization from which they derive their existence, i.e., the Communist party. The soccer players' organization has a central committee, presidium, control commission, secretariat, etc., exactly like that of the writers', artists', chess players', canoeists', or circus performers'. But they are quite deceptive as far as the concept of a smooth-functioning Stalinist pyramid is concerned. Their activities are reduced to the activities of an apparatus, approved once a year by "elected" (delegated) organs. They are considered just another type of state agency funded by the state. Its employees are state employees. All funds are paid into a common treasury that decides their allocation. But sports, in particular, are an interesting sphere of social activities where the application of the principles of the Stalinist pyramid poses some difficulties. Sports events take place in full view of the public, even international public. Results cannot be camouflaged (though, as proved by the reporting in Soviet media, this is not always true). Everything is much more public than are, for instance, economic and political matters. It was on sports pages that journalism first—after the restrictive Stalinist period of the fifties—returned to its normal purpose: objective and current reporting, explicit critique of individuals and their achievements, the right of the criticized persons to reply, etc. It was in the world of sports where democratic elements first began to assert themselves. Sports events became the locus for a mass outlet of suppressed feelings and attitudes (as is common at other latitudes and longitudes of our world). In the absence of a public political life, sports events assume a disproportionately large role in the life of a nation. This is, of course, true of all regimes that employ sports as an instrument of state policy to foment chauvinistic passions.

Sports were under an increasing public control for a long time and therefore played an important part during the first stage of the so-called "democratization" process. In analyzing the development in Hungary prior to 1956, Tibor Mérai, once a Stalin Prize laureate, writes how in Hungary a passionate interest in sports, soccer in particular (traditionally the most popular sport in the country), became a substitute for political activity, and how in 1954, after the defeat of their national team in the finals of the world championship, Hungarians for the first time in years became aware of a possibility to publicly and spontaneously demonstrate their approval or disapproval, enthusiasm or dismay. Mérai regards this phenomenon as the first step in the political activation of the population in the subsequent period.

Top achievements in sports, which are in the state's own interest, require more financial aid and lead to professionalism. This development, no surprise in a capitalist society, creates a number of problems in the Stalinist society. The official pyramid is largely based on all kinds of social privileges and privileged financial rewards. But the law of the pyramid demands secrecy in the name of national defense. (Kremlinologists in the West become sometimes so fascinated with the pyramid that the real, parallel structure completely escapes their attention.) Professionalism in sports is permitted *de facto,* but must not be admitted publicly, which would destroy the myth elsewhere as well. It is important for preserving ideological purity. However, the relative freedom of the press in sports reporting does much to compromise this ruling mythology. By attacking the jungle of professionalism, free of public control, sports reporting touches on the crux of the matter, the existence of a double reality. Seemingly on the periphery of society, it is in sports where the public is first confronted with the conflict between the parallel and the official reality, between the pyramid and real life. How this conflict evolves in sports is an indicator of what will happen in other areas.

In Czechoslovakia the existence of parallel structures became most evident in the cultural sphere. After 1948, this sphere was supplied with the same transmission belts as other spheres. The voluntary Czechoslovak Writers Syndicate was replaced by the Writers Union, with a presidium, central committee, secretariat, control commission, and a congress. The same happened in music, theater (though, surprisingly, not in the motion picture industry, probably because Soviet filmmakers themselves had no union at that time), and fine arts. Profusely funded by the state, this entire area became the center of extraordinary attention, which, for some time, Czech and Slovak intellectuals considered due them by right and tradition. Books were published in numbers never before attained (shortage of consumer goods and the low price of books ensured a continuous interest and market). The state supplied large funds for establishing permanent repertory theaters in all the larger towns. A number of new permanent opera companies, orchestras, and other art establishments were created, and, following the Soviet model, folklore ensembles were founded (on the other hand, old choral societies practically disappeared, and for many years amateur theatricals, representing a from-below initiative, were paralyzed). Motion picture production grew tremendously and was free of marketing problems.

Following the Soviet example, an academy of sciences was established and organized according to the pyramid model. Only organizations were allowed to publish, on approval of the pyramid, which also regulated the publishing programs. The small number of specialized publishing houses facilitated a strict control over the publishing programs. Their monopolistic position yielded them growing income. One such organization was the Czechoslovak Writers Union, which was to play an important role later. But the Czech and Slovak cultural establishment soon became aware of the other side of the coin of that gigantic structure spending huge sums of money, granting rewards, and providing glory. They realized that the entire cultural scene was being subsumed by the pyramid and that it would only further the tension, which the arts are so sensitive to, between the official pyramid and the parallel reality.

The first stirring occurred shortly after 1953. In 1955 and 1956, a similar process of growing awareness was also taking in Poland, Hungary, and the USSR. But Czechoslovakia was, at that time, still free from the economic difficulties Hungary and Poland were experiencing. The voices of intellectuals remained therefore isolated as compared to the other two countries. But they were basically the same. Significant was a debate in *Literární noviny,* a weekly of the Czechoslovak Writers Union (a faithful copy of the Soviet writers' weekly by same name, it replaced *Lidové noviny* seized in 1948 from its liberal publisher). Its topic was one typical of that time: ideology and politics. The theoretical point of departure was the young Marx, and it stressed the growing discrepancy between theory and practice, between official theory and official policy. Marx's classic tenet of their interdependence and his qualification of ideology as false consciousness was very relevant, and it formed the ideological ground for the first open conflict between Czechoslovak intellectuals and the power pyramid.

This occurred at the Second Congress of Czechoslovak writers. The pyramid's reaction was slightly delayed, but this time it managed to quell an incipient rebellion. The editorial board of *Literární noviny* and the leadership of the Writers Union was changed. Authors of polemical articles, Ivan Sviták and Karel Kosík first of all, were punished. The same happened in cinema and theater, where the main victims were Karel Kraus and Otomar Krejca, under whose management the National Theater in Prague became the center of the Czechoslovak cultural scene and true heir of the Czech avant-garde theater tradition. Music and the fine arts were also not unaffected.

Of more importance were the sources of controversy: the philosophical and sociological implications of the young Marx in Germany and his conflicts with the feudal conditions in Baden-Hessen; Krejca's classic, but emotionally relevant, presentation of Chekhov, the sad accusation of a semi-feudal society killing everything good in man and offering him no future as an individual; Kadár's and Klos's film, *Three Wishes,* or Danek's and Krska's *Here Are the Lions,* a defense of humane individualism, individual conscience, and morality, and of a man thrust, by a strange social metamorphosis, backward, not forward, who is forced to fight battles seemingly long-won. A long time before young radicals in the West began claiming their rights nobody bothered to ask what the meaning was of that strange parallel between a long-gone past and the present. The question was asked much later.

The first normalization was soon followed by a crisis of the Czechoslovak economy that undermined the very foundations of the pyramid and strengthened the autonomy of the real structures. On the cultural scene this was also the beginning of a remarkable process within the pyramid itself, which years later culminated in the so-called Prague Spring.

Czechoslovak culture entered "socialism" through a pompous gate—castles became recreational facilities for writers and musicians, and there were titles, financial rewards, lucrative offices, and fiefs for their services. The patron's hand was generous, overly generous, but there was a *quid pro quo.* As compensation for support and an elevated position within the pyramid the patron expected an unconditional subservience to the pyramid.

At first, the pyramid seemed to achieve that new society in which the historic connection between art and politics reached fruition. But illusion disappeared fast, first subconsciously, inexorably, because of the invincibility of art. In hindsight, there were only two possible outcomes. In the first, socialistically-minded artists, who sympathized in good faith, and with the best intentions, with the regime and offered their talents to the pyramid, would have to suppress themselves. The irreconcilable contradiction between the pyramid and ideas killed either their work or them, or both. Very few survived. In the other outcome, the artists' conviction, talent, and belief in truth would be stronger than their sincere desire to serve the pyramid. They would find their work and themselves in conflict with the pyramid unwittingly. But the conflict with the pyramid was the conflict with the patron, and it meant the loss of material support, privileges, offices, and fiefs. Consequently, many behaved as their precursors in the Italy of the Renaissance with its popes and local princes patronizing arts. They dressed reality into the religious garb of the pyramid and rendered tribute to its themes and myths. But the similarity ends there. They, at the same time, sought to gain a growing independence on its patronage. This autonomy is called freedom of artistic expression or simply freedom of expression. And we may be witness once again to how members of the "new society" stormed gates that they had only shortly before opened.

How was this accomplished? There were two, actually three, ways. It seemed most simple in cinematography. A film artist is not, in contrast to writers or musicians, a one-person producer creating a work of art in the hope of winning the favor and approval of the patron. A film artist, like his predecessors centuries ago who created the Sistine Chapel, David, and Moses, requires patronage before he can start his work. When the motion picture industry was nationalized, it was unnecessary to create a mechanism of the pyramid as elsewhere. It sufficed to change film workers into industrial employees, that is, into state employees, with fixed salaries, bonuses, pensions, and steady work without the danger of being fired. The industry took care that its products conformed with official norms and distanced themselves from the parallel reality. But artists, unlike others, cannot be state employees. Their work must be independent of their ideological affiliation and goals. But in motion pictures the pressure was more intense than where an artist worked alone. The industrial machine had to turn out products. Autonomous work was practically impossible and schizophrenia was unavoidable.

Some destroyed all their past work. Others simply stopped creating altogether.

The only films in the fifties whose importance extended beyond the country's border were animated cartoons, especially those by Jiří Trnka and Karel Zeman. The nature of their work excluded large-scale industrial production. Under Central European conditions, animated cartoons could be produced only by small studios because of their arcane complexity of work; and the expensive and unprofitable products were guaranteed a market by the patron. In their poetic uniqueness, untainted by the pressure of the market, works by Jiří Trnka and Karel Zeman are pure products of a patronage system (not just the Stalinist one), and I dare say they are impossible without it. But they served as a model.

Even after 1956, cinematography was aware of the practical impossibility of producing artistic films outside of the patronage system. It therefore tried to create small studios that would gain some degree of autonomy within the system because of their number and decentralization. It was done at a time when the pyramid began showing signs of weakness, due to economic difficulties in the country. Their role gradually increased, small studios began to contradict the pyramid, which was, in the beginning of the sixties, no longer strong enough to dispel the dispute at its onset as in 1958.

The dispute persisted and generated calls by the pyramid for an organization and solidarity. As a result, under the pretext of filling the gap, the Union of Film and Television Artists was launched, much later than other unions. In actuality, the pyramid was not closing a gap but the parallel reality was making itself felt. For the first time, a so-called social organization was born within the Stalinist system that was not a transmission belt; it was one designed to defend the interests of its creators, not merely professional interests, but artistic and ideological ones as well, i.e., political interests. Gradually, and especially in 1968, the new union became the focus of political activities on the cultural front. It was unnecessary to overcome the old habits of unions long integrated as a transmission belt into the pyramid. The boom in Czechoslovak motion picture production was, in the first place, caused by the weakening of the patronage system, yet, at the same time, preserving its positive aspects. It made possible the creation of artistic films that would have been destroyed by the reintroduction of the market system.

The Writers Union, in contrast, was created as a classic transmission belt, complete with all the other components of the pyramid. Its task was to supervise the whole literary scene on behalf of the pyramid and its policy. For that purpose the pyramid equipped the Union with the structure of a political organization and with material means. It had its own publishing house and for a long time practically a monopoly in publishing original Czech and Slovak literary works and magazines. It managed the so-called Literary Fund, collected from compulsory contributions of writers' royalties and, above all, from payments by all publishing houses of their income from publishing classic works. The Union used the "Litfund" to cover the cost of facilities at the disposal of its members and to grant loans, rewards, and stipends. The fund was part of the pyramid, and corruption was a primary goal.

The first restiveness occurred within this colossus in the years 1953–1956, culminating during the Second Congress of Czechoslovak writers. Stalin's death, the exposure of Beria's crimes, and the Twentieth Congress of the Communist Party of the Soviet Union affected the intellectuals at a time of still relative economic stability in the country. The majority of Union members were Communists. The entire leadership was exclusively Communist until the Fourth Congress in 1967.

The first actual conflict was a typical dispute within the pyramid, not a revolt against it. The question was how to make the functioning of the Union more "socialistic." But the pyramid is instinctively defensive against any attempt to reform its own structure. Being a Stalinist power system it began to realize that any kind of autonomy would weaken its structure and possibly lead to its disintegration and was therefore intolerable. But it could no longer enforce unconditional obedience short of a brutal administrative intervention, which was not in line with the situation at the beginning of the sixties.

The Twentieth Congress definitely politicized the entire intelligentsia. It is always the first to become politicized under circumstances of such a dearth of information, and its mainly communistic character provided it with a limited political platform. On the literary scene the situation was unique and more favorable then elsewhere. Practically all disputes in the scientific and artistic areas immediately became political, but the only weapon available to the scientists and artists was their personal prestige and reputation.

They were limited by being employees of the pyramid and therefore fully dependent on it for their livelihood. Writers were in a different situation. They were practically the only ones who worked independently. They owned and managed a publishing house, which guaranteed them a market for their works, and their control of the Literary Fund ensured the survival of those among them who got involved in a conflict with the pyramid over matters of principle. Above all, they had at their disposal (and through them the whole intellectual front) a magazine that exercised an influence over the entire intelligentsia and a growing segment of the public. Consequently, writers, not directly dependent on the pyramid, began unconsciously to transform their organization and the struggle for their rights in their struggle for the Union's own politically influential magazines. Gradually, their organization changed from a transmission belt and an institution representing the cultural patronage system (ensuring the loyalty of a traditionally influential segment of the intelligentsia by granting social and material privileges) into a political organization that became the champion of the political struggle within the pyramid.

It took some time for the pyramid to realize its mistake, but by that time it was too late and therefore necessary to turn to the material basis of the revolt, the economic independence of writers. In this regard the following story circulated in Prague. At a reception in the Kremlin Khrushchev expressed his shock to Novotny over the Czechoslovak leadership's ineptness in dealing with the writers' resistance. "You have them as sparrows in a bag. And what do you do with a sparrow you have in your pocket?"

Eager and with revolutionary obedience as always, Novotny replies, "I would squeeze it firmly, comrade Khrushchev."

"Well," says Khrushchev unconvinced, "but watch out, if you suffocate it, you'll be left with nothing."

"Of course, of course," Novotny corrects himself. "I shall squeeze it, but will leave my palm slightly open so it has enough air . . ."

"And how will you make sure the sparrow won't fly away?"

Novotny is embarrassed. "I tell you how. I would hold the sparrow by its feet and pluck its feathers out one by one. Then, I open my palm—and what happens? The palm is warm, the sparrow is naked. He will love to be cuddled . . ."

The pyramid began to levy unusually high taxes on writers (interesting was the conservative nature of the new taxation system with its unprogressive scale in higher brackets so as not to affect at least the most widely read writers). But it was too late. The solidarity of the Union as an organization was already consolidated. The Writers Union became the first autonomous part of the Stalinist pyramid, a social organization that ceased to be a transmission belt. The significance for a society in a profound crisis was obvious. Writers proposed to the pyramid that the Union be used as a model for a reform of the system. . . . They did not realize that the pyramid had become a self-serving system set only on strengthening its own mechanism and not on what would be self-superseding reform. As the conflict intensified, the existence of the parallel reality became ever-more apparent. The pyramid had no choice but to attack. It divested the Union of *Literární noviny* and threatened to seize its publishing house and the Literary Fund. But once again, it was too late. There was no longer a sufficient number of communists in the Union willing to sanction punitive actions against other members. It was necessary to resort to the Central Committee of the Communist Party, the very summit of the pyramid. Though this disciplinary action was the last example of anti-intellectualism in this period, it incensed most of the Union members, who would now rebel at any future suitable occasion.

The gradual transformation of the Union of Czechoslovak Writers into a political organization is important for understanding the process of the sixties that culminated in 1968. Initially, social metamorphosis was not its goal. The majority of members, and the leadership in particular, did not contemplate a reform of the Stalinist society. They claimed the right to manage their own affairs within the structure of Stalinism. The Union was part of the pyramid, but, at the same time, was the part most sensitive to the parallel reality. Exposed to the discrepancy between the pyramid and the parallel reality, the Writers Union underwent a change, striking a blow to the pyramid from which it never recovered. It could no longer remain as simply a professional organization, and therefore liquidated itself as a Stalinist institution. In the spring of 1968, together with other arts unions, it established the so-called Coordination Committee of Arts Unions. It was a political body in which the leading role of the Writers Union dissolved. Its congress was to take place in the autumn of 1968 and, as an expression of the disintegration of the Stalinist pyramid, the Writers Union was to dismantle its transmission-belt structure, returning its castle, a symbol of Stalinist privilege, to the public and transforming itself into a voluntary association of groups of writers with the purpose of defending the freedom of their creative work.

There was also a struggle in process elsewhere on the cultural scene in the sixties. The struggle was for abolishing monopolies and for defending individuality and standards of artistic creation. Only social organizations within the pyramid were entitled to operate cultural facilities. And the pyramid could exercise control by granting or withdrawing subsidies. Consequently, there had been within the cultural sphere a persistent struggle for decentralization and economic emancipation. In the dramatic arts, it finally became possible to form theatrical companies independent of the system of state theaters. They were organized as cooperatives. In the same way, new exhibition galleries were opened. Fine artists and musicians were in a similar situation as film workers. They were state employees with a guaranteed employment, but very limited creative freedom. It was no secret that the most profitable performance was a conventional one. The only escape was to find a new market. The new galleries offered works for sale and helped to renew private interest in buying pictures, also stimulated by inflation. This was a market in its classic form, which for years had been the sole privilege of foreign diplomats.

Theaters faced yet another problem, one that was typical of all social and economic activities. Even after the small companies were formed, the overwhelming portion of theatrical workers remained state and municipal employees protected by a single labor union. It was almost impossible to fire them, which proved to be a dubious advantage. Theaters became crowded with low quality personnel, actors in particular, and they blocked the hiring of new, young people. It was another heritage of the Stalinist cultural policy. When, at the beginning of the fifties, state repertory theaters were established everywhere, there was a shortage of suitable personnel. Almost anybody was hired, but on the basis of one's politics rather than talent. Within ten years, theaters became overstaffed and were competing for additional subsidies. The country was oversaturated with theaters and attendance was lagging. As a result, demands grew for softening the contracts and abolishing provisions for practically guaranteed life employment.

In regard to nationalized movie theaters, the whole network was taken over by the Czechoslovak State Film Agency, which was also in charge of the distribution policy. In the fifties it was a perfect tool of the pyramid, but was abolished after 1956, during the first wave of the so-called decentralization. The State Film Agency relinquished its theaters to local national committees. As a result, any kind of centrally-directed policy in film distribution ceased—nonadministrative tools of cultural policy were unknown to the pyramid. Theaters became a source of profit to the national committees. But no investments were made and they soon began to deteriorate. Profit became the only concern and consequently the only criterion for the selection of films. A search for a solution started in the sixties, when the situation became serious from both the financial and cultural viewpoint. Film clubs or movie theaters featuring artistic films simply did not exist at that time. The national committees were ready to return theaters to the state, but, owing to the huge expense required to rectify a decade of neglect, the state refused. Plans were proposed for preferential treatment to those theaters that would present better films and organize other cultural activities, but such plans went against the pyramid concept.

In the middle of the sixties, artists had learned how to use the Stalinist patronage system to its own advantage. The absence of a free market and the weakened control of the pyramid facilitated a rapid development of avant-garde trends in all areas. However, the question was how to inject a democratic spirit into the economic sphere as well and to find a genuinely socialistic form for its existence. The pyramid, which regarded this area as the most politically threatening of the parallel reality, supported this movement but for different reasons. It opposed the reintroduction of a market economy on a wide scale but was willing to apply it in the cultural sphere. It relied on the conservative taste of the audience enhanced by the Stalinist cultural policy of the fifties. It hoped a free competition would gradually sweep away the avant-garde and replace it with cheap, slightly erotic, entertainment. The pragmatism of neo-Stalinism, its desertion of ideological principles in the interest of the pyramid, became here evident much earlier than in politics and economy. What happened most clearly in the Union of Czechoslovak Writers, took place at the beginning of 1968 less conspicuously and within a shorter time in all segments of the pyramid, within the whole system of the transmission belts. First came the intellectuals' and students' organizations. Gradually, organizations of blue and white collar workers and farmers joined in to pierce the armor that kept them prisoners within the power pyramid, to become real, elected representatives of group interests.

The struggle for freedom of the press was instrumental in the transformation of cultural pursuits into political ones, and for which the Writers' Union and other publishers of cultural magazines fought for decades. They also fought for the freedom of association and of managing their own affairs and electing their representatives. But it was not necessarily a conscious struggle. As in all societies where political activity is temporarily banned, culture became a substitute for politics. In the end, all activities became cultural only in appearance and political in substance.

The abolition of press, radio, and television censorship at the beginning of 1968 was, for all practical purposes, the end of the pyramid. In its final, neo-Stalinist phase the pyramid controlled the state apparatus only. Political channels and transmission belts were paralyzed, and at last even the pyramid's own representatives revolted against it. For months, the press, radio, and television belonged to those who worked there. Except in a few rare and marginal instances, there was no demagogy or sensationalism, no cry for revenge or for settling old scores. Thousands in the press, radio, and television showed not only a high degree of competence but also a high degree of responsibility for the fate of the nation and society. They knew that for twenty years the country had been without adequate information and any possibility to influence policy from below. It now had to find its bearings in the dark. For several months, information media helped to dampen accumulated resentments, always in danger of erupting. They blocked demagogues on both sides and sought to circulate as many facts as possible, leaving it up to the people to come to their own conclusions. And they barred quacks, who at such times always come up with some panacea. But most of all, the media resurrected people as citizens, citizens of a new type, who felt a direct responsibility for society and acted accordingly, citizens who were fit for self-government. Everything in the media was conducted on a highly professional level. A thorough study of this phenomenon would not only make a contribution to Czechoslovakia, but one to the world.

Another important achievement of the press, radio, and television was the renewal of horizontal channels. Direct contacts between the individual segments of the pyramid were viewed by the pyramid with suspicion. They smelled of conspiracy and were explicitly forbidden. Contacts ran only vertically. Society was perfectly atomized. The absence of uncontrolled information rendered individuals, groups, and even whole strata of the population completely isolated from each other without even the slightest opportunity for mutual consultation, confrontation, or, of course, a common action.

Most important were the links between the intellectuals and workers. A common front with mutual exchange and solidarity was born, which was anathema under the pyramid, where contact between intellectuals and workers threatened to expose the lie of the workers' rule at the heart of the ideological monolith. Contacts were established even among the individual labor unions of factories on the basis of the most varied national, regional, and local interests. Only then could there be said to be citizens of a socialist state, citizens who slowly assumed the rights they theoretically had been granted in the past. The masses of the "peoples democracy" truly began to stir.

When the Manifesto of 2,000 Words reminded the pyramid of the necessity of providing concrete expression of the democratic movement establishing autonomous local institutions, the remnants of the pyramid realized it was the end. And they acted accordingly. They requested a foreign armed intervention.

translated by Dr. Vilém Brzorad

THE LEGACY OF 1968

MILAN HUBL

On the threshold of 1978, I, as one of the active participants in the Prague Spring and as an historian, would like to express some of my observations concerning why Czechoslovakia underwent social changes, the conditions under which the progressive movement in the Communist party was formed and operated, why the post-January politics failed, the reformers' goals, the obstacles they encountered, and why their activities were not crowned with success. In addition, I would like to address those ideas and events of the Prague Spring that I consider urgent problems of our time (ten years later) and for the future.

WHAT WE WANTED

The profound crisis of the whole society, precipitated by the regime of A. Novotny, inevitably led to a polarization inside the Communist Party of Czechoslovakia (CPC) and in the society. The opinions of the Communists concerning the causes of the crisis and its solution, were particularly clear-cut. On the one hand, there was a movement striving to preserve the status quo—even by means of force and the suppression of all criticism. On the other hand, there was a movement that recognized the necessity for change and for resolving the crisis with the aid of political reforms; in 1968, this movement was called the progressive movement of the CPC. The first prerequisite for any kind of genuine change was in administratively changing the leadership of the party and state. When First Party Secretary Novotny was replaced by Dubcek, many regarded this as merely a "palace revolt," whose consequences would not be

---

Milan Hübl is a Czech historian and a former rector of the Higher Party School in Prague who was also a member of the Central Committee of the Czechoslovakian Communist Party. An active participant in returning Husak to political life after his release from prison, Hübl was rewarded for his pains with imprisonment when Husak won control of the party and State after the 1968 occupation. He currently resides in Prague.

particularly significant in the political life of the country. Only later, when this was followed by other changes in the leadership, did its importance become clear. By this time, a significant portion of the previously passive party and wide circles of the society had already become much more active.

In the beginning of 1968, the party developed an "Action Program," which, as its name suggests, was to tackle vital problems; but, in addition, it attempted to prepare fertile ground for long-range structural solutions. Providing an analysis of the current situation in Czechoslovakia, it stated that Czechoslovakian society had entered the phase calling for the rapprochement of all social groups, that old methods of organizing society, its economy and culture, had outlived their usefulness. The Action Program called for a wide-ranging societal initiative, for an open exchange of opinions, and a democratization of the entire social and political system. The Action Program also supported the thesis that political deformations, which result in the conversion of a revolutionary dictatorship to bureaucratism, were obstacles to the development of all aspects of social life. These structural problems in society and in the party were cited as dangers to the future of socialism in Czechoslovakia, to its humanitarian message and human face. The absence in the party of socialist democracy and the cruel suppression of criticism hindered independent actions and prevented the timely and consistent correcting of mistakes. These deformations prompted an inquiry into state and party leadership and the monopolistic position of certain leaders in the ruling elite.

The Action Program spoke of the necessity of a new constitution for the republic and of revising the legal code accordingly—in order to secure the complete equality of citizens, their rights, and the rights of nationalities and national groups living in Czechoslovakia.

The constitutional enactment of the federation, adopted after the occupation on October 27, 1968, was the only judicial enactment of one of the 1968 reforms: neither a federal constitution, separate constitutions for the two republics, nor new laws securing criminal and civil rights were enacted.

One of the most important postulates of the Action Program was contained in the demand for a division of power and control. Nowhere, not in any facet of economic and political life, should power be concentrated to such an extent that, in the hands of an apparatus or individual, it could be wielded to prevent the exposure of mistakes and exaggerated facts. Only when complete power is divided and there is a system of mutual control can there be a guarantee that power will not be abused. The Action Program provided for the division of state security organs into two independent parts—civil and state. In the future, the program stated, it would be forbidden to use security organs to resolve internal political issues and the contradictions of a socialist society.

I do not intend to go through all of the areas of the Action Program. But I will recite the points of two more. The section on science and culture established professional autonomy and abolished censorship in scientific publications, works of art, and the mass media.

The program stated that entrance of youth into educational institutions should be governed only on the basis of merit. Restrictions in the use of foreign magazines and literature were lifted for those receiving permission to study abroad and for professional purposes. Each citizen received the right to a passport for trips abroad.

The foreign policy of Czechoslovakia in the Action Program was formulated as the politics of a socialist state—as a member of an association which Czechoslovakia not only intended not to destroy, but, on the contrary, sought to perfect by affirming the spirit of its principles—of mutual respect, respect for sovereignty, equality, and solidarity, within Comecon as well as the Warsaw Pact. A new direction in foreign policy was indicated by the anxiousness to conduct a more active political role in Europe and demonstrate independent initiative in international affairs. In 1968, the first steps were taken in the direction of normalizing relations with the Federal Republic of Germany. The importance of this step was later evidenced when, after the occupation, those who accused the post-January government in Czechoslovakia of having betrayed the people and failing to carry out inter-allied obligations were the same ones who had implemented this step. The same held true for the settlement of disputed issues with Austria.

All of the positions listed here from the Action Program as well as many others, began to be implemented immediately—and under extremely complicated circumstances, since the government of Dubcek was not politically homogeneous. The changes were not only aimed at rectifying errors in the development of the state. They were primarily confronting the entire social life. The history of revolution, including the English and French revolutions, gives us very few examples of a revolutionary democratic transition without internal shake-ups and external conflicts.

We, in Czechoslovakia, tried to put forth goals that could be implemented gradually without extending beyond the limits of what was possible during this period. And only after achieving these goals would the consequent, more profound changes be implemented. The conservative wing of the CPC, by nature an antidemocratic group, exploited the democracy of 1968 to its own ends. But, if in that period any segment of the population would have been deprived of the opportunity to exercise democratic rights, our credibility would have been compromised, and, besides, the regulation of one group would have set a bad precedent. This was where the complexity of 1968 lay, but since the overwhelming majority of the population supported the post-January government, even this problem was not insurmountable.

The CPC, which itself changed in the course of 1968, undoubtedly endured a great deal during this active and varied period. In certain discussions, rash statements and extreme opinions were occasionally allowed but, as a rule, they were motivated by the desire to bring the party and society out of a deep deadlock. Impatience and one-sidedness were the punishment for the sins of the past, for the absence in the past of an open and free exchange of views.

In 1968, the Communists demanded an extraordinary congress, resulting from the profound, internal need to freely elect a new leadership of the party as a guarantee, it was hoped, for the implementation of the post-January political views. The draft of the new statute of the CPC, which was prepared before the congress, provided for secret elections of all party organs—from the local party organization up to the Central Committee and its Presidium, the Politburo. The party statute also provided for freedom of discussion, which was already in effect at the district party conferences in March–June, 1968. After the discussion period, the will of the majority ruled, but the minority retained the right to its opinions, and later, on the basis of new facts, to demand a reopening of discussion.

The decision makers in the CPC had been elected by the party organs, while the task of the apparatus was only to implement these decisions, not the other way around—for example, when the party machinery rules the entire party and imposes its will on the members. The extraordinary Fourteenth Congress, scheduled for September 9, 1968, was to have approved the new statute and elected a new Central Committee and Politburo, ending the *transition* period of the post-January epoch.

The conservative forces spoke out against all of this, attempting to secure a return to the former status quo. Later, when they lost influence in the party, the program of the conservative forces became the restoration of the "old order." The extraordinary conferences of the district and regional party organizations—where delegates to the congress were chosen—clearly demonstrated that opponents of the post-January politics found themselves in a scant minority. These people understood that neither in open discussion, nor at the congress, would they prevail, and that they would have to be prepared for the likely results of the congress, or prevent the congress from taking place. Unable to prevent the convocation of the congress by their own strength, they secured the military intervention of five of the Warsaw Pact countries under the pretext of a victory of the counterrevolution.

In Czechoslovakia, it was later often debated why Dubcek and his collaborators did not recognize the danger of intervention. Even Gustav Husak accused Dubcek of this lack of foresight; although Husak, even as late as August 20, 1968, had spoken at a meeting without in any way hinting he was aware of any danger only a few hours before the occupation.

The intervention of five countries was intended to prevent the extraordinary Fourteenth Congress from being held. But, in spite of the occupation, delegates assembled at a Prague factory in Vysočany and, with a quorum present, adopted the resolution supporting the decision of the Politburo of the CPC, formulated on the night of August 21 and condemning the entry of soldiers as an act of violation of international law and the principles governing relations between socialist states. The holding of the Party Congress at Vysočany prompted the release of the prime minister of Czechoslovakia, the chairman of the Czechoslovakian Parliament, the first secretary of the Central Committee of the CPC, and other political leaders who had been removed to Moscow and who were threatened with the same fate that befell the Hungarian leaders during the events of 1956. The Czechoslovakian leaders were freed under the pressure of Czechoslovakian and world public opinion. Nonetheless, before leaving Moscow, they all, with the exception of Kriegel, signed the so-called Moscow Protocol, which tied all of their hands.

The occupation of Czechoslovakia refuted all of the positive assertions made by the Warsaw Pact countries in the so-called Warsaw

Letter (July 15, 1968), stating that the signing countries did not intend to interfere in the internal affairs of Czechoslovakia and violate the principles of equality and independence. Military intervention was a direct contradiction of both the announcement by the Soviet government on October 30, 1956 of the principles of mutual relations between socialist states and the signed Final Act of the Helsinki Conference.

WHY WERE OUR ACTIONS NOT CROWNED WITH SUCCESS?

Many ask themselves this question, not only communists, but socialists, democrats and others as well; amateurs and professionals, persons with no direct connections with what occurred in Czechoslovakia and accidental observers. And there are many answers to this question, often contradictory; given the complexity, it really could not be otherwise. From a long list of explanations, let us consider only a few.

"They arrived in the nick of time" (to stop the counterrevolution?) the official press asserted as well as those who earlier shouted: "Nobody asked them to come here."

- Were the communists-intellectuals to blame because of their excessive radicalism and the maximalist tone of the demands? There were many intellectuals who did understand the uniquely complex situation in the country and the limited possibilities due to the geographical position of the country.
- Were the impatient youth, whom no one warned of the possible consequences, to blame?
- Or the journalists, who rashly published extreme points of view and unrealistic demands?
- Or all the Communists now excluded from the party, who did not realize the danger of intervention and, therefore, encouraged the illusions?
- Perhaps, the party and state leadership, headed by Dubcek, was to blame because it was not unified and, therefore, indecisive?
- Perhaps, Dubcek himself was to blame? Dubcek, who, in spite of all his humanism and personal integrity, lacked the traits of a clear-minded and purposeful leader who understood the vital importance of events and their consequences.
- Perhaps, all the people could not stand the test?

After the defeat of any movement, the same discussion surrounding an eternal theme is conducted: Who is to blame? These discussions are positive when not aimed at finding a scapegoat, settling personal scores, or becoming a springboard for personal ambition.

This kind of discussion is positive only when conducted peacefully, in a business-like way, without hysterics. The historian is obligated to review the complexities and causes of historical phenomena and not to seek only one ultimate reason or explanation, buried behind successive locked doors, for an event. In this case, not even a master key will help.

The prologue to 1968 was 1956. Then, discontent, provoked by the Twentieth Party Congress in USSR, was stirred in Czechoslovakia. But it quickly abated.

In comparison with Czechoslovakia, the Polish October was more productive and decisive, as demonstrated in the speeches and actions of Gomulka. The Poles—with the support of China—averted military intervention by Soviet divisions, which were within the country. Gomulka and his companions very skillfully contained discontent in Poland within certain limits, and, consequently, Poland was able to avoid an armed confrontation with the USSR. But when the excitement cooled, there remained the peelings of unfulfilled slogans. The uncorrected mistakes of the past caused a new crisis in 1970, which resulted in the ouster of Gomulka himself.

Thus, we see that when a proliferation of reforms from above are executed inconsistently and without support from below, the situation not only does not change but worsens.

Hungary, already in 1956, employed almost all of the tactics that many contemporary critics of Czechoslovakia counsel, in retrospect, for the Prague Spring. The government of Nagy liquidated the monolithic system of one-party supremacy; it allowed the resurrection of the social-democratic party and the agrarian party and included representatives from each in a coalition government. When this demonstration of Nagy's "decisiveness" prompted a second Soviet intervention, the government of Hungary declared its country's departure from the Warsaw Pact and its country's neutrality and turned to the United Nations for help. The government of Hungary called upon the population to defend the country. Organized resistance continued for several hours. A general strike continued for two months. There was no help from anyone. A period of repression, deportations, and mass emigration followed.

Poland and Hungary in 1956 both exemplify the historical

dilemma of such isolated experiments. Minor or token reforms run aground; decisive actions run up against a wall, which, if not noticed in time, will completely crush them. The limitations of a small country, its relative geographic position, the international alignment of forces, and the bipolarization of the world cannot be overcome alone. Aroused discontent in several East European countries simultaneously might have a better chance of success and force the superpower to pay more attention to the interests of small states and realize that the old form of relations is no longer adequate and that change in the internal politics of these countries is necessary. It is in the interest of the great power that small countries should not be prevented from living as they choose. And only when the continually repeated and swelling conflicts will be ended, only then *viribus unitis*.

THE LEGACY OF 1968

I am convinced that permanently recurring problems, crises, and conflicts will force Czechoslovakia to find a solution. In such a recurrence, people will seek inspiration in the events of 1968. The trauma of failure has yet to be exorcised; but a new generation, not active in the period of the Prague Spring, may only repeat the mistakes of the impatient, previous generation. However, retrieving the lessons of 1968 does not at all imply any return to the point where events were interrupted, and binding of the broken thread. The years of so-called consolidation have made their imprint on the consciousness of *all* generations, even to the extent of proclaiming the slogan, "I do not think, therefore I am." The new generation can be inspired by the freedom of speech and of the press achieved in 1968 and be aware of the consequences of becoming intoxicated by that freedom; they are open to a lively political dialogue in the society as well as between the society and powers-that-be, a return to the life of parliament, self-governing enterprises, the development of science and the arts and much, much more.

The legacy of the past becomes the political strength of all eras. And, therefore, the best of what 1968 offered will influence the actions of thoughtful people until the time when this legacy will be realized in a new, liberated society.

translated by Cynthia Stone

THE NATIONALITY PROBLEM

FRANTISEK SILNITSKY

Following the collapse of the multinational Austro-Hungarian Empire, as a result of the First World War, several new states arose. One of these was the Republic of Czechoslovakia. Czechoslovakia was formed not simply due to the crushing defeat of the Austro-Hungarian Empire, but because the division of Austro-Hungary into separate, independent states was part of the agreement between the victors. In addition, the population favored the creation of their own state and a political representation of the national groups was organized. The Bolshevik Revolution in the neighboring multinational Russian empire and its defense of national self-determination also had an effect on the creation of new European states. (It certainly should not be forgotten that the Bolsheviks maintained and stressed this slogan in response to the politics of President Wilson, as witnessed by the debate of "the nationality question" at the Eighth Congress of the Russian Communist Party [Bolsheviks] in 1919.)

The Czechoslovakian Republic was itself a multinational state. The Czechs inhabited the historical lands of the Czech kingdom—Czechia, Moravia, and Silesia—and they based their striving toward an independent state on "their historical right to statehood." It was quite different for the Slovaks. Linguistically, the Slovaks are very similar to the Czechs. However, after the fall of the Great Moravian State in the tenth century, the Slovaks became a constituent part of Hungary—though, despite the thousand-year national dependence and strong Magyar influence, the Slovaks were not subdued and survived as a nation.

During the First World War, the Czechs and Slovaks joined forces to form a common state. The landmark in this process was the Pittsburg Agreement, signed May 30, 1918 by representatives of Slovak organizations active in the U.S. and T. G. Masaryk, the Czech representative. According to this agreement, the new state was to include the Czechs and Slovaks, since the Slovaks preferred to enter the new, democratic Czechoslovakia, rather than remain constantly subject to the Magyar threat.

According to the Pittsburg Agreement, the Slovaks were to be afforded a relatively large amount of national autonomy: a Slovak government, a Sejm (Polish parliament), and a court. The Slovakian language became the official language, to be used in the schools and universities.

Formed in 1918, the Czechoslovakian Republic became a truly democratic state, but the government was centralized. Consequently, a nationality problem arose, which persists to this day. Besides the Czechs and Slovaks, who in 1921 made up 65.5 percent of the country's population, there were also some additional minorities. (The term "national minority" includes citizens of this state who belong to a nationality located primarily in another multinational state or in an independent national state.) In Czechoslovakia, the national minorities were: Germans (22.3 percent of the population), Hungarians (4.8 percent), Rusyns (3.8 percent), Jews (1.3 percent), and Poles (0.6 percent). In general, those of Jewish heritage numbered more than 2.6 percent, but half of these claimed another nationality—the decision was voluntary. (At that time, official anti-Semitism in Czechoslovakia was nonexistent. This situation changed only after 1948, when the Communist Party of Czechoslovakia, in obedience to Stalin, waged anti-Semitism campaigns.)

The statistics cited above are from 1921. But, according to data collected in 1930, Czechs and Slovaks within Czechoslovakia already comprised 66.9 percent of the population and national minorities, 33.1 percent.

With the creation of the Czechoslovakian Republic came the national idea of "Czechoslovakism." According to this idea, Czechs and Slovaks were considered one national group. And this was, at that time, not a political invention. To the contrary, this was the result of joint actions by the Czechs and Slovaks against the "Magyarization" of Slovakia, and it embodied an entire set of attitudes —from the view of the Slovaks as a branch of the Czech people who lived under Hungarian rule, to the concept of the Czechs and Slovaks becoming unified in one state. At the same time, Czechoslovakism necessarily served as a means of stabilizing the new state whose fundamental national groups (i.e. at that time, "Czechoslovakian") were able to counterbalance or even outweigh the strengths of the national minorities, who, from their experience before 1918, associated all nation-states with national oppression.

In the new Czechoslovakia, the Czechs promoted the development of Slovak culture; the union of Czechs and Slovaks in one state put an end to the threat of Magyarization and fostered the development of a Slovak national consciousness. But, the extent to which this new national consciousness developed made it clear that the idea of Czechoslovakism, the idea of merging two neighboring nationalities into a unified whole, could not satisfy the Slovaks.

Resolving the nationality problem in multinational Czechoslovakia became significantly more complicated before the Second World War. There were several reasons for this: the world economic crisis, which particularly affected the industrial Czechia; the activities of Hungarian irredentists; and the aggressive nationalism of neighboring Germany, where the Nazi party proclaimed itself the representative of all ethnic Germans. Alone, multinational Czechoslovakia could not withstand German aggression. And the outcome is familiar to us all. Great Britain, Italy, and France signed the Munich Agreement with Germany, and Hitler's troops occupied Czechia and Moravia (which in March, 1939 was what remained of territory inhabited by Germans that was not annexed to Germany in 1938), and Slovakia became an independent state.

After the Second World War, securing national existence was a first priority of Czechoslovakians, and they continued to perceive German nationalism as their major threat. Czech and Slovak politicians did not take the world changes into account, that atomic weapons now existed, nor did they consider that a vanquished Germany was no longer an aggressive, nationalistic, and fascist state. For these reasons, the political parties of Czechoslovakia strove to guarantee the national existence of their peoples through a union with the USSR. (The Munich Agreement of 1938, and the consequent belittling of national interests, as well as the political notion, generally accepted at the time, that small states required the defense of a world power all played a part.)

At the same time, the Czechoslovakians had come away from the Second World War convinced that cooperation between the nationalities was essential to legitimate and viable political organization. They were disposed to meeting a major precondition for a solution to the nationality problem: to respect the unrestricted equality of the different national groups and national minorities and to create institutions of national autonomy. After the war, Czechs and Slovaks alike were striving toward integration, although the idea of Czechoslovakism was this time completely abandoned. The problem of a major national minority—the Germans—also ceased to exist after the war, since the Germans were deported to Germany. Indeed, this did involve some unresolved and potentially inflammable problems of international relations and morality, but the Germans were no longer relevant to the internal state affairs between national groups.

In 1945, a new system of political pluralism, with the multi-partied government of the National Front, was created in the reconstructed Czechoslovakia. In Slovakia, the highest political organ was the Slovak National Council, and the legislative organ was the College of Deputies. In accordance with the new Košice government program*, it was stipulated that the activities of the central and Slovak political organs would be coordinated. Initially, there had been a supreme political organ for the Czech lands—the Czech National Council—but it was disbanded as early as May 11, 1945, and was incorporated by the central government of the Czechoslovakian Republic.

In this manner, the central Czechoslovakian government became, at the same time, the government of the Czech people. On June 2, 1945, an agreement was reached between the Czechoslovakian government and the Slovak National Council stipulating that executive and judicial power in Slovakia should reside in the Slovak National Council and that state legislation proposed by the government and approved by the Slovak National Council, be executed by means of decrees by the president of the republic. This agreement was completed in 1946, but arguments arose repeatedly between the state government and the Slovak National Council; these arguments mainly concerned personal politics, the jurisdiction of the central government, and questions relating to legislative matters. Thus, we see that as early as 1945, inequity existed in the regulation of national relations in multinational Czechoslovakia. Because of the absence of Czech national political organs, the state government automatically identified with the Czech people. Moreover, the power of the Slovak national political organs was always being restricted. The unique opportunity to harmonize national relations was slipping away.

In 1946, the head of the Communist Party of Czechoslovakia,

---

*The program agreed upon at the meeting in the town of Košice in eastern Slovakia between the two Czechoslovakian governments in exile (located in London and Moscow).

Klement Gottwald, became prime minister of Czechoslovakia. By this time, the Communist party already controlled all of the key political organs of state power. And, in spite of the fact that the Communists received only 30.4 percent of the vote in Slovakia in the 1946 elections, the government of Gottwald succeeded in dissolving the College of Deputies (which was a coalition headed by the Democratic party and which received 62.5 percent of the vote) and appointed a new College of Deputies headed by the Communist, Gustav Husak, on November 19, 1947. In February, 1948, political pluralism was liquidated. Czechoslovakia had become Communist and in the course of one year laid the foundations for a Soviet-type society. In the area of foreign relations and culture, Czechoslovakia broke its traditional, centuries-old ties with the West and was now manifestly under the thumb of the Soviet Union.

What did the construction of a Soviet-style society signify in resolving the nationality problem in Czechoslovakia? Namely, that there would be no truly national solution—decisions on all critically important problems in Czechoslovakia would be made in Moscow. And since the inequitable regulatory organs conformed to the Soviet model, this issue was considered settled. Formally, the differences between Czechoslovakia and the Soviet Union were preserved. The USSR was nominally a federation, an association of sovereign republics headed by national political organs and with a federal government. Whereas, in Czechoslovakia, the Slovaks but not the Czechs, had these political organs. Yet, in the building of the actual ruling party, the situation was identical. In the USSR, each had its Communist party, but the Russian Communists were identified with the Communist Party of the Soviet Union (CPSU)— the all-state organization to which the republic Communist parties were subjugated. This was also true for Czechoslovakia: there was only the Communist Party of Slovakia, while the Czech Communists were members of the Communist Party of all of Czechoslovakia. As a result, in the multinational countries of Czechoslovakia and the Soviet Union, a national Communist party represents a sort of second-class organization.

Marxism-Leninism does not consider a nation to be pluralistic, and thus it goes against man's multifaceted nature. For Marxism-Leninism, for the Communist Party of the Soviet Union and other Communist parties associated with it, the important element is class, the working class. Translated into practical language, communism means that the working class is manipulated for the purposes of securing the Communist party's own power. What results is the destruction of the socio-political structure of the people. The Communist party does not allow ideas in society which diverge from communist ideas; therefore, national consciousness and a striving to develop one's people are irreconcilable with communism and with so-called proletarian internationalism. The program of Marxism-Leninism is denationalization.

As a result of Czechoslovakia's adoption of the Soviet model—in complete disparity with its history—the Jewish question, beginning in 1949, came into the foreground as an aspect of the nationality problem. It was bequeathed to Czechoslovakia as a part of the imperialist conspiracy, and Jews were, consequently, charged with subversive activity. In the "Report of the Commission of the Central Committee of the Czechoslovakian Communist Party on Political Trials and Rehabilitation in Czechoslovakia in the Period from 1949 to 1968," it is stated that the secret security service in Czechoslovakia cooperated with Soviet security organs and "stressed the danger of Jewish bourgeois nationalism and Zionism." There were political trials and many of the defendants were condemned to death and executed. Simultaneously, a campaign was being conducted in the Soviet Union against so-called cosmopolitanism, a campaign which, in common human terms, could only be called anti-Semitic.

The Soviet model for dealing with the nationality problem was also used in Czechoslovakia in the campaign against the so-called "bourgeois nationalists"—notably directed against Slovak Communists. It was primarily against Communists because, in the process of creating the so-called "classless society," all other non-Communist Slovaks had been quickly removed from political life. Therefore, somewhat later, in accordance with the urgent political needs and with the Stalinist model, the party began to expose enemies in its own ranks. In the history of the Communist Party of the Soviet Union, the struggle against the "bourgeois nationalism" of non-Russians is a central motif. The term itself came about, not by accident, but in accordance with communist doctrine, in which national sentiment and consciousness is defined as a historically limited phenomenon, inherent only in bourgeois society. For this reason, a nationalist is a two-fold enemy—as a nationalist and as a bourgeois. At the end of April, 1953 (Stalin died in the beginning of March of that year), charges were brought against a group of Slovak "bourgeois nationalists." On March 31, 1954, with the charges having undergone three revisions by the Politburo, the so-called Slovak nationalists (members of the Communist party) were sentenced. The most severe sentence—life imprisonment—went to Gustav Husak.

At the end of the 1950s and beginning of the 1960s (the constitution of the Czechoslovakian Soviet Socialist Republic was adopted in 1960), the Slovak national political organs were deprived of practically all of their most essential rights. This was justified on the grounds that socialism was now a reality in Czechoslovakia, and the crossover to communism was beginning, in which nations and their cultures converge and a nationality problem ceases to exist. This period of intensified centralism in Czechoslovakia occurred when, in the USSR, Khrushchev was conducting the politics of rapprochement of nations towards a complete merger. At the time, in the beginning of the 1960s, Slovakia was undergoing intense economic development, which received a great deal of help from the Czech lands. Paralleling economic growth was a strengthening of Slovak national consciousness and the demands for an analysis of national relations within the Czechoslovakian state.

In 1963, after 15 years of suppression of their national consciousness, their criticisms of political trials in Czechoslovakia and their demands for justice for those sentenced erupted. The fight against so-called Slovak bourgeois nationalism created one of the most important issues in the country. In 1963, it was already clear that the issue was not the rehabilitation of one or another Slovak Communist accused of bourgeois nationalism but the problem of the Slovak national group as a whole and of national relations with Czechoslovakia. Only in January, 1968 was the rehabilitation not only of certain individuals but of the national consciousness of the Slovaks carried out.

In September, 1967, Aleksandr Dubcek—then, the First Secretary of the Communist Party of Slovakia—attacked the economic plan of the Czechoslovakian Republic; in particular, for its investment of capital in Slovakia at a rate lower than the state plan provided. The mood of the Slovaks, aroused by the contemptuous attitude of President Novotny towards Slovak culture, played a definite role. The developing national consciousness and its political transformation by the national Communist party into a force for a new system respecting the rights of nations and citizens was an absolutely unique phenomenon in the history of Communist-run states. In the multinational Soviet Union, where the suppression of non-Russian national groups is typical, there was no instance of a national Communist party protesting "against accusations of bourgeois nationalism made against its leaders or the national group it represented," i.e., there was no instance of any national Communist party representing the will of its national group in criticizing the central powers. What occurred in the autumn of 1967 in Czechoslovakia completely departed from this framework of the Soviet model, the model of association by silent peoples.

In stating national needs and creating a unified Slovak people with its own political leadership, the Slovaks contributed to the fall of Antonin Novotny. But they were not alone. The examples of the Czechoslovakian SSR and the USSR show that nationalities of a multinational Communist state cannot speak out on their national needs when the central power is supported by the dominating nation in the country and is free to use force. But at the end of the 1960s, the former dominating Czech nation did not afford any support to the center. Serious political abandon could be observed during those years in Czechia. Political terror, anti-Semitism and its tragic consequences—the persecution of the so-called Slovak bourgeois nationalists—all led the Czechs to raise the issue of morality and conscience in politics. Moreover, the politically active part of the Czech nation supported the Slovak demands. As a result of this respect for national rights, an overall democratization of the country followed. In fact, in a multinational state the transformation from totalitarianism to democracy, to a society which respects the rights of man, must begin with a review of national relations. If a state is not in a position to guarantee the rights of nations, it cannot guarantee the rights of individuals. The privileged position of one of these nations in the state automatically leads to a violation of the rights of other nations.

The USSR followed very intently what was happening in Czechoslovakia. The national demands of the Slovaks, formulated by the Slovak Communist leaders, did not fit the framework of the Communist Party of the Soviet Union (CPSU). In 1968, Czechoslovakia's Warsaw Pact neighbors expressed their view of the Czechoslovakian reforms on several occasions. And this was cause for concern. The need for shifting away from the Soviet model was expressed in an article I published in early 1968 on the resolution of the nationality problem in Czechoslovakia (in the magazine of the Central Committee of the Czechoslovakian Communist Party, *Zivot Strany* [*Party Life*]). In this article, I issued a warning concerning the reevaluation of the method of ruling the state and, most important, concerning the reevaluation of the Soviet form of federation.

> After the war, Czechoslovakia sought its own path to socialism, but without success. It, consequently, looked to Soviet society as a model.... But it was during the time of Stalinism.... The new People's Democracies were unable to depend upon their traditions, on their national development and the precepts of their forebearers. To the contrary, the interests of a universal, stereotyped socialism demanded the liquidation of the most expressive national traits.
>
> We adopted not only Soviet theory, but Soviet practice as well; we adopted the Soviet model as a whole without even asking ourselves the question of whether our conditions are compatible with the use of this mold, or whether something acceptable under one set of conditions can be acceptable under other conditions, let alone whether this system is appropriate even under Soviet conditions. We apparently forgot that to create a cultivated country, to develop democratic forms of life in society, to overcome the negative sides of national life—such as great power chauvinism, authoritarian forms of government, etc.—is more complicated than merely suppressing national life.

Marx drew attention to this when he wrote concerning the liberalization and economic reform in Russia, "Civilization—it is a plant which must be fostered and nurtured for centuries."*

> The Renaissance of Leninism, which began after the Twentieth Party Congress of the CPSU [1956], was favorably received in Czechoslovakia. But, it soon became clear that this, too, was no clear-cut matter. A detailed study of the works of Lenin and his period of leadership revealed that even Leninism is no panacea for Czechoslovakia's ills.... Let us consider, for example, the nationality problem. Until October, 1917, Lenin was a staunch adversary of a Russian federal state. He was, in essence, an advocate of the unitary state. But, after October, 1917, when the national movements in Russia threatened the unity of this state, Lenin agreed to the idea of federation.

---

*Karl Marx, *Collected Works*, vol. no. XVI (Prague, 1965), p. 235.

The federation became a state form of multinational association. . . . Lenin was concerned not with the federal nature of the state, but with preserving the unity of the state and the economic resources of the former Russian empire, and strengthening the military-political foundation of the Revolution. . . . For Lenin, federation was a means, not an end. . . .

And if we proceed at the present time to transform the relations between the Czechs and Slovaks into genuinely equal relations and believe the federal rule of the state can guarantee this equality, then we must also understand that the Soviet type of federation was created under entirely different conditions. We cannot forget that the USSR was formed as an instrument of the central apparatus of the RSFSR, emphasizing the dominating role of the Russian nation. Public opinion in the national republics on this subject was never requested. The formation of the USSR was an act of the ruling political power.

The federal form of state rule in the USSR did not at all hamper the creation of an absolute, centralized state. We should therefore be warned not to attach too great an importance to the form of the state. When Czechoslovakia becomes a federal republic, it will be necessary to devise a system of guarantees, insuring that national relations will be such as to prohibit the rise of a dominating people and to secure genuine equality among nationalities. Czechoslovakia, therefore, faces the task of creating its own model for a solution to the nationality problem . . .

Let us consider for a moment why the CPSU, after the occupation of Czechoslovakia, allowed only one of all the reforms of the Czechoslovakian Spring to become legal—the establishment of a federal republic.

The need for changing national relations in Czechoslovakia was recognized in 1968 by Slovaks and Czechs alike. And, for this reason, the nationality problem ceased to be simply of local concern in Czechoslovakia and became important for the Soviet Union as well. There was not only the clamoring of the Slovaks for a national political government constituted from among the ranks of the Slovak Communist party, there was the support of the Czechs, a nationality formally identified with the government of the state. Czechoslovakia thus became an example for the non-Russian nationalities in the USSR as well as for the Russians—an example of another and different alternative to the Leninist-Stalinist multinational state.

In 1968, a certain portion of the Slovak federalists from the ruling echelons of the Communist party and intellectuals closely identified with them backed the position of self-rule for Slovakia, but their basic goal was not the democratization of the government but greater authority for the government of Slovakia. The Czechs not only did not object, but, on the contrary, many Czech spokesmen proposed a federation on even more liberal foundations—a federation whose framework would provide only for a common defense and a consistent foreign policy. In other words, the Slovaks, were, in fact, offered complete national autonomy. It was the Slovak federalists who refused this kind of "free federation," opting for economic cooperation with the Czech regions (the specific input of Slovakia into the gross national product of Czechoslovakia at that time was 25 percent).

As a result of this situation, the same Slovak national movement that in the autumn of 1967, to a significant extent, prompted the fall of Novotny and the beginning of democratization, at this point, acted as a brake to the platform that brought the Slovaks—Gustav Husak, Vasil Bilak, and others—to the foreground.

The Soviet occupation of Czechoslovakia put an end to the reform movement. Of all the reforms produced in the period of the "Prague Spring," only the federal reorganization of the state became law (in October, 1968, two months after the occupation). According to the federation law, Czechoslovakia presently consists of the Czech and Slovak Republics. But, the Communist parties, as the sole organization of political power in the state, continued in accordance with the Soviet model: for the Czechs, the CPC (Communist Party of Czechoslovakia), the all-state party; but for the Slovaks, the Communist Party of Slovakia. Thus, the creation of a federal Czechoslovakia was accompanied neither by political pluralism in general, nor by guarantees of civil rights. Federation did not disturb the Soviet Union. By suppressing democratic reform, federation was simply not a threat to the ruling clique of the CPSU. The formal federation could still be manipulated. And so, the nationality problem in Czechoslovakia continues.

translated by Cynthia Stone

OPPOSITION

JAN STAREK

To free oneself of word-symbols imbued with so much chiliastic faith, pragmatic effort, so much hate and anger, hasn't been easy. It isn't easy to free oneself of words that once were the key to power and all sorts of advantages, or words that embodied impotence and sometimes were the accompanying passwords to prison: communist, non-party person, anti-Communist, "merely" socialist, follower of socialist democracy or democratic socialism, social democrat, Masarykite ... These and similar words were, and for some still are, far too compromising for safe navigation in the waters of political life: even an innocent confession of socialist convictions can be considered a display of outmoded Old Communism or cunning anti-Communism, whichever one prefers. But such confessions are becoming more and more rare.

Sometimes the sparks fly between us, but only briefly. The disputes are most likely only echoes of ancient and recent traumas, a relic of the past and not any sign of a seriously considered future. It often happens that peers, of similar experience, thinking, and political (let us assume "oppositional") orientation suddenly engage in a sharp, breathless, and unreasoned dispute over who is more socialist, who more radical, and whether one was always against the Communist party, or perhaps for it, or in it.

The present situation so far as programs are concerned also pertains to political or ideological labels. Few people have any interest in them, and no one has enough desire to work out detailed programs, form groups, and create a united front on the basis of them. It's true that in Czechoslovakia you can hear people say: "We know what we don't want, but don't know what we do want! We have to work this out." But despite this, programs, or simply actions—short-term or long-term, minimal or maximal—are not multiplying. Judging only by this, not just the opposition would be given up for

---

The author, who has written this excerpt under a pseudonym, presently resides in Prague. The following is part of an article whose complete title is, "Emigration and Opposition."

lost, but political thought in general. However, closer observation shows that judgments on the basis of the programs (their numbers and quality) are unreliable. Could this programmatic vacuum not testify to the complete opposite, that we are finally beginning to convalesce from ideological fever and its accompanying political lethargy?

By the standards of the program-building Western Communist parties, the ideological New Left, and the soberly pragmatic, yet conceptual and thereby programmatic, social democrats, the degree of Czechoslovakian skepticism toward any program, declaration, and political promise engendered by ideology, no matter how reformed the ideology, is most likely unacceptable, inexplicable, and politically misconceived.

Nevertheless, Czechoslovakian political reality is much more dynamic and varied than a few years ago, when clandestine groups spent late nights over programs and declarations and attempts were made to create some kind of national liberation front. An emergent pragmatic "opposition" in Czechoslovakia has rather mysteriously appeared. But let us be careful: opposition is still used in quotes (for obvious reasons), and a few sober words must be said concerning the new phenomenon of pragmatism. First of all, it has not yet completely formed from the embryo it was in the traumatic experiences of 1968 and 1969. And consequently, *pragmatism* is not yet a complete world view. "The Pragmatists" know little about the rules of genuine pragmatic behavior, on the basis of which many intellectual norms would have to be rejected; it is doubtful that they have any awareness of a corresponding ethics to pragmatic behavior and of its social demands.

"No more programs—at least for now!" can also be a program or at least the common denominator, especially when this slogan emanates from what was formerly an overly ideologized and politically aggressive movement. The nonelaboration of programs could be progress, if it encourages more respect for reality. Of course not all programs are constricting, deceiving, or make false claims. Our moderately optimistic reasoning is in fact based on the appearance of such programs in the future.

The reluctance to decide questions of principle, even in conversation among friends, to define what socialism is and isn't, to decide once and for all whom one is for and whom one is against, to summarize programs and hang out political banners, even the most unsullied, is typical for present-day Czechoslovakia. The language that for decades expressed our specific aspirations is disappearing, and not only in Communist-reformist circles—ideological charades interest even intellectuals less and less. Every day the totalitarian regime confronts the thinking person, the person with a conscience and a sense of honor, with a dose of practical, politically tinged, problems. Daily compelled to take some kind of personal stand on these problems, he begins to perceive all ready-made recipes and simple solutions as pointless.

Our people are repelled by everything recalling the past, but also by anything completely new and shocking—even novelty reminds these skeptical Czechoslovakians of something suspiciously familiar. People persistently, even subconsciously, seek values in everyday life. Ideological styles are out of vogue: one more advantage of our misery. And this is why people seek something with at least a glimmer of hope, but just a glimmer, and, if possible, with no promises. The thinking of a thoughtful Czechoslovakian certainly takes the world prize for "greyness." But it also takes first place for sobriety, caution, critical character, and possibly self-critical character. Demagogues and orators of all possible creeds would have no easy time attracting a crowd of us by words alone.

Every well-thought-out political program (which, in the final analysis, one can't do without) presupposes a certain stability, a tradition, if only a certain historical association of thought and action, a background of established political culture. And if such conditions exist, to endlessly interpret the program's individual words, refute vague suspicions, ponder the philosophy's premise, refer to the classics, etc., is all unnecessary. In short: in our time, and under our circumstances, the effort to be exact, comprehensible, and literal quite paradoxically leads to ideological confusion, semantic disputes, and recriminations.... We finally grasped that one can write whatever one likes, it can even be done well, but there is always the hang-over. It becomes clear that the formulated program is not a nexus of thought and action, of the desirable and possible, but simply something skillfully written on paper. We still haven't acquired the skills of political conduct, and they cannot be compensated for by radical criticism of the causes for the Communist movement's bankruptcy, by intellectual brilliance or sincere repentance: *Mea culpa, mea maxima culpa!*

People, including those who are far from indifferent, have realized that programs are not on today's agenda. I think that this is not only liberating, but, above all, politically valuable.

Meanwhile, the ideological ice has begun to break. Thought is gradually freeing itself, and the dark corners of the recent past are opening up. True, the ice melts slowly, but just think how long it took to freeze! And so though it is *already* passed the point of drawing up another program, it is not *yet* time for a program of political action, nor for determined leaders; passed the point of ideology, yet not even time for realistic guidance in change.

The practical prospects for progress reside in the sphere of real political power. I agree that when the representatives of the regime do act, it will often be unsettling, and I suspect these representatives fear this themselves. But when the moment comes, one will need a very clear head and strong stomach, and should help them, each as much as possible, with all their critical faculties and sense of caution.

And now, turning to prophesy: it will be Communist-reformists and former Communists who will bring about the change. It will not begin on a D-day, but is a slow process and has already begun—and it cannot be stopped.

Certain people will be haughtily skeptical of their actions, others will yawn from boredom, still others will be rudely indignant. But the simple fact of the matter is that those who will act and influence events will not be those in the right, who will have the right ideas and ideals, but those who simply start acting. Though this truth is elementary, it is a closely guarded state secret—the consequences in mere nonobedience towards authority would be enormous.

The anti- and non-Communist opposition is as refined as it is incapable of action. Considering its bitter recollections of the fifties, its caution is understandable, though, and let's be truthful with ourselves, it frequently verges on fear, the basic human fear, for one's peaceful existence. This pertains also to those who managed to become part of the establishment, and there are no few such people.

I have no illusions that the mainspring of future reforms will stem from any sense of guilt or of historical responsibility. It's important to remember that reformists know how to manipulate the regime's mechanism (or at least its components), they know its shortcomings, understand its secret code. They are sensitive to the apparatus's vacillations, know its secret passageways leading to those who make the decisions, they know how to retreat and how to navigate in the ideological fog. These people know the apparatchik's psychology and psychopathology; and the reformists will be the ones to act—they simply can't help it!

Their truth is more limited than the truth of others, but they will attain the maximum number of more or less significant, practical successes. They will not aim at changing the structure of society: they are more interested in tangible success than principles. In the final analysis, they will create enclaves, purify the air, and supply the stimulus for movement and change. They will make diversity possible, although the path to all this will be very difficult. They will not be so ambitious as to apply logic or geometry to problems, nor will they attempt to square the circle, but they may achieve something that will at least resemble a rectangle. They will not attempt to "lie their way" to the truth—which is, in any case, futile—but will, rather, bring it about that many current truths will again publicly be called lies (or mistakes, excesses, or deformations...). These people will not implement "de-totalization of totalitarianism," but they are the ones who will initiate the process.

These people have no illusions about themselves: many would rather have been liberals, democrats, statesmen, or leaders with much greater pleasure... though it's only talk and nothing else. Yet in the political game, in the power struggle, at the moment of truth, they become the reformists that they are, even if they are confined to the regime, ruled by the party, which is still, to some small extent, their party.

But now, seriously and without irony, isn't there something ethically respectable in all of this? Shouldn't one reject the more attractive but amateur role of democrat or liberal and return to what he knows, to the professionalism of a reformist or even reformist apparatchik? And isn't it true that after so much disillusionment this is the most responsible position?

The Soviet military presence in Czechoslovakia is not the cause but the effect of a prolonged political era, a consequence of the war, of February 1948. But life could become more human as a result of modifying this effect, even in the event that the causes themselves remain, that 1948 is not reversed, or "played back." It is not at all necessary to unwind the whole ball of history back to the "original mistake" in order to make amends. We won't lie to ourselves, but let's conceal the truth for a more favorable time. It remains to have faith that some day some people will be able to *act* in the regard to the truth in history, rather than merely talk about it. After all, truth is something that eventually makes itself known.

translated by Liza Tucker

POLAND

THE CHURCH AND THE LEFT: A DIALOGUE

ADAM MICHNIK

In what follows, I will be using the term, the "Secular Left." Because of the imprecision of this phrase, I should first explain how I understand this concept, with reference to four dates in modern Polish history. They are: 1936, 1946, 1956, and 1966—each date a decade apart.

It is quite easy to determine who was on the Left in 1936. The essential characteristics of a leftist position at that time were: antifascism; support for a planned economy and land reform; and the doctrine of the separation of church and state. The structure of the Polish Left resembled the classical West European patterns; and the same was true of the Polish Right. However, ten years later the picture was far more complicated.

We are accustomed, following the official historiography, to identifying a leftist stance in 1946 with support for the "new reality" and the new government established by the Red Army. Many at the time, especially among the intellectuals, also adopted this view. The ideologists of the communist Polish Workers' Party (PPR)—Jerzy Borejsza, Wladyslaw Bieńkowski, and Stefan Zólkiewski—appealed to the ideals of the Left; and an appeal to those same ideals was made by the leaders of the "official" Polish Socialist Party (PPS)—Julian Hochfeld, Oskar Lange, and Adam Rapacki—who called for cooperation with the Communists. Nevertheless, a majority of the

---

Adam Michnik was born in 1946 to Communist parents. In college he became an organizer and leader of the student opposition and in 1965 was arrested and was later expelled from the university. However, in several years he was admitted to the correspondence department of Poznan University and completed his degree thesis on "Selected Historical Problems of Polish Political Thought in Emigration, 1864-70." Adam Michnik is a prominent lecturer at the Flying University (which is an unofficial institution intending to fill the gaps in the official educational system) and a leader of the Committee for Social Self-Defense—KOR (KSS-KOR), set up by intellectuals in 1976 in defense of workers persecuted by the government for their participation in the Radom and Ursus demonstrations of the same year. The following are excerpts.

leaders of the prewar PPS (e.g., Puzak, Zdanowski, Zaremba, Dziegielewski, Ciolkosz, Zulawski) took a stand against the "new reality." A similar opposing position was adopted by such leftist intellectuals as Maria Dabrowska, Maria and Stanislaw Ossowski, and Jan Nepomucen Miller. A specific split occurred within the traditional formation of the Left. *Kuznica,* under its editor-in-chief Zólkiewski, stressed the PPR's progressive program of social reforms, while the leaders of WRN (Wolnosc, Równosc, Niepodleglosc—Freedom, Equality, Independence), Maria Dabrowska and Zygmunt Zulawski, stressed the backwardness and totalitarianism of these same reform methods. This bifurcation on the Left deserves to be remembered. Too many publicists, quite hastily, I believe, equate the official party system with the political programs of the entire Left—which, as experience shows, are by no means identical with the advancement of despotism and lies.

Ten years later, in 1956—the year of the Polish October* —the Left defined itself through a double negation: against the conservative and regressive forces within the Communist party (especially against the pro-Soviet Natolin group), and also against the traditional Right, personified above all by the Catholic Church. The reformist and official youth weekly *Po prostu* simultaneously attacked the Stalinists and the Catholic clergy. Leszek Kolakowski, who, as the ideologue of the October Left, was systematically accused of oppositionism, revisionism, and various other heresies by the party leadership, was at the same time active on the weekly *Argumenty,* the organ of the Association of Atheists and Freethinkers, a periodical which engaged in a persistent polemic with the Catholic Church and religion. The so-called revisionists were, as a rule, ex-Stalinists who rebelled against the party orthodoxy. In the wake of October, they gradually developed closer affinities with members of the anti-Stalinist Left, like Maria Dabrowska and Maria and Stanislaw Ossowski. The Secular Left had at that time two enemies: the central committee of the party, and the Catholic Church. The negative effects of this situation became apparent only after the next ten years.

Nineteen sixty-six witnessed an acute conflict between the leadership of the United Polish Workers' Party (PZPR—the Communist

---

*Rebellion of intellectuals and party members for liberal reforms, which Khrushchev's revelations of Stalinism at the Twentieth Party Congress in 1956 inspired. It was as a liberal that Gomulka came to power at this time.

party formed in 1948 by uniting the PPR and PPS) and the episcopate. This was the most important political conflict since the dissolution of the weekly *Po prostu* (1957). Yet not one of the revisionists, including a group of young people congregated around the program of Kuron and Modzelewski [which called for the replacement of "class rule" of the Communist bureaucracy by "workers' democracy"]—people of unquestionable honesty and courage—raised his voice in protest. All of them considered it fitting and proper to read and listen without protest to the heaps of rubbish dumped on public opinion by the party propaganda machine. Neither Leszek Kolakowski, nor Wlodzimierz Brus, nor Maria Ossowska, nor Antoni Slonimski, nor any other of the moral leaders of the leftist and secular intelligentsia opposed the patently false propaganda campaign against the bishops, nor did they speak out against the absurd accusations that the bishops were betraying the national interest. The attitude of the revisionists (and this applies as well to the group of leftist students mentioned above) is perhaps best described by the jocular *bon mot* of one of the more eminent representatives of this circle: "Finally both sides [i.e., the party and the church] are satisfied, since each has found in the other an adversary on its own level." To the author of the joke, both sides of the conflict appeared equally foreign and hostile. A similar attitude was demonstrated at the time by Leszek Kolakowski. In a sermon delivered at the end of 1965, Cardinal Wyszynski quoted approvingly from Kolakowski's essay, "Jesus Christ—Prophet and Reformer." Kolakowski's essay and the well-disposed commentary of the Primate of Poland could together have formed the first step toward a reconciliation between the church and the secular intelligentsia. But this was not to be. Kolakowski denounced in the press the Primate's interpretation of his essay. Throughout the entire period of conflict, Kolakowski remained silent. He interrupted this silence in October 1966, when, on the tenth anniversary of the Polish October, he delivered a commemorative lecture to the students of Warsaw University. In this brilliant and incisive speech, Kolakowski analyzed the effects of the party leadership's ten years in power. In his analysis, conducted from the point of view of the dissident intelligentsia, there were judgments so critical and so radically formulated that they led to Kolakowski's expulsion from the party. However, in this speech, otherwise so severe and far-reaching, there was not one word touching even remotely upon the party's politics with respect to the church and religion. The Secular Left understood the need to struggle for an extension of democratic freedoms, but it did not regard the church as an ally in these desires.

And so, a decade later, I ask again: What is the Left today, in 1976? I cannot answer this question unequivocally. During the past several years, as a result of the failure of the official communist ideology, nationalist feelings have become stronger and more popular. This is apparent in government circles as well as in the dissident milieu. Both the government and the dissidents are divided, though I am more concerned with the divisions among the dissidents. Borrowing a formulation from one of my friends, I will say that the dissident movement is composed, on the one hand, of those who believe in the superiority of the capitalist system, and, on the other, of those who claim as their program the idea of democratic socialism. I am aware that this is oversimplified, but I will nonetheless adopt it and claim that I identify the Left with the latter group. Understood in this fashion, the Left propagates ideas of freedom and toleration, ideas of the sovereignty of the individual and of the liberation of labor, ideas of a just distribution of the national wealth and of an equal chance for all; it combats chauvinism and national repression, obscurantism and xenophobia, lawlessness and social inequality. The program of the Left is that of antitotalitarian socialism.

* * *

Relations between the Catholic church and the socialist movement were very bad from the very beginning. The hostility was mutual, as were the recriminations. Today, years later, it is still difficult for many to judge these recriminations objectively. The church viewed the program of the socialist movement as an infringement of the natural law of God and a harbinger of moral nihilism. From a historical perspective, it appears that in many of the opinions of Catholic writers ridiculed by the socialists, there were rational elements and reflections that even today deserve careful consideration. The socialists, in turn, charged the church with hostility toward social reforms, a close alliance with the rich and the powerful, a desire to dominate and absorb all spheres of secular life, and, finally, a lack of tolerance towards those of other faiths and towards nonbelievers. Both the socialists' hostility towards religion as such and their programmatic atheism were consequences of their negative attitude towards the political role of the church. Marx, for example, had understood religion as an ideological justification of the *status quo,* to be interpreted solely as hypocrisy.

The anthropocentrism and materialism of Marx are in response to the specific social functions to which religion was occasionally reduced throughout the centuries. This is not to say that I claim there is a place for a God—Christian or otherwise—in the entire historiographical construction of Marx and Engels; what I do want to claim, however, is that the strong atheism of Marx followed not so much from his hatred of the very idea of transcendence as from the conservative social teachings of the church of his times.

In our own Polish conditions, the mechanism of these relations was similar. Dispensing with an erudite historical argument, I will quote instead the testimony of an, by all accounts, impartial man. Jerzy Zawieyski wrote:

> What was the church and Catholicism for us, former socialists and believers, in the twenties? Ruefully, I have to admit that the church, in the persons of its official representatives, or of the clergy, constituted for us the greatest obstacle on the road to Catholicism and faith. Catholicism [as it was practiced at that time] was for us synonymous with anti-Semitism, fascism, narrow-minded bigotry, fanaticism, and all that was antiprogressive and anticultural. In the Diet, the priest-deputies of those days fought with indiscriminate words and methods. The anti-Semitic activities of Father Trzeciak, filled with venom and hatred, were generally repulsive. The program of the so-called "all-Polish youth" took up the slogans of God and Fatherland—meaningful words that were made to signify all that is reactionary, aggressive, fed with hatred. The fights at the universities and among the young people brought only disgrace to the Catholic youth. From among their ranks, after all, came those with the razor blades and brass knuckles.
>
> A certain part of the Catholics supported the nationalist, even fascist movements, conducting their battle with "the enemy" on all fronts of secular thought—fighting with an imaginary enemy, a reluctant enemy and one who very often abstained from the fight.*

---

*Jerzy Zawieyski, *Droga katechumena* (Warsaw: Biblioteka "Wiezi," n.d.), p. 35.

The conflict between the Secular Left and the Catholic Church was total in the years of the Second Republic [between the two world wars].

* * *

After the war, there occurred not an ideological or a political dialogue, but rather a sharp political conflict between a fairly conservative Catholic Church and a totalitarian government brandishing radical and progressive slogans.

Without denying the necessity of social reform, the church strongly defended its property. The episcopate consistently attacked all actions by the new government which aimed at secularizing public life. For example, the introduction of civil marriages and divorce laws provided the subject of numerous critiques by the church. The antichurch and antireligious policy of the government on the one hand, and, on the other, the opposition of the episcopate to the separation of church and state were the principal issues behind the formation of the political division. This was a denominational division, though obviously not a strict one. There were many who rejected the new government without belonging to the Catholic Church, e.g., the aforementioned leaders of the prewar PPS and the circle of intellectuals gathered around Stanislaw Stempowski, Maria Dabrowska, and Maria and Stanislaw Ossowski. There were also Catholics—or, rather, those professing Catholicism and describing themselves as the Catholic Left—who accepted the new order and the rule of the Communist party. Although it sounds paradoxical, the leaders of this group, who congregated at first around the periodical, *Dziś i jutro,* and were later known as Pax, were the same people who, before 1945, had directed a right-wing extremist faction and were akin to the fascist ONR-Falanga (Radical-Nationalist Camp). It was much easier for Boleslaw Piasecki, and others like him, to accept totalitarian state control than it was for the inheritors of the cooperatist ideas of Edward Abramowski, or for the socialists who had formed their political identities in the fight against the Sanacja [government of Pilsudski, 1918–35] for an authentic parliamentarian system.

Therefore one can speak of divisions and conflicts of two types. One source of conflict was the resistance of the church against the secularization of public life and the separation of church and state, a postulate which for decades had constituted a permanent element of the programs of the Secular Left. On the other hand, the Catholic Left, ignoring the denominational division, was defined primarily by its positive attitude towards the policies of the new government—a government which from week to week revealed more openly its totalitarian character.

A great majority of the leftist intelligentsia—and not only of the Catholic Left—supported the ruling Communists. For proof of this fact, it is enough to browse through the volumes of such periodicals as *Kuźnica, Twórczość, Odrodzenie,* or *Myśl współczesna.* The intellectual and political conceptions of those first years contain the seeds of the later moral and political failure of the Polish Left. They precipitated the steep decline that led noble and just people to condone Stalinist lies, violence, and crimes.

This is a separate subject, and an important one which deserves profound reflection. I do not want to accuse thoughtlessly (as has recently become fashionable) nor to excuse thoughtlessly (as has also become fashionable) those who identified with what was generally considered to be the Left. They probably had various motives. For me, however, it is beyond doubt that fear of the clerical right, a fear conditioned by the specific image of Polish Catholicism, and one often justified by the real backwardness of the Catholic clergy during the Second Republic, was one of the important factors influencing the ideological decisions made at that time. For the members of the traditional Left, it was easier to accept violence when it served a cause as obvious as the secularization of public life.

* * *

This argument returns often in conversations with the followers of the PPR. They justify the ideological choice they made at the time with their apprehension of the strength and influence of the reactionary camp. "There was no third choice," they say. "We were not able to predict what would happen later, but we remembered well the political practices of the Catholic Church before 1939." On the other side, the Catholics, those who since 1945 remained in strong and unwavering opposition to Communist rule, say today: "How can we trust those who at that time trampled over our basic rights? How can we cooperate with those who were aligned with lies and violence, and who never faced up to their own past deeds?" These two stereotypes were not without consequences: the harmful silence of the Secular Left in 1966 during the campaign against the episcopate, and the painful reticence of the Catholic groups in 1968 during the pogrom against the secular intelligentsia. (The "Znak" group was a praiseworthy exception.)

To a significant part of the secular intelligentsia, the postwar reforms brought hope for the eradication of social and cultural backwardness, for the realization of a vision of a just and modern, a tolerant and democratic Poland. The ideal of the separation of church and state was an important element of this vision. Accordingly, all the legal reforms furthering this separation met with the approval of the secular leftist intelligentsia, as was the case with the introduction of civil marriages and the divorce law as early as 1945.

The episcopate took a stand against these reforms. It should be noted that the position of the episcopate was not intended to apply only to Catholics (which would have been understandable); the bishops stood against the right of divorce for all citizens of the Polish state, including those outside the Catholic church. From the point of view of a nonbeliever, the matter would appear easy to explain: the church was simply defending its privileged position. The positive attitude of the leftist intelligentsia towards the Communist government's policy of secularization seems in this case unassailable.

Still, I believe that the case was neither simple nor unequivocal. The entire political context of those years amply demonstrates that the legal reforms were aimed not at the separation of church and state, but rather at the subordination of the church to the state, whose policy included the "atheization" of the entire nation. The attempt to subordinate the church was part of an overall policy aimed at the complete subordination of the entire society to the regime, at the destruction of any possibility for social independence. In a word, it was one element of the policy of "totalitarianization."

One could argue that the separation of church and state is always a positive step, even if it is enforced by an otherwise unsavory government. I will answer this with the claim that there exists a fundamental difference between, on the one hand, the desire to secularize public life (i.e., to bring about a situation where, from the point of view of the state, religion is a private matter of the citizens) and, on the other hand, the desire to make society atheist (i.e., to destroy the church and religion). One of the conditions for the separation of church and state is the separation of the state from the church, rather than a situation in which the church is an obedient tool in the hands of an atheistic government (as happened, for example, in the Soviet Union). The separation of state and church is dependent on the full freedom of religious worship. This separation does not mean that the nonbelievers are second-class citizens, but it also does not mean that the believers become second-class citizens. It is also completely false to identify secularization with the state propaganda of the gospel of Marx and Lenin according to Stalin. This ideology, passing itself off as a science, fulfills all the functions of an official state religion. If one accepts the view that the worship of God should be a matter of indifference to the state, then the state should be equally indifferent whether or not one worships the idols of the party, history, or progress.

One should note in this context the accurate formulation of the French intellectual Jean-Marie Domenach, who wrote "Strictly speaking, secularism means that a situation in which one idea can monopolize the state is inadmissible. It is apparently for this reason that secularism contains in itself the best protection against the hypertrophy of political consciousness, defending society from idolatry." According to Domenach, secularism is an "insurance, created by believers and nonbelievers together, against the seizure of the state by totalitarian philosophies."*

I cannot add anything to Domenach's incisive formulation. I will only note marginally that the members of the Left who went through Marxism should easily comprehend the fact that truth is concrete. It is possible to understand the great illusions of 1945, but today, thirty years later, there is no excuse to maintain unchanged opinions. In other words, the evaluation of certain ideas depends on the context in which they are voiced. Thus, during the Second Republic, an anticlerical (although not antireligious per se) attitude was an expression of progressive and democratic aspirations. And although it is with rue that I read today a prewar opinion of then Rev. Stefan Wyszyński, who claimed that "our intelligentsia often ... prepares the ground for Communism—and a scaffold for itself,"†

---

*Jean-Marie Domenach, "Swiadamosc religijna i swiadamosc polityczna," *Więź*, no. 6 (1968): 18.
†Stefan Wyszyński, *Inteligencja w przedniej strazy komunizmu* (Katowice, 1939), p. 3.

still I believe that the resistance against the prewar political practices of the church was, at least from the viewpoint of the Secular Left, both understandable and reasonable. My point is that the same anticlericalism took on a totally different meaning when the church resisted the attempts of the state to assume totalitarian control over the spiritual life of the nation.

What yesterday was progressive and democratic, what seemed to lead to freedom and tolerance, today, in a different situation, serves the reaction and opens the road to violence and blind fanaticism. Those of the Secular Left—and the author counts himself among them—should always remember this. We became an unconscious tool in the hands of a totalitarian power which, acting on a foreign mandate and with foreign help, worked against the Polish nation. As long as we are not willing to admit this clearly and openly, we cannot count on the trust and understanding of those whose biographies were different from our own.

* * *

Confronting my own tradition and my own past, I feel obligated to explain here what prompted the fundamental transformation of the image of the church in the eyes of people like me, those who were completely dissociated from—not to say hostile to—the church and Christianity. I am thinking here of the role played in our intellectual lives by the periodical, *Więź*. Certain characteristics of the editorial policy of *Więź* need to be mentioned here: the stubborn and consistent attempts to conduct a dialogue with those who thought differently, the tenacious effort to bridge the gap separating believers from nonbelievers, the constant overstepping of denominational "chalk circles."

Więź spoke a compelling language and constructed a new type of ideological links. Nevertheless, the editors of *Więź* did not have an easy life. They were fiercely opposed by PAX; they were mistrusted in the secular milieu and in the episcopate. PAX saw the collaborators of *Więź* as followers of humanistic forms of socialism, while PAX preferred totalitarian Stalinism. The clergy accused *Więź* of being a Trojan horse filled with subversive, modernistic novelties. The opposite was true. If *Więź* sowed the seeds of ideological subversion anywhere, it was in the atheistic and anticlerical circles. With a patient and far-sighted policy (so patent from the articles of

Tadeusz Mazowiecki and his collaborators), the editors of *Więź* were able to reveal to us a different and far more accurate face of the Catholic church; they were able to show us the deep sense of the Catholic bishops' attitudes; and finally, for some of us, they were able to reveal the secret of the supernatural. It is thanks to the intellectual experience of reading *Więź* that I am able to now appreciate the entire past of the church and especially the role the church played during the last thirty years of Polish history.

* * *

During the period of intensified Stalinist terror (1948–55), Poland was a country of lawlessness; the constitution was nothing but a scrap of paper; religious freedoms were a fiction. The actions of the church did not differ fundamentally from those recommended in the encyclical of Pope Pius XI. The church defended its faith and its right to preach the Gospel.

Let us try to reconstruct the main lines of action of the Catholic church on the basis of the contemporary church documents and pastoral letters of the episcopate and the Primate.

In the "Episcopal Letter to the Catholic Polish Youth" dated April 15, 1948, we read:

> The new needs arising from the desire to rebuild our fatherland, and the necessary changes in social and economic life, are coming hand in hand with the intensified propaganda of the materialist philosophy. There are many voices, anticipating that an upbringing based on Christian principles will become outdated, which claim it is necessary to search for new methods of raising new generations. The slogan of a "total reconstruction of man" is spreading, and it is taken to mean that our youth should be raised according to the materialist world view. The new arrangement of the world and the preparation of man for new deeds is supposed to take place without God and religion, and outside of the national Christian tradition. The church cannot agree to the upbringing of Catholic youth without God, with His teachings silenced, with His commandments ignored. The church does not dissuade you from your earthly duties, but, at the same time, it wants to raise you in the consciousness of your high dignity as rational and free children of God bound to the fate of this earth but aimed at eternal destiny. You are to aspire to the knowledge of all truth, both natural and revealed. You are to realize yourselves as whole human beings.

Maintain a clear stance toward views that degrade man, who is God's creation. Resist, in the light of your knowledge and in the spirit of faith, all attempts to convince you that man has nothing to do with an act of creation by an eternal God; that man simply "descended from a tree." Repulse this attack by means of your living faith.

Treat the entire flood of propaganda and the apostles of materialism with special calm; behave with goodness and understanding. Most often, they know not what they do. Harden yourselves against the attacks of error. Repulse the flood of materialist literature. But, work eagerly and systematically in school. Thorough studies will gradually reveal to you wide domains of life, in which economic matters occupy an important part. However, these economic matters are not everything, since they cannot fulfill all of man's cravings.... Do not be offended by the materialism of some of your elders, and respect the good will of those among the materialists who sincerely work for a better future for the working masses.... Be realistic in life, but remain within the bounds of God's law and never deny your Christian ideals. Vow to work well not only for the well-being of the country but also for its Christian culture and for the Christian spirit....

Materialism does not recognize God's commandments, nor eternal moral laws, nor Christian ethics, nor any other constant moral norm. It professes the cult of worldliness and sensuality, of the struggle for survival, of hatred. You ... have the honorable task of preserving the principles and practices of Christian morality in your own life and in your environment.... Have a pure heart. Respect in your customs the holy order of God and your human dignity. Love your neighbor with all the sincerity of evangelical love.... Guard yourselves against hatred, which emanates from hell. In the face of the postwar collapse of honesty, beware of every injustice to your brothers, and avoid selfishness.... Love the truth. Become disciples and apostles of truth. Mendacity depraves the soul and contradicts both the moral principles and the conditions of national rebirth.*

In the "Pastoral Letter of the Polish Episcopate on the Celebration of Christ the King," the bishops wrote, in part:

Do not send your children to schools from which religion has been removed. In Poland there is no law forcing you to send your children to nondenominational schools....

We call on everyone to engage in creative endeavors. We all must conscientiously fulfill the duties of our professions. Let the farmer con-

---

Listy pasterskie Episkopatu Polski (Paris, 1975), pp. 63–66.

scientiously sow the fields. Let honest work, which is the calling of man, flourish in foundries, mines, factories, offices, and stores. Let us work harder and harder to reconstruct our Polish life, our capital and our cities, our farms and our churches. Let us retain trust and a complacent spirit, retain the sense of personal, national, and Catholic dignity. Let no one be provoked to irrational deeds by irresponsible elements. Our Polish life should be dear and holy to us. We cannot jeopardize it in vain. We cannot squander Polish blood in aimless confrontations. The nation must remain strong, vital, able to realize what will constitute its grandeur in the future.*

This describes the situation and the antimaterialist resistance of the church, as contained in the church documents of 1948. The program formulated by the bishops emphasized the struggle for the right to teach religion, for the right of the youth to receive a Catholic education. The recommendations for action involved appeals for fidelity to the principles of Christian morality and the cultivation of Christian virtues. The call to resist the materialist currents (i.e., the communist ideology) was accompanied by warnings against collaboration with the armed underground. It was a call not for political, but rather for, so to speak, moral and philosophical resistance. This program was dictated by the situation of the country at the time. In 1948, a year after the rigged election to the Diet, the remnants of any authentic political pluralism had already been destroyed. In September, 1946, before the elections, the bishops still called on Catholics to vote "only for such persons, groups, and electoral programs that do not oppose Catholic teachings and morality."† In 1948, all possibility of choice was gone. By then, the rule of the Communists, both in reality and in the social consciousness, had solidified and was implacable. The program of the bishops was a program of moderation and survival. Their letters are subdued in tone; they appeal for conscientious work, a hope of stability and of a relatively quiet existence for the Catholic society under its new conditions.

By 1949 the tone of the letters changed. During the course of a single year international relations suddenly worsened. The conflict between Stalin and Yugoslavia began. In Poland, PPS and PPR were

---
*Ibid. pp. 70–71.
†Ibid., p. 42.

united, and a violent campaign against the so-called "rightist-nationalist deviation" was inaugurated. A policy of collectivization and intensified party watchfulness was widely propagated and meant an increase of police terror. This new policy was also reflected in the policy of the state towards the church, evident in government publications and church documents. "On March 14, 1949," we read in Mikolaj Rostworowski's book, "the secretary of the Polish episcopate, Bishop Zygmunt Choromanski, received a declaration from the minister of public administration concerning the relations between the state and the church. This declaration compiles a series of complaints in order to prove an 'increase of hostile activity towards the government and the people's state by certain sections of the clergy.' The declaration further states that 'the government will not tolerate any seditious activity.' "*

The program of the bishops was doubtless one of defense of the church. Many of the postulates of this program may appear backward and unacceptable to us. Let us, however, be careful in passing judgment on their reactionary character, since it is easy here to indulge in nonsense. One single example of this pitfall will illustrate my point, one which seems to be fairly widespread in the circles of the secular leftist intelligentsia. In 1964, a certain journalist, discussing the episcopal policies, wrote:

> During one of the meetings of the episcopate, in May 1946, the church authorities took a stand in support of a series of antisocialist demonstrations in our country, including the incidents organized by the traditional reaction under the banner of anti-Semitism. When the League to Combat Racism turned to the episcopate to condemn these incidents, the episcopate resolved that the Polish League to Combat Racism be answered by the Primate, who would declare that the Jews are dying, not because of anti-Semitism, but as the avant-garde of communism. The episcopate thought it unnecessary to make a public appeal, since such an appeal would be political in nature.†

So much for the journalist. The question of anti-Semitic incidents (the most widely known of which took place in Kielce) is too complicated to be discussed here. It is difficult to engage in polemics with

---
*Mikolaj Rostworowski, *Slowo o PAX-ie* (Warsaw, 1968), p. 47.
†Wojciech Pomykalo, in *Dialog i wspoldzialanie* (Warsaw, 1970), p. 63.

the episcopate based only an account by an ill-disposed author; but it is also difficult not to call attention to the fact that the circle of Catholic intelligentsia assembled around the periodical *Tygodnik Powszechny* published a declaration unequivocally condemning the anti-Semitic incidents. One must also note the often-repeated opinion (shared by, among others, Stefan Korboński) that these incidents were instigated by the UB (Urzad Bezpieczenstwa—the Office of Security), which complicates the picture even further. I mention this opinion to alert the reader to the fact that the author of the article cited above is Wojciech Pomykalo, a man known for his anti-Semitic pronouncements, especially in 1968, and the editor-in-chief of the biweekly, *Wychowanie*. The accusation that the Polish bishops are anti-Semitic sounds so grotesque coming from Pomykalo that any polemical commentaries are unnecessary. The context in which these charges of the reactionary character of the church were made needs to be always kept in mind. We may be offended today by the persistent defense of the principle of teaching religion in schools, but let us note that the bishops, recalling the sad fate of the church and of religion in the Soviet Union, were right in thinking that the liquidation of religious instruction in schools would only be the beginning of a total prohibition. We may be shocked when the church calls on believers "not to read impious books, etc.," but we have to remember that it means fidelity to the principles of Christian ethics is categorically and emphatically incompatible with participation in the official public life of the totalitarian state and with support for totalitarian political ideologies. And this is hard to deny.

* * *

On April 14, 1950, the government of the People's Republic of Poland (PRL) signed an "agreement" with the episcopate. It was preceded by the government's decision to take over the mortmain property of the church. Whatever we may think today of this decision, it is difficult to deny that, at the time, it represented only another means of strengthening the totalitarian power. In light of these facts, the "agreement" was a desperate attempt on the part of the episcopate to find a *modus vivendi* with the state.

The text of the "agreement" reads in part:

In order to insure for the nation, for People's Poland and for its citizens, the best possibilities of development ... the government of the Republic, which respects religious freedom, and the Polish Episcopate, which has in view the good of the church and the contemporary Polish state prerogatives, will regulate their mutual relations in the following manner:

1. The Episcopate will call on its clergy, in their pastoral office, to teach the faithful to respect the law and the institutions of the state, in accordance with the teachings of the church.

2. The Episcopate will call on its clergy ... to encourage the faithful to intensify their work toward the reconstruction of the country and for the increase of the national welfare.

3. The Episcopate of Poland proclaims that the economic, historical, cultural, and religious laws, as well as historical justice, require that the Regained Territories belong to Poland. Acting in accordance with the assumption that the Regained Territories constitute an integral part of the Republic, the Episcopate will request of the Holy See that the church administrations now under the law of the residential bishops be changed into permanent ordinary dioceses.

4. The Episcopate will oppose, as far as possible, all activities hostile to Poland, and in particular it will oppose anti-Polish and revisionist pronouncements on the part of the German clergy.

5. The principle that the Pope is the highest and conclusive authority applies with reference to matters of faith, morality, and church jurisdiction, whereas in all other matters the Episcopate will base its actions on the Polish state prerogatives.

6. Acting in accordance with the principle that the mission of the church can be realized in various socio-economic systems constituted by the secular powers, the Episcopate will explain to its clergy that they should not oppose the extension of the collectivization of agriculture, since all cooperatives are in their essence based on the ethical principle of human nature, which aspires to voluntary social solidarity and has as its goal the common good.

7. The Church, in agreement with its principles condemning all anti-state actions, will specifically oppose the abuse of religious feelings in antistate activities.

8. The Catholic Church, condemning in accordance with its assumptions all crimes, will also oppose the criminal activities of the underground gangs and will condemn and punish with canonical consequences those members of the clergy who are guilty of any underground or antistate activity.*

---

* *Listy pasterskie,* op. cit., pp. 91-92.

In exchange for these obvious concessions from the church hierarchy, it was agreed that:

> ... the state will insure the teaching of religion in the schools, religious practices for school youth, freedoms for the remaining Catholic schools, and religious care in the army, hospitals, and prisons. The Catholic University in Lublin is accorded the right to remain in operation. The right of the church to conduct further philanthropic and educational activities is recognized. Students of the seminaries receive the right to continue their theological studies without hindrance. The convents receive the assurance of free work and the right to the material means for a humble livelihood.*

* * *

After the "agreement" was accepted, the tone of the pastoral letters became much more guarded. In the official church documents, we find nothing about the state breaking the law, about lawless arrests, about the torture of prisoners, about sham trials. The only issue defended consistently is the unity of the clergy, for the sake of which constant appeals were made to the clergy to relinquish all political activity.

* * *

On October 19, 1956, began the deliberations of the Eighth Plenary Assembly of the Central Committee of the PZPR, which elevated Wladyslaw Gomulka to the position of First Secretary. One week later, two close associates of Gomulka, Wladyslaw Bienkowski and Zenon Kliszko, arrived in Komancza to visit Cardinal Wyszynski, who was imprisoned there. As a result of their conversation, the Primate of Poland returned to Warsaw and—after a three-year interruption—resumed his post.

Freed from prison, the Primate of Poland abstained from the political arena. The only area in which the church tried to exert pressure was in the matter of teaching religion in the schools. As Mikolaj Rostworowski writes in the book cited above:

---

*Ibid., p. 96.

On December 8, a verbal agreement between the government and the Polish Episcopate was reached. As a result of this agreement, the teaching of religion was to take place in the schools as an elective subject for those students whose parents expressed individually in writing the desire that their children be taught religion. On December 31, the Council of State passed a decree concerning the establishment and staffing of church positions. When this decree was announced ... it superseded an analogical decree of February 9, 1953.*

These concessions to the church had important political consequences.

Immediately after assuming power in the party, Wladyslaw Gomulka undertook the pacification of a "politicized" public opinion. Already in his first speeches, attacks appeared against the so-called "revisionists," against their program promoting power for the Workers' Councils, independent trade unions, the abolition of preventive censorship, and pluralism in the youth movements. Intending to make the church and the Catholic milieus politically neutral during the conflict with the revisionists, the new leadership, in addition to the already mentioned concessions, agreed to reactivate *Tygodnik Powszechny* with its "old" editor-in-chief, Jerzy Turowicz. (The periodical had been shut down in March 1953, and then taken over by Pax.) These tactical moves were of great value to the government.

Shortly after the restoration of religious instruction in the schools, articles began appearing in the revisionist papers—in *Po prostu,* among others—attacking the intolerance of the Catholic priests and discrimination against children who did not participate in religious instruction. A critical attitude toward the very idea of religion in the schools was apparent in these articles. These critiques are quite understandable given the ideological background of the revisionists. Atheism and anticlericalism were permanent elements in the ideology of Polish revisionism. The Stalinist persecution of the church and religion was not condemned in even the sharpest critiques conducted by the revisionists; at most, it was regarded as an inappropriate tactic which, by pushing the church almost to the edge of the catacombs, strengthened "religious prejudice." I would hazard the opinion that many revisionists believed

---

*Mikolaj Rostworowski, op. cit., pp. 115-16.

that effective limitation of the influence of Catholicism and the church constituted one of the very few merits of the period of "errors and deviations." It is significant that in their criticisms of the party and of party orthodoxy, the revisionists often employed analogies with the Catholic church. One could say that the more repulsive the party was to them, the more it reminded them of the church. In their denunciation of the irrationalism and blind faith pervading the confused constructions of the Stalinist version of "dialectical materialism," the revisionists were the inheritors of the ideas of the rationalist philosophers. They contrasted the "fanatical faith" of the Stalinists with reason and tolerance.

There was surely some truth in the revisionist attacks on the bad atmosphere in the schools. It is difficult not to accept the postulate of the separation of church and state on the French model. The problem, however, lies in the fact that these attacks and arguments must have sounded equivocal and false to Catholic ears. "How is it," they asked, "*now* they defend toleration? Where was their beloved toleration when religious instruction was hindered, when the Catholic Church was persecuted, when *Tygodnik Powszechny* was closed, when priests were being imprisoned?" One can imagine that to a bishop who only yesterday was persecuted the revisionists must have appeared an especially repugnant group. Only yesterday they attacked religion and the bishops, only yesterday they were the activists of the ideological front of the party, the eulogists of the regime when this regime was especially cruel, and today—still not considering themselves guilty—they shift the responsibility to the objective conditions and to others, blaming others for their own deeds, while at the same time passing themselves off as moralists, reprimanding the intolerance of others, of those who only yesterday were being persecuted. "Whence comes this moral rigor among those who wrote apologies for Bierut's (Gomulka's predecessor's) policies? How can one explain their steadfastness against the relatively liberal policies of Gomulka, who declared his desire to save the nation from Russian intervention, from a repetition of the Hungarian tragedy in our country?" That was precisely the meaning of the violent polemic between Stefan Kisielewski and Wiktor Woroszylski concerning the attitude of the government towards the Hungarian uprising—a polemic in which Woroszylski was, morally and politically, absolutely right. Through concessions to the church, the government prevented all possible attempts at an understanding between the revisionists, on the one hand, and the church hierarchy and the traditionally Catholic milieus on the other.

* * *

The public pronouncements of the episcopate during the first years following the Polish October (1956) are characterized by political disengagement, moderation in all formulations, and even a certain friendliness towards the regime. Among the recurrent topics in the episcopal pronouncements were appeals for a Catholic upbringing of the youth and attacks against abortion. But none of these appeals had an antigovernment character. On the contrary, in the "Pastoral Letter for the New Year of Educational Work," dated September 3, 1959, the fifteenth anniversary of the manifesto of PKWN (The Polish Committee of National Liberation—provisional government set up by the Soviets, July 22, 1944, after their liberation of Poland) was referred to by the bishops as "The Fifteenth Anniversary of the Restoration of Polish independence." This letter calls for the cultivation of such virtues as family life, sobriety, humility, cleanliness, diligence, and frugality. The return of religious instruction in the schools was called a "great proof of the wisdom" of the government.* In "The Report of the Polish Bishops to the Clergy Concerning Pastoral Efforts," dated March 17, 1960, similar formulations can be found. Here the bishops call for diligence and conscientious work and condemn "laxity and laziness, drunkenness, and the theft of public property." "We work a lot," wrote the bishops, "but not always conscientiously; we know how to respect our own goods, but we do not respect the common property of the nation. We do not remember that sabotage at work, destructiveness, the theft of social wealth, and defective production hurt us and retard general economic progress."† This concern for the social and economic situation of the nation, together with the simultaneous omission of all oppositional or polemical accents, effectively complemented the aspirations of material welfare promoted by the party press and the propaganda slogans of "good

---
*Listy pasterskie, op. cit., pp. 184-88.
†Ibid., pp. 197-98.

work." All conflicts between the government and the church hierarchy remained concealed.

This does not mean, however, that such conflicts did not exist.

* * *

Starting in 1960, the conflict between the church and the state government steadily intensified. In June, 1962, the episcopate published a document entitled "Contemporary Secularization." In this document, full of patient and thorough analysis, a distinction was made between secularization understood as an objective characteristic of our epoch, and secularization understood as "an organized activity accelerating and administering secularization." According to the authors of this document, the movement of secularization in Poland, consistent with the second meaning of the term, is:

> a political movement, since it is encompassed by political planning and is directed by political institutions, while being supported and executed by administrative means.... It is a totalitarian movement, because it aims to influence all manifestations of social, familial, and personal life, and to exclude from this life all judgments and evaluations based on religion. It is a movement that does not allow for the possibility of choice. Every child and every young person can only attend schools that programmatically aspire to secularization.*

I will return later to the merits of this case (i.e., to the problem of secularizing). Here I wish only to draw attention to the decisive and uncompromising tone of this document as evidence of the intensifying conflict. The same tone can be found in the proclamation of the bishops "concerning religious education" from March 1963. In this proclamation, the bishops sharply attacked the policy of the state, which hindered, and in some cases simply prevented, religious instruction. The administrative difficulties consisted of a prohibition for nuns, friars, and laity to teach religion.

* * *

It seems that Gomulka's team never seriously considered permanent coexistence with the church. The declarations and concessions

---

*Ibid., p. 263.

of the period following October 1956 were only tactical maneuvers to overcome the complicated political situation and the weakness of the new leadership. Together with the progress of political stabilization came an increase in antichurch repression.

*   *   *

The intensification of the conflict between the state and the church followed from the government's policy limiting democratic freedoms. This policy was aimed at the revisionist circles (i.e., the secular intelligentsia) and was subsequently applied to the church.

The retreat from the slogans and practices of the Polish October began immediately after Wladyslaw Gomulka assumed power. Following attacks in the press against the revisionists, the government resorted to administrative procedures. Exactly one year after the Eighth Plenary, which installed Gomulka as First Secretary, the popular weekly of the young intelligentsia, *Po prostu,* was closed. The police brutally dispersed the demonstrations of protesting students. At the same time, a literary periodical, *Europa,* was shut down before the first issue was released. This action led several eminent writers —including Jerzy Andrzejewski, Mieczyslaw Jastrun, Adam Wazyk, Pawel Hertz, Juliusz Zulawski, Jan Kott, and Stanislaw Dygat—to renounce their party membership. Early in 1958, another periodical, *Nowa Kultura,* was practically liquidated. When Andrzej Werblan, representing the party leadership, moved to impose a new ideological line on the periodical, Wiktor Woroszylski, Tadeusz Konwicki, Wilhelm Mach, Marian Brandys, Leszek Kolakowski, Witold Wirpsza, and Jerzy Piorkowski all resigned from the editorial board. By 1961, politicians representing the liberal wing of the party had been removed from leadership positions. Wladyslaw Bieńkowski lost his position as minister of education, Stefan Zólkiewski was no longer minister of higher education, and Julian Hochfeld ceased to be director of the Institute of International Affairs. Antoni Slonimski was no longer the chairman of the Writers' Association. The political police and the prosecutor's office became much more active—the trials of Rzewska, Konracki and Rudzińska, and the mysterious death of Henryk Holland all bear witness to this change. At the beginning of 1962, the government, using police provocation as an excuse, closed the Crooked Circle Club, one of the last relics of October and one of the last authentic examples of freedom of expression. In 1963, the regime closed the weekly *Przeglad Kulturalny,* which was edited by a group of secular intelligentsia and maintained a certain independence from the growing nationalistic and repressive tendencies of the party apparatus. At the Thirteenth Plenary Assembly of the Central Committee of the PZPR (July 1963), a battle with the "hostile tendencies" in science and culture was proclaimed. The discussion club at Warsaw University and the so-called "Contradiction Seekers Club," a circle of high-school students, were also dissolved. The growing censorship restrictions led to a sharp conflict between the leadership of the party and the intellectuals. The uproar surrounding the so-called "letter of the 34" [open letter to Prime Minister Cyrankiewicz from intellectuals concerning censorship in Poland] was a public manifestation of this conflict. The fall of 1964 witnessed the trial of Melchior Wankowicz, and during the following summer Jan Nepomucen Miller was tried. The famous case of Kuroń and Modzelewski [concerning the promulgation of a political declaration by young communists] also began in the fall of 1964; they were tried in July 1965 and received sentences of three and three and a half years, respectively. Shortly after their trial, disciplinary action was taken against their students.

All these repressive acts elicited protests from the intelligentsia. Many took a public stand against the policies of the government; among them were Maria Dabrowska, Antoni Slonimski, Maria Ossowska, Tadeusz Kotarbiński, Edward Lipiński, Leopold Infeld, Leszek Kolakowski, and Wlodzimierz Brus. By 1966, the intellectual circles of the Secular Left were fundamentally at odds with the government. Moreover, in this conflict the party leadership showed no tendency toward concessions. The official government policy allowed no one to hope for a real compromise.

* * *

In the late fall of 1965, during the final days of the ecumenical council, the Polish bishops addressed a message to the German bishops, one which shortly became the focus of a controversy.

In the message of the Polish bishops I find today almost none of those statements I consider objectionable in the ideological line of the primate and the episcopate. (Of those objectionable statements I will speak later.) "The Christian symbiosis of church and state," we read in the *Message,* "existed in Poland from the very beginning, and the two never really became separated. In time, this led to an almost unanimous way of thinking among the Poles: what was 'Polish' was also 'Catholic.' From this way of thinking there developed a Polish Religious style, in which the intertwining of religious and national elements included positive as well as negative aspects." It is not often that I am able to find in church documents such an open admission of the shortcomings of a "Polish Catholic's" attitude.

A little further, writing of the medieval contacts between Poland and the West, the bishops emphasized the participation of foreigners in the development of Polish culture. "Poles deeply respected their brothers from the Christian West, who came to Poland as ambassadors of true culture. Poles were not unmindful of the foreign descent of these visitors. We really are very indebted to Western culture, and that includes the German culture." This view of the nation and of the national culture, free from chauvinism and xenophobia, should seem close to that of the secular leftist intelligentsia. It differs completely from the nationalistic view of Polish culture to be found in many Catholic milieus. It was, therefore, no accident that the bishops emphasized both the libertarian and tolerant traditions of Poland and the Polish slogan, "For your freedom and ours."

Seeing themselves as participants in this tradition of liberty and tolerance, the bishops had the courage to draw from it a practical conclusion. They made an attempt to distinguish Nazism from the German nation as a whole.

The bishops wrote in part:

> We know well how large a part of the German population was under the inhuman, national-socialist pressure. We are familiar with these terrible internal sufferings, to which, at the time, righteous and responsible German bishops were subjected; it is enough to mention Cardinals Faulhaber, von Galen, and Preysing. We know of the martyrs of the "White Rose" and of the resistance fighters of the 20th of July; we know that many people and many priests sacrificed their lives (Lichtenberg, Metzger, Klausner, and so many others). Thousands of Germans, Christians as well as Communists, shared the same fate in the concentration camps as our Polish brothers....
>
> And this is why we must try to forget. Let us have no more polemics, no more cold wars, but rather the beginning of a dialogue, one to which Pope Paul VI and the members of the Council aspire everywhere. If on both sides we find good will . . . then a serious dialogue will be successful

and fruitful. . . . This is why, during the Ecumenical Council, it seems important to us that we begin this dialogue on the pastoral platform of the bishops . . . so that we can become better acquainted with each other —with our folk customs, religious rituals, and life styles, which have roots in the distant past and are conditioned by this cultural past.

We ask you, Catholic priests of the German nation, to celebrate with us, in your own way, our Christian Millennium—whether with prayers, or by designating this celebration as a special day. For every gesture of this kind we shall be grateful. . . . In this Christian and humane spirit we extend our hands to you . . . , we forgive and ask you to forgive. And if you . . . will accept this brotherly embrace, we will be able to celebrate our Millennium with a clear conscience and in the most Christian manner.*

The following decade confirmed the humanistic sense and the deep political wisdom of the *Message*. Events confirmed the correctness of the bishops' position: Poles have no choice other than to engage in a dialogue with democratic German opinion and to achieve a common surmounting of the effects of the Nazi Apocalypse. Inciting and cultivating national hatred cannot lead anywhere. And that is why today, no one with a modicum of common sense will accuse the bishops of questioning the stability of Polish borders and of "forgiving" Fascist criminals. We read today with disgust and embarrassment the arguments of Zbigniew Zaluski, filled with lies and progovernment servility, about the "repentance of the innocent and the absolution of the unrepentant." At the time, however, even the right of the bishops to write the *Message* was questioned. "By whom and at what time," asked *Trybuna Ludu*, "was the episcopate given the right to these sorts of demonstrations and actions?"

The unrelenting criticism of the church in the media was accompanied by administrative repression. The tone of the propaganda and the practices of the regional administrations suggest analogies with the persecutions of the church during the time of the *Kulturkampf*. The polemical methods resembled the worst patterns of Stalinism.

Faced with this situation, the Secular Left behaved, at best, passively. Why? The people associated with the Secular Left tended to interpret the fight of the church as a fight for its own concrete

---
*Ibid., pp. 830–36

privileges. At the same time, the government was not at all concerned with any privileges of the church—those were already long gone—but rather it wanted to further terrorize society, to infect the nation with xenophobia, to bring about a national integration by appealing to chauvinistic slogans, and, in the popular consciousness, to identify humanitarian and Christian values with the ideology of national treason. From then on, what was antitotalitarian was supposed to be associated with what is antinational. In a word, what was at stake was the further spiritual and political totalitarianization of Polish life. The next stage of this process, this time aimed against the secular intelligentsia, took place during the "March events" of 1968.

* * *

This is not the place to describe in detail the March events and the anti-Semitic campaign against the secular intelligentsia. However, we are interested here in what attitude the episcopate conveyed towards these events. The episcopate was generally felt to view the behavior of the intellectuals and the youth as a reflection of Communist infighting, and the anti-intellectual pogrom and anti-Semitic demagoguery as a further extension of party conflicts.

From the actual documents it is obvious that the bishops openly sided with the persecuted individuals and the values under attack, and stood against the persecutors, that they tried to defend the dissident intellectuals and the young people protesting at rallies, that they condemned violence and deception. It is impossible—without ill-will—to interpret the letters of the episcopate and the sermons of the primate of Poland in any other way. At most, these letters and sermons can be criticized for a certain lack of concreteness, for vague generalizations, and understatements. One may recall other occasions when the Polish bishops had the courage to present their views far more explicitly and directly. But all of us, we leftist and secular critics of the episcopate's position in 1968, should remember our reactions in 1966 during the antichurch campaign; and we should compare our behavior at that time with the behavior of the bishops during the March events. Maybe this will lead us to see our own complaints in the proper context. Before we point to a mote in someone else's eye, let us remember the beam in our own.

Having stated these shortcomings in my own position and that of my ideological colleagues towards the church, I believe that honesty demands that we also acknowledge the shortcomings of the episcopate. Let me say flatly: what was lacking in the pronouncements of the bishops was the unequivocal condemnation of an officially propagated anti-Semitism. I believe that under the prevailing circumstances, mere allusions were not sufficient. I want to be perfectly clear: I do not believe that the Jewish question was the most important and central issue in 1968. It simply could not be in a country where there were practically no Jews. The enormous anti-Semitic campaign was promulgated not primarily in order to strike against those remnants of Jewish society that survived the Holocaust, but it was supposed to unleash nationalism and xenophobia among the people, to mask the real causes of the social crisis, to dissuade Poles from thinking rationally and to make them accomplices of a crime. This is why anti-Semitism was such an important problem.

I am trying to understand the sources of the church's reticence. First there is the lack of trust. One should admit that the bishops had no reason to sympathize with the intellectuals, who before October had not only fought the church and Christianity and spent good portions of their lives as members of the PZPR, but even immediately before the March events had not hidden their mistrust of the church; not only had they not protested against the repression aimed against the church, but they also wrote for programmatically atheistic periodicals. There was also no reason for the church to sympathize with the group of students gathered around Kuroń and Modzelewski, since the main programmatic statement of this group, the so-called "open letter to PZPR," had all the characteristics of antichurch obscurantism (besides church obscurantism, there also exists such a thing as antichurch obscurantism). Both the secular and leftist intelligentsia and the above-mentioned group of students (the so-called "commandos") represented much that was foreign and hostile to the traditional model of the "Polish Catholic." Thus, for example, they had a "derisive" attitude towards tradition, aversion to the glorification of the past, and this occasionally led to an exaggerated "pessimism" about Polish history; they made light of and occasionally completely ignored the role of Catholicism in the national culture and the function of the church in social life. These elements, admittedly, played a secondary role in the ideology of these students and were not considered crucial. But in this rather confused situation, none of them made any attempt to inform the church circles of their real antitotalitarian, rather than antichurch attitudes.

I suspect that the conflict between the leftist secular intelligentsia and the regime was, indeed, seen by the bishops as an external manifestation of some acute intra-Communist power struggle. They probably viewed also the anti-Semitism propagated from above in the same terms, since it had been used before in internal party struggles. If we assume that this is how they viewed the situation, their reticence no longer appears strange. It is not surprising that the bishops did not want to jeopardize the long-term interests of the church by entering into the muddy fights on the side of one of two equally untrustworthy party matadors. It is probably in this way that one can best explain the fact that the concrete political and ideological context is ignored in the pronouncements of the episcopate, which are limited to rather general declarations about the fundamental right of the students to protest, and the equally fundamental right of the dissident intellectuals to the freedoms of science and culture.

Nevertheless, keeping in mind all these explanations, I am still inclined to believe that the moderation of the church was a serious mistake. Because, quite apart from factional struggles, the racist demagoguery victimized real people, both those who were persecuted and those who were degraded and made accomplices by being pushed into the anti-Semitic vendetta. An unequivocal pronouncement of the bishops about anti-Semitism was badly needed for both of these categories of people.

In 1968, the dark elements of the Polish tradition crashed to the surface. Communist obscurantism, equipped with anti-intellectual and racist demagoguery, struck against the Polish adherents of democratic socialism; and, by so doing, the government also trampled and destroyed values dear to Christianity: truth, freedom, and solidarity. This was well understood by the progressive intellectuals of the Catholic circles, who, without regard to old quarrels, made their position clear, unequivocal, and concrete. I have in mind here the attitude of the deputies from the "Znak" circle. The speeches of Jerzy Zawieyski and Stanislaw Stomma during the debate in the Diet carried tremendous moral and political weight. A voice from the episcopate would have been even more important.

* * *

One should remember, however, that the position of the bishops was clear to the party and state apparatus. In the opinion of the party leaders, it was precisely the bishops, and Cardinal Wyszyński, in particular, who had inspired the interpellation of the "Znak" deputies. Let us recall the events.

On March 16, 1968, Radio Free Europe broadcast the text of the interpellation of Józef Cyrankiewicz [Prime Minister of Poland from 1948–70] by the deputies of the "Znak" circle. The interpellation was dated March 11.

> Deeply moved by the events of March 8 and 9, which took place at Warsaw University and at the Polytechnic, concerned with peace in our country in the context of a complicated international situation, and concerned about the proper atmosphere for the education of youth, on the bases of Article 22 of the Constitution of PRL and Articles 70–71 of the Rules of the Diet of PRL, we ask: 1) What plans does the government have to restrain the brutal actions of the police and ORMO (voluntary police) against the students, and how does it plan to investigate who is responsible for the brutal treatment of these young people? 2) What plans does the government have to solve the burning questions being posed by the students, questions which concern wider public opinion as well and address the problems of individual freedoms and the cultural policies of the government?

> *Justification*
> The demonstrations of young people studying in Warsaw were caused by certain apparent mistakes of the government concerning cultural policies. The young considered the removal of *Dziady* [*Ancestors Eve*, by Adam Mickiewicz, nineteenth century play dealing with the traditional Polish opposition to Russian chauvinism and imperialism] from the stage a painful and dramatic interference that threatened the freedoms of cultural life and insulted the national traditions.
> We also believe that on Friday, March 8, it was possible to have avoided the events that took place at the university. During the demonstration, buses of ORMO entered the university, inflaming the situation.
> On March 8 and 9, the demonstrating youth were beaten with extreme brutality, often in a manner endangering lives. There were cases of students who were seriously mistreated, among them women.
> Society was enraged by these actions.

We appeal to the prime minister to urge the government to undertake immediate action to ease the situation. This requires that the brutal actions of the police be stopped. And those who protest when faced with these brutal forces should not be considered enemies of the regime.

Neither students nor the rest of the society took a hostile position towards socialism during these events. The irresponsible shouts, which also occurred, were provoked by the actions of ORMO and the police and should not be used as a basis for judging the attitudes of the young.

We also wish to express our concern about interpretations of this kind in the press, which further inflames the situation. Neither crushing the demonstrations nor forsaking communication with society will provide a correct solution. We appeal for your consideration of this.

Konstanty Lubieński, Tadeusz Mazowiecki, Stanislaw Stomma, Janusz Zablocki, Jerzy Zawieyski.

Let us try to appraise the significance of this interpellation of the "Znak" deputies. The most important aspect is of course the moral one. The demonstrative interpellation of "Znak" was a defense of those who were persecuted and needed defending. Taking the side of people who were beaten and reviled, defending their honor and the honesty of their intentions, the "Znak" deputies accepted the priority of ethical over tactical or political considerations: they were not trying to feather their own nests in the political turmoil, and they gave priority to fundamental moral values. Especially important were Jerzy Zawieyski's attempts to defend the moral and intellectual qualities of the attacked writers. I am not referring here to the fact that Zawieyski called Antoni Slonimski a "distinguished Polish poet," which in the atmosphere of those days was a beautiful act of courage and solidarity, nor am I concerned here with the following fragment of Zawieyski's defense of Kisielewski:

> I know Kisielewski, and I know that under his jester's mask he is not cynical, that, on the contrary, he is a man deeply involved in the life of People's Poland, a righteous, honest, and courageous man.... Stefan Kisielewski, who in the fervor of a speech used some unfortunate phrases [involving the word "dim-wits"], was in fact defending issues he considered important and right.

Let us repeat here that, in 1968, such a defence of Kisielewski required perseverence and determination.

I believe, however, that the greatest moral significance of Zawieyski's action lies in his defense of writers who long ago were involved with socialist realism. They were defended by a writer who paid with years of silence and poverty for his dissension from this kind of literature and for his loyalty to his own religious world view. With the stand he took in 1968, Zawieyski showed that the ex-Stalinists were genuine enemies of the Stalinists (e.g., of Putrament and Czeszko).

Zawieyski's gesture also had a political dimension. By their interpellation and their later actions, he and the other deputies from "Znak" deflated the carefully orchestrated propaganda campaign, according to which the "March" dissident movement was composed only of Jews, cosmopolitans, and ex-Stalinists. Even the most horrendously shameless and false propaganda could not fit Stomma or Zawieyski into one of these categories.

The interpellation and the attitude of "Znak" had tremendous long-range significance. They showed that political divisions are not always identical with denominational divisions, and that the old lines of demarcation were out of date. This was proven once again by Tadeusz Mazowiecki, when, during the deliberations of the Diet's Commission on Science and Education (March 1968), he defended the persecuted students and intellectuals, thereby invoking the wrath of Andrzej Werblan.

Thus, we find the leaders of PZPR and the Catholics from "Pax" and ChSS (United Christian Society) on one side, and the Secular Left and the "Znak" Catholics on the other. In this manner the interpellation gave substance to the articles written in a similar spirit and from the same viewpoints in periodicals like *Tygodnik Powszechny* and, more frequently, *Więź*. Moreover, the interpellation of "Znak" marked a new stage in modern Polish history. Though, we need to remember that, in the eyes of the general public, the interpellation derived the greatest part of its significance from its reflection of the attitude of the episcopate and of the primate of Poland.

* * *

During recent years, the leftist secular intelligentsia has changed its attitude toward the church. The secular intellectuals have stopped opposing the church and propagating official atheism.

Many of them have publicly admitted this change in their point of view.

When Antoni Slonimski was asked why he, a liberal and a rationalist libertarian, was continually publishing in a Catholic periodical when he could choose from so many different magazines, he replied: "Before the war, the church was reactionary and communism was progressive; today, it is the other way around."

This complete shift in attitude toward the church and religion is also demonstrated in the recent writings of Leszek Kolakowski, who is silently considered the principal ideologue of the secular leftist intelligentsia.

Moreover, we should note the fact that the principle of religious freedom found expression in an open letter concerned with the situation of Poles in the Soviet Union (the so-called "Letter of the 15" of December 1974), as well as in a letter critical of proposed changes in the constitution (the so-called "Letter of the 59" of December 1975). Both of these letters were signed by persons connected with leftist intelligentsia circles. But both were also signed —*signum temporis*—by Catholic priests. I consider this change one of the most important in Polish ideological life.

* * *

Still, many of my friends will claim that the church now supports freedom of conscience and belief, freedom of the press and of scientific research, freedom of association and opinion, only because it is itself deprived of these freedoms. But did the bishops defend these freedoms with equal vigor when Catholicism was dominant, during the Second Republic? And will they defend them with equal vigor when Catholicism is once again acknowledged by the state government as the dominant religion, when the altar is once again beside the throne? I will answer that only a blind man can ignore the changes taking place today in Polish Catholicism. In order to see the enormity of these transformations, it is enough to compare the style and the intellectual level of the prewar Catholic press with those of such contemporary periodicals as *Tygodnik Powszechny, Więź,* or *Znak*. A careful reading of the pastoral letters of the episcopate will reveal new, promising elements. However, the fact of a change in the church does not seem to me to be the most important thing. What is most important is not even the fact that the attitudes of the church and the Secular Left toward each other have converged. I am concerned here with matters of principle. Our attachment to human rights would be doubtful if we wanted them only for ourselves. That is why we have the political responsibility of defending the freedoms of the church and the human rights of Christians independently of what we believe the role of the church to have been 40 years ago, or what we believe it will be in another 40 years. Human rights are for everyone or they do not exist for anyone. This is beyond debate.

* * *

However, this does not solve the problem. It is one thing to know the social and political responsibility of the Secular Left, which, under the threat of spiritual self-destruction, must promote the idea of the indivisibility and universality of human rights and must defend all those who are persecuted. But its concern about the actions of the church and the church hierarchy are quite a different thing. These people claim very often with Simone Weil that the church again wants to become "the strongest," that it wants to return to the "Constantine method" of wielding spiritual power. I will explain this notion by citing the arguments of Bohdan Cywiński, who contrasts the idea of a "Constantine Church" with the idea of a "Julian church":

> The idea of Constantininism derives ... from the name of the emperor Constantine, under whose rule the theory of the dual powers, the spiritual and the temporal, found expression for the first time. Julianism [from the name of the emperor Julian the Apostate, who "rejected Christianity and sought to destroy the church"] offers a model of a political situation which is diametrically opposed to the Constantine model. Instead of the collaboration of the dual powers, there exists a conflict. The church finds itself in the opposition. It is deprived of political power, but it retains its moral authority and derives its strength from this fact. There is even, perhaps, a general law describing the situation of the church in a state: its moral authority is inversely proportional to its participation in political power.... Moral authority is the foundation of the Julian church, in the same way power is the foundation of the Constantine church. The Julian church is morally pure, since persecution purges it of opportunists and surrounds it with a special halo: the tradition of Julianism is both indestructible and beautiful. At the same time, Julianism is

certainly related to Constantinism, and they share some common characteristics, especially where the mentality of the clergy is concerned. There is a noticeable temporal connection between the two.... Julianism does not develop by itself; it is rather a contested form of Constantinism, arising where the state has rejected its previous idea of collaboration with the church. It is wrong to claim that the Julian church has spurned political power; it is a church forcibly removed from participation in this power. This fact is important because it determines mentality. During the reign of Julian the Apostate, the Constantine period was probably remembered as a time of correct social organization, and the possibility of a return to the previous patterns was probably awaited with eagerness. The legality of this arrangement introduced by the renegade emperor was never accepted, and the difficult times were endured so the church would later be able to resume its proper social position. Alliance with the state was not renounced; but one waited for the return of a government which would be more appropriate for such an alliance. In the meantime, because of its lack of political power, the church had to be satisfied with its moral authority as the leader of the spiritual opposition. This authority had something in common with the authority of an exiled king, but it was authority nevertheless.

... Constantinism is a participation in power; Julianism is characterized by regret and indignation over the loss of this power, and never by a free renunciation of this power. That is why, for all its spiritual power, the Julian church is never in complete solidarity with society, or fully identified with it. Indeed, it does want society to identify itself with the church, but this is not the same thing. Having been deprived of political power, it fights to retain spiritual leadership over the nation. Thus it does not recognize the existence of other means of achieving the spiritual or ideological integration of the nation, nor does it admit the existence of other forms of opposition against the secular power in addition to those controlled and instigated by itself. If the presence of such outside opposition becomes evident and creates some other ideological alternative for society, allowing the dissidents to organize apart from the church hierarchy, then the Julian church condemns this opposition, or refuses to treat it seriously and disparages it publicly. The Julian church is never eager to collaborate with independent centers of dissident thought. In its conflict with the secular government, the church wants to act alone, without partners, for whom it can feel no solidarity.*

Not one of the members of the Secular Left was able to formulate his concerns with comparable clarity and precision. Our fear is a fear

---

*Bohdan Cywinski, *Rodowody Niepokornych* (Warsaw, 1971), pp. 262–64.

of the Julian politics of the church and of their possible consequences.

This is a serious matter. None of us can deny the enormous contributions of Julianism to the resistance of the church against official violence and lies. However, we should remember that the negative consequences described so well by Cywiński also apply to the church in our own times. Julianism is not only a sequel to Constantinism; it is also the result of loneliness. For as long as the Polish bishops stood alone against the "leading ideology," not only in their defense of the church and religion, but also defending elementary human rights and fundamental humanitarian values, for just so long was Julianism the only possible course of action. As long as the secular opposition expressed its hostile attitude toward the church and religion, Julianism was unavoidable. However, this seems to be changing.

An opposition is slowly crystallizing which, while still proclaiming the traditional values of the Left (freedom, equality, independence), at the same time rejects unequivocally—and hopefully for good—political atheism.

This is an important novelty. Faced with this situation, the Catholic Church will have to decide whether, in the temporal order, the aim of the church is to defend itself or to defend human rights. Does the church desire an authentic freedom for all, including those of other faiths and those who do not believe, or does it want only freedom for itself, for its own educational goals and its own press? Does the church feel freedom for Catholics can be separated from the wider sphere of fundamental freedom for all? Furthermore, does the church desire—and I repeat again that this concerns only the worldly and temporal order—to defend all those who are wronged and humiliated, all who are persecuted and who suffer, or does it seek only the restoration of its own privileged position in the nation? And finally: does the church, separating that which is Caesar's from that which is God's, want to limit its political role to recommendations as general as those contained, for example, in the encyclicals of Paul VI, or does it want to support only confessional political parties? In short, does it want to fulfill its apostolic mission within the framework of the separation of church and state, or does it want to rule over the nation together with the state government?

It is not for me to answer these questions. I should note, however, that for the Secular Left, and perhaps also for the Catholic Left, these questions are not theoretical but absolutely concrete, as concrete as the vision of Poland for which we are fighting.

* * *

To tell the truth, I find the following argument not very convincing: Catholics deserve freedoms (religious, cultural, political, etc.) because they constitute a majority in Polish society. And if they were a minority? Would they then have the right to less freedom, even a little bit less? The rights and freedoms of Catholics should, I believe, be totally independent of the number of people proclaiming themselves Roman Catholics; in any case, Catholics should enjoy the same full rights as Protestants, Muslims, or atheists. The law of the state should regard faith as a private matter.

This is how I understand the principle of secularization: the full separation of church from state, the full separation of state from church, and the full recognition of civil rights. This principle is defined quite differently by Cardinal Wyszyński, who believes secularization to mean a "purging of the faithful citizens and of Catholic religious elements:"

> It is a current that developed toward the end of the eighteenth, and became powerful at the beginning of the nineteenth century. It aspired to the creation of a secular school and morality and, with the state's help, to the secularization of all its political and social institutions. Its phraseology is dragged in from French literature.... Expressions like "école laique" and "morale laique" are from the freemasons and the political-economic liberals when, without consideration for any moral principles, they were lending their strength to this tendency, especially in France. So if we read so much nowadays about the secular state, this is only a warmed-over offering of old stale dishes, which a modern man cannot even swallow. These are outmoded conceptions. The state power has no right to forcibly promote, with the help of public institutions, the so-called secular morality, or secular ritual, especially in a thoroughly Catholic society.*

Perhaps this is a misunderstanding of terminology. If secularization is taken to mean censorship and the decimation of the national culture by the elimination of all religious traditions; if it is under-

---

*Stefan Cardinal Wyszyński, *Kazania Świętokrzyskie* (Rome, 1974), pp. 51–52.

stood as including the use of force by the state to combat Catholic customs and impose different ones; then it is difficult not to agree with the primate. Such "secularization" is then only one more devious mask to conceal the true totalitarian face of the state. However, the arguments of Cardinal Wyszyński can also be understood as a critique of the very principle of the separation of church and state. This confusion of terms in our language is terrible; thanks to the official propaganda, there are more and more words that render comprehension more, rather than less, difficult.

The People's Republic of Poland is not a democratic or a secular country; it is subject to a definite state totalitarian idea. The necessary precondition for the secularization of this country is the elimination of the totalitarian political structure. A secular country is thus a country in which a Christian would not have to "make the terrifying choice between God and Caesar." The idea of a secular country means that "those who choose God would not be tortured by the idolatrous Caesar," and, at the same time, that no one else would be "subjugated to a supposedly Christian Caesar."*

We should recall in this context that, in April 1962, the Polish bishops wrote: "We have no means or riches; we have no material force; and for this lack we thank the Lord, for it frees us from even the temptation to use them."†

In August 1963, the bishops declared:

> We have listened long enough to complaints that in previous generations the hierarchy and the clergy supported the temporal thrones and "bathed" in their glory. Perhaps sometimes it was that way. As a consequence of these past experiences, we should remain as distant as we can from the thrones of the powerful of this world.**

If we could regard these declarations as proof that the church has abandoned all desire of gaining material power in the future, then these statements would correspond to the deep desires of the members of the Secular Left and assuage many of their worries. In that case, I would gladly admit that, in contrasting the opinions of the primate with those of Domenach, I have been tilting at windmills.

---

*Domenach, op. cit., n.p.
†*Listy pasterskie,* p. 258.
**Loc. cit.

I wish it were so. But this does not alleviate other doubts suggested by the above-mentioned fragment from Cardinal Wyszyński's *Kazania Świętokrzyskie.*

I do not understand the argument that some ideas were "dragged in" from France. I believe that our isolation from, and hostility toward, foreign ideas, per se, is a tradition unworthy of continuation. It is only a small step from this to the accusations of cosmopolitanism which are so highly favored by totalitarian dictatorships. These accusations were also used against Christians, and let us recall that the Christian religion is in its origins neither Polish nor Slavic, and was also once "dragged in" to Poland from somewhere else.

It seems to me that Wyszyński's evaluation of liberalism is also unfairly one-sided. It is true that liberal ideas found themselves in conflict with the church in the nineteenth century, but it is rather problematic to reduce all of liberalism to this one position. The anticlericalism of the liberals was probably determined by the position of the church. However, in times of totalitarian dictatorship, this is not the most important point. What is more important, I believe, is that the liberals formulated in a secular language the principles of freedom of conscience and belief, of human rights, the ideas of tolerance and of the parliamentarian system. It is no accident that the accusation of liberalism constitutes the strongest invective in the language of Communist propaganda. The leaders of this system understand very well—often better than the leaders of the church—that the ideas of the followers of Mill undermine totalitarian rule, which breaks the will and destroys the conscience, and that these ideas are not aimed at the Christian religion and the church. An open conflict between the liberal secular intelligentsia and the church is now a closed chapter, hopefully for good, of European history. The ideas of the church, of the Ecumenical Council's constitution, *Gaudium et spes,* and of the encyclicals of Popes John XXIII and Paul VI do not in any way threaten those who believe in the liberal conception of the rights of man. On the contrary, with respect to the main problems of the temporal order, and especially concerning the attitude towards the fundamental rights of man, Christians share identical aspirations with the students of Mill.

Whoever today, here in Poland, combats the Catholic Church in the name of human freedom is either ignorant or is not a liberal. Only ignoramuses or knights of the totalitarian, atheistic reaction armed with liberal phraseology are capable of this. For the true liberal is always on the side of those who defend the rights of man.

I should also briefly mention the masons in this context. Cardinal Wyszyński also slighted them in his sermon. It seems that he was influenced by a very old and even more unjust stereotype. The freemasons were liberals. They aspired to a democratic and secular state, which evoked the hostility of the church hierarchy. But let us repeat: an attitude towards the church should not be the only criterion for judging an ideological movement; and this applies as well to the bishops. One should not forget that, while the freemasons were active in Poland, there was much that was questionable in the attitude of the church. Incidents of "supporting the throne"—and I am using here the formulation of the bishops—were not uncommon. And the church was not always on the side of the defenders of the rights of man in worldly matters. The freemasons, oppressed by the church, contributed to Polish history both through their cultural products and by their uncompromising struggle for the rights of man and of the citizen. This is why they deserve respect and objective judgment. On the other hand, the destruction of national culture and customs carried out by the Communist government under the banner of secularization has nothing to do with masonic traditions.

I am not engaging in this quarrel for historical or erudite reasons. Nor is it because the masons are in need of any defense today: there have been no masonic lodges in Poland for nearly forty years. There is, however, something in our country that is far more dangerous —the myth of an omnipotent masonry. In a situation in which there are no masons, anybody can become one by nomination in the press, just as everyone could become a Jew in 1968. The myth of an "omnipotent freemasonry" may prove to be very convenient for the Communist power elite as a surreptitious mafia responsible for the next "temporary difficulties" or economic crisis. It is a dangerous myth: it cultivates thoughtlessness and strengthens obscurantism. And it may become especially dangerous in crisis situations; it might, just like anti Semitism, inflame anti-intellectual emotions; it may further the search for scapegoats, and encourage totalitarian demagoguery. In conclusion, I will say that the attacks of the church against "liberals and masons" represent a bad tradition. They are associated for the Secular Left with attacks against its most cherished values: freedom, tolerance, and the rights of man. In these attacks we again hear the voice of a past filled with conflicts and rancor.

The values of the Secular Left, as has often been said, grew out of the Christian tradition. These values are today voiced and defended by the church: exemplified by the constitutions of the Ecumenical Council, by the pastoral letters of the Polish bishops, and by the often lonely but always unyielding defense by the primate of Poland of freedom, tolerance, and the rights of man. For many years, however, the Secular Left and the church had understood these values and their defense in very different ways. In the view of the Secular Left, these values had to be defended against the church, since the ideals of the rights of man and the aspirations of the church seemed to be in opposition. As a result, Polish culture underwent a split: the "radical Pole," equipped with secular ethics and the ideas of the rights of man, diverged from the "Catholic Pole," who was conscious of his responsibilities towards God and the Fatherland. These were dramatic and long-lasting conflicts. Only Communist totalitarianism and the consciousness that common values were being threatened led to an eventual rapprochement. These values proved to be common indeed, despite the fact that both the Secular Left and the church had denied this for a long time. And I cannot believe that anyone from the church would deny this today. For it was precisely in defense of these common values that many spiritual children of the "masons and liberals," together with priests, signed letters concerning the proposed amendments to the constitution based on the Soviet model (the so-called "Letter of the 59" and the "Letter of the 101"), which were, incidentally, similar in their basic postulates to the pronouncements of the episcopate. This similarity is spectacular evidence of the rapprochement. At the same time, the church made a noble and far-sighted gesture: the episcopate defended the repressed signatories.

The road towards this rapprochement has been complicated, crooked, full of zigzags and misunderstandings that cannot disappear overnight. The easing of past tensions and prejudices will take time. If, however, the encounter of the Secular Left with Christianity is to be authentic, then both must strive for the truth. Hopefully it will be so; though the historical sense of this encounter may be understood in different ways. For some, it might be "a temporary cease-fire," or a tactical alliance. But for others, including myself, the encounter of the Secular Left with the church and Christianity constitutes, above all, a great opportunity for Polish culture. It creates hope for overcoming the ghetto mentality, for a permanent overstepping of the "chalk circles." It creates hope for eliminating the strict division into two camps, secular and Catholic, and replacing it with a pluralist unity within our culture. All will benefit from it. Catholics will remain Catholics, while the nonbelievers will remain nonbelievers; but the destructive ghetto climate will at least lessen. In this unified but by no means homogeneous culture, there will be a place for both Catholics and liberals, since both are necessary. This explains why the Secular Left must be concerned about the church's attacks on freemasonry.

It can be said that this argument is nothing but a utopian fantasy. However, as Antoni Slonimski says, what would life be like without such fantasies?

* * *

It is not for me to advise the church about its attitude toward secular circles and secularization, but I do feel justified in supposing that the church will speak with authority to these circles only if it addresses the problems of concern for this community, and if it replaces its position of defensive hostility with an attitude conducive to well-meaning dialogue.

* * *

We have used the word "dialogue." The word is ambiguous, often misused, and variously interpreted; an idea easy to explain but difficult to realize.

* * *

When I speak of a "dialogue" with Christianity, I do not have in mind intellectual sword play or a tactical power struggle; instead I am concerned with elementary human values. From the encounter of the Polish Secular Left with Christianity in an antitotalitarian resistance came their dialogue.

This encounter has three dimensions: as an encounter with God, with the church as an institution, and with Christianity as a system of values. From the Catholic perspective, the most important of these is doubtless the encounter of many former atheists with God, which often leads to their conversion. These are difficult personal and private matters. I do not feel qualified to write about them. I cannot interpret these phenomena. However, to completely omit this dimension would impoverish and falsify the problems with which we are concerned.

Speaking very generally, we can observe in recent years an increase in religious interest, and a turning towards religion on the part of many people who, until recently, were nonbelievers. This phenomenon is not a kind of tactic or an attempt to subordinate religion and the church to definite political goals. I will address this problem in a moment. Here I am writing of those who are seeking an internal moral order in transcendence, of those whose encounter has given new meaning to their lives.

This dimension of the new situation is most important for the Christians and generally most difficult for the nonbelievers. It is easier to accept the presence of the visible church than the sphere of invisible and incomprehensible phenomena. Yet, without the acknowledgment of this sphere, real pluralism is impossible. Otherwise, the Christian will view the nonbeliever as a cripple or a cynic, while the nonbeliever will see the Christian as a charlatan or a dim-witted simpleton. Denominational and ideological ghettos will continue to exist. Our lives will be impoverished by ignoring what might serve to encourage a fruitful confrontation of ideas among people who think differently, but who aspire in their different ways to similar goals of humanism and truth.

*　　*　　*

The second dimension of the new situation, insofar as it stems from the historical vicissitudes of the encounter between the church as an institution and the Secular Left, has been our main subject. Before we can examine what the expectations of the Secular Left should be with respect to the church, we need to clearly specify what they should not be.

The change in our orientation toward the church and our rejection of political atheism should not be confused with an attitude of total apostasy. A man of the Secular Left is not a renegade from the entire system of values he previously espoused. Such renegades, and many of them exist in our intellectual circles, switch from one extreme to another, damn all that is leftist, and affirm the classical schemes of conservative thought. Yesterday a member of the PZPR, today he sings the praises of the Middle Ages; in his hatred of communism he espouses the virtues of serfdom; he replaces, as someone aptly put it, "yesterday's foolishness with the one from the day before yesterday." He is more popish than the pope and more Catholic than the primate of Poland. However, at the same time, he demonstrates an open aversion to public actions in defense of human rights, and carefully avoids them.

I do not question the personal honesty of some of the representatives of this tendency, but I hold a very different position. I am prone to see numerous dangers in the ostentatious anti-Communism and philo-Catholicism of the former PZPR members. I believe that their anti-Communism is not equivalent to antitotalitarianism; it reflects conservative paternalism in social life and thus disguises hostility to democratic principles and social equality. This kind of ideological construction makes it extremely easy for one to reconcile simple conformism with patriotic phraseology. According to this view, the Catholic Church is the only defense of the nation against sovietization, and therefore the nation should restrict its opposition to religious practices. I believe that this is a dangerous attempt to reduce religion to its nonreligious functions, and a dangerous abrogation of one's own responsibility for the fate of one's country. For it is not true that the mission of the church can replace political and social activism; while it is true that the desire to make this substitution indicates a completely utilitarian attitude toward the church and religion.

The current change in attitudes should not mean that we will begin to regard the church as a political ally. The church is not a political party, and it is both unrealistic and harmful to expect it to act like one. This is independent of whether we see the church as progovernment, rightist, leftist, conservative, or revolutionary. The task of the church is to teach the gospel, and no unequivocal political program can be derived from the gospel without abuse. A contrary point of view must lead to an exploitation of religious institutions and of religion itself. The teachings of the gospel are something different, something both greater and more narrow than any political ideology; they are neither leftist nor rightist. There exists a definite current of rightist thought that refers to these teachings and strives to remain loyal to their principles; and there also exists such tendencies in the leftist camp. The principles of the gospel were inscribed on the banners of both the Right and the Left, and were also trampled by governments of both the Right and the Left. The gospel does not belong to anyone. For Christians it is the revealed Word; for nonbelievers it should represent a code of inviolable moral principles. Thus, if the Left is loyal to the teachings of the gospel, then the gospel will be on the side of the Left. In this sense we can speak of a basic community of fundamental human values shared by the church and the Secular Left, but this community is by no means identical with a political alliance and it would be wrong to understand it in this way. Such a misunderstanding would represent an attempt to identify religion with politics, to subordinate the transcendent functions of the Catholic Church to the temporal and worldly plans and political interests of the Left. We know from the past that such attempts have never led to anything beneficial for either religion or politics.

What, then, can the Secular Left expect from the church? First, the Left must accept the specific suprapolitical and transcendent apostolic mission. This is not a call for conversion, but for the acceptance of reality. As long as the Left views the apostolic mission of the church as charlatanism, it will not find understanding among church members. Conversely, as long as the church judges people only according to their participation in religious worship, it will find the Left its principal adversary. This is unavoidable unless both sides are willing to accept pluralism as a lasting element of Polish reality. The Secular Left needs to understand that the church and religion are not outmoded relics, that they are not diminishing and temporary phenomena, but rather an indispensable part of the social, moral, and intellectual reality of Poland.

In Poland, the Secular Left is in a very difficult situation. It must defend its socialist ideals against an antinational totalitarian government brandishing socialist slogans. It seems, therefore, that precisely because of this, the defense must be unrelenting, consistent, and uncompromising. It must be free of sectarianism, fanaticism, and outmoded schemes. Leftist thought must be open to all ideas of independence and antitotalitarianism, open to Christianity and to the entire spiritual wealth of the Christian religion. The members of the Secular Left should welcome fraternization with all men of good will, including Christians—not despite their faith, but thanks to this faith. Believers in humanist socialism should wish for every persecuted Christian to see in them his closest and most honest friends. Only then will they become worthy of their great predecessors from the early years of this century; only then will they live up to their principles; only then can there be a rebirth of authentic Polish socialist thought. Socialism, which I understand as an intellectual and moral movement, can be reborn in Poland not as the result of unsavory alliances and equivocal compromises with one or another faction in the party, but only through an uncompromising struggle for the freedom and dignity of man and a thorough and honest reevaluation of the past.

For us—the Secular Left—the encounter with Christianity, centering on such values as tolerance, justice, human dignity and the search for truth, opens the way for encounters free from material interests, and it promises an ideological community in a new dimension, important for the formulation of the direction of our struggle for democratic socialism. The Polish experience in these matters, our ability to live together in mutual respect, solidarity, and community as a Secular Left free of thoughtless atheism, with Christians free of religious intolerance, may also be helpful for other antitotalitarian leftist movements in other countries and other parts of the world.

*translated by Olga Amsterdamskaya
with assistance from Gene Moore*

HUNGARY

PREFACE

In the wake of the political upheavals and economic setbacks suffered by most countries in the Soviet bloc since the 1950s, a growing intellectual ferment has been taking place in some—if not all—Communist countries. Next to Poland, this is perhaps most prominent in Hungary. The Czech experiment of 1968, which tried to give a "human face" to Communism, was something quite different; in contrast to Hungarian and Polish intellectuals, who criticized the regime from the outside, the Czech Communist party tried to reform itself.

Following the tragedy of 1956,* the Communist regime pursued a policy of gradual reconciliation with the sullen and disillusioned Hungarian people. While their real power base has remained the Soviet military power, they succeeded in gaining—sometimes grudging, sometimes cynical, sometimes simply resigned, but, to a significant extent, genuine—acceptance of their rule.

The introduction of the "New Economic Mechanism" in the sixties allowed a measure of decentralization, a partial application of the profit motive, a limited freedom for small-scale private enterprise, leading to a not insignificant and quite broadly-based rise in the standard of living. Perhaps for the first time in modern history, a large majority of the Hungarian people has a disposable income —and the goods to spend it on. Even Miklós Haraszti, one of the prominent opposition critics of the regime, admits, "The material satisfaction of the masses is an undeniable achievement of Hungarian post-Stalinism."

The editors would like to acknowledge their gratitude to George Schopflin (son of Julian Schopflin—author of this preface and translator of this section) for his kind assistance in the selection of the following articles.

*In October–November 1956, the Hungarian people rose in spontaneous revolt against the oppressive and economically disastrous regime, swept away Communist party rule, forced the Russians to withdraw from the capital and part of the country, and, within the scope of a few days, tried to set up a pluralistic political system based on neutrality. However, the Russians returned and crushed the freedom struggle by overwhelming military force, reinstating a Communist puppet government, which, in turn, carried out a savage retribution, executing thousands—among them Imre Nagy, the erstwhile Communist prime minister of free Hungary during its brief existence. About 200,000 people fled from Hungary during the conflict.

Part of the price paid for this modest affluence is heavy indebtedness to Western finance. This, in turn, leads to increased sensitivity by the regime to Western public opinion, which has to be balanced by unquestioning obedience to the Soviet Union, especially in foreign affairs, but also in maintaining the rigid primacy of their own Communist party.

The government has also, to a modest extent, loosened its grip on the intellectual life of the nation. Their slogan is, "Whoever is not against us, is with us." Debate and argument became somewhat freer, artistic life was allowed to range more widely, limited contacts with Western cultural life were permitted, travel to Europe and elsewhere has been facilitated, visits by exiles, and others, to Hungary encouraged. Historical and sociological studies (the latter were practically forbidden in the Stalinist period) could be undertaken beyond the limits of previous orthodoxy, as long as they paid a minimal lip-service to Marxism.

However, some deliberately vague and unwritten rules remain in the form of "taboos" (e.g., frank criticism of the Soviet Union, or questioning the legality of Communist rule). For someone who oversteps these hazy boundaries, official measures are applied without hesitation: loss of jobs, confiscation of manuscripts, police and court action, occasionally forcible exile. All this is done, however, in a slightly gentler and sometimes more sophisticated manner than the crude repression of Czech intellectuals and Russian dissidents.

One remarkable feature of this reconciliation has been the acceptance—often quite wholehearted—of the status quo by a fair number of opinion leaders, economists, scientists, publicists, writers, and artists. They consider their circumscribed freedom for expression (sometimes allowing them even more moderate and "constructive" criticism of abuses or shortcomings) as a valuable achievement. Many of them have become spokesmen for the regime; thereby contributing to the good press enjoyed recently by Hungary in the West. And they consider any attempt to extend these limited liberties as dangerous.

Their concern is, perhaps, understandable. Democratic traditions in Hungary have always been very weak; at the same time, the state —semi-Fascist under Horthy, Stalinist under Rákosi—has almost always been a strong force for progress, against a rather conservative society. The intellectuals have, therefore, always served in advisory or managerial positions, with the accompanying privileges.

Meanwhile, a number of young intellectuals—writers, philosophers, economists, and so on—who grew up and were schooled in strait-laced Marxism, have begun questioning the validity and relevance, both in theory and practice, of the official creed. Often they still retain Marxist concepts and methodology (and jargon); but their dissatisfaction with the state of affairs, the spiritual lassitude, and social immobilism—also their reaction to the above-mentioned intellectual conformity of formerly revered masters—have, nonetheless, led them increasingly to a trenchant criticism of Marxism. They have read widely, going back to the original writings of Marx and his followers, studying Western Marxist literature, and following with interest similar attempts in the Soviet Union and other Communist countries.

In attitude they range widely: some of them, at first, try to salvage and rejuvenate Marxism (Márkus, in his 1968 treatise published here) or at least make practical use of its concepts (Bauer); at the other extreme, some reject it completely (Endreffy, Haraszti). A few of them may search for a solution in spiritual fields, touching on the religious (Endreffy), but this does not seem to be deeply significant to their general stance. (It might mirror certain stirrings in Hungary: while the established churches are quiescent, having made some sort of peace with the regime, a number of religious sects have become more active; such as Jehovah's Witnesses, Nazarenes, Methodists.)

The writings of those who tackle Marx and his school head-on manifest an apparent dichotomy, insofar as they tend to limit themselves to theory and disregard, or only touch on in passing, its practice. This may be partly due to their general conclusion—which many, like Márkus, came to after first attempting to recreate and expand a Marxist framework for philosophy—that Marxism (and its integration of theory and practice) is irrelevant. What is more, they have found it also to be irrelevant to the Communist regime in its largely pragmatic policy making, beyond the ceremonial obeisances to certain convenient tenets of Marxist dogma.

The aftermath of 1956 and the suppression of the Prague Spring in 1968—which shattered their hopes of reform and constructive change from inside any Communist party and ended any political "loosening-up" among the constituent countries of the Soviet empire—taught them the bitter lesson that neither revolt nor thoroughgoing reform can be expected to solve the problems of their society in the short run. They themselves have felt the heavy hand of the regime when they occasionally violated the "taboos." (The *cause célèbre* was the sentence of Haraszti in 1973 for his, at that time unpublished manuscript, *Worker in a Worker's State* [New York: Universe Books, 1978], dealing with the parlous state of the working class in Hungary.)

So it is ironic that, on the one hand, they demand more freedom of expression and communication—in particular, the freedom to abandon any kind of self-censorship—on the other hand, they are cautious in their statements, use a somewhat circuitous, oblique style, heavy with hints, inviting the reader to "read between the lines." They generally reject any solution that, in their eyes, may lead to "catastrophe" (i.e., to a new Soviet intervention or war; see the Bence and Kis essay).

For much the same reasons, they do not try to form organized groups (which could be accused of "factionalism" in Marxist parlance, immediately subject to suppression by the party and the state) but operate as individuals or, at most, as loose debating societies with ever-shifting personnel.

What are, then, the aims of this disjointed opposition (if it can, indeed, be called an opposition)? Their aims are modest: to be free of the need for self-censorship (at least in the theoretical field); to establish a network of communications, by distributing their works in manuscript—this is the meaning of *samizdat* (literally "self-publication" in Russian)—to meet in occasional discussion groups without fear of police raids; to reach that 0.1 percent of the population that might be interested in their ideas. Their hope is that in this way they may gradually, almost imperceptibly, push further back the limits to freedom of expression.

In addition, they want to remain within the bounds of legality, partly to avoid any pretext for state intervention, partly to exert some moral pressure on the regime, so that it too should observe and honor its own laws and the constitution. (The Hungarian Constitution, on paper, is quite liberal but with a number of catch-all loopholes, such as the statute against "bringing the State and the Government into disrepute," etc.) In this, they parallel the tactics of the Czech "Chartists" and Russian dissidents.

Politically speaking, their impact is rather limited. In contrast to Polish intellectuals, they seem to have no links with the working class or the peasantry (the remnants of the Hungarian populist movement—quite significant in the prewar period and some time after—have been largely coopted by the regime). They do not see themselves as a powerful social catalyst; the *samizdat*—in Haraszti's words—is not an answer to a crisis, only to the deadening of sensitivity born of conformism. They have somewhat vague ideas about a "more democratic" socialism; but it should be noted that, generally speaking, they do not consider capitalism a satisfactory alternative.

The regime, of course, keeps a watchful eye on their activities but, in the present social climate, does not see much relevance in their doings (as long as they "don't rock the boat"). After all, a wise tyranny will allow a measure of *ius murmurandi* (the right to grumble).

The price they have to pay for their dissent is "marginalization." This is a comparatively recent phenomenon in Eastern Europe: those who come into conflict with official ideology, or simply want to opt out, are not actively persecuted but tolerated "on the margins" of society. The official media may be denied them, they may not work in their own profession in official posts; but they are allowed to take subordinate jobs, intellectual "piecework" (such as translations, data collection, some fieldwork), and are allowed to express their views in *samizdat* form.

In Hungary, true *samizdat* did not arise until the early seventies (the Márkus treatise included here, for instance, was published in an officially sponsored quality literary magazine in 1968, *Kortárs—Contemporary*). At first, it included mainly translations from Western political and sociological literature, then the fruits of the Polish opposition were distributed in manuscript form; gradually, however, original essays, discussion papers, answers to questionnaires appeared in growing numbers (the essays included here by Bauer, Bence-Kis, Endreffy, and Haraszti appeared in a larger collection titled *Marx in the Fourth Decade*, which consisted of replies to the question put by András Kovács: "What does Marxism mean to you today?").

In view of their dilemmas and of their situation, it is no surprise that many of the writers in this selection are somewhat pessimistic. Nevertheless, their work is both proof of the dead end at which Communist societies have arrived intellectually, and a testimony to the unbreakable human spirit, offering some modest hope for the future.

Julian Schopflin

DEBATES AND TRENDS IN MARXIST PHILOSOPHY

GYORGY MARKUS

The revivalist activity, promising the beginnings of a renaissance in Marxism, that has been going on in philosophical thought throughout the world in the last decade or so, cannot be divorced from a significant change in viewing this philosophy. The monotony of the period of the "personality cult," which led to a complete "depersonalization" of philosophers—when "debate" simply meant, in the majority of cases, the unanimous condemnation of "mistaken views," defined as such in advance—changed to a mien of creative argument. In this very moment, debates are going on in practically all areas of international Marxist literature—from the definition of the concept of "matter," to an interpretation of historical determinism; whether the "negation of negation" is truly a law of reality; whether a Marxist "anthropology" can exist or not; what is the basic social/spiritual function of art; and so on.

Thus our philosophy is today rich in arguments. But can we talk about *trends* within Marxist philosophy as a whole, apart from technical questions? It is a fact that there are nowadays several schools of thought, especially in specialist philosophical disciplines such as aesthetics and the theory of logic, which accept the general principles of Marxism and its conceptual apparatus, but approach the problems of their own field in contrasting ways, often arriving at contradictory results. It is also accepted that a *Gleichschaltung* (a term originally used by the Nazis meaning "enforced conformity" or "leveling") of these different viewpoints, or indeed their "adminis-

---

György Márkus (1934–   ). Graduated from the Lomonosov University, Moscow, in the fifties. Assistant Professor of Philosophy, University of Budapest, 1957–59. On staff of the Institute of Philosophy, Hungarian Academy of Sciences, 1960–68. Expelled from Communist party and dismissed from his job in 1968, following a joint protest against the Soviet occupation of Czechoslovakia. In 1973, Márkus coauthored with György Bence and János Kis "Anti-kapital," a critique of Marx's theory distributed in manuscript. It earned the official condemnation of the Communist party. And in 1978, Márkus emigrated to Australia.

trative" liquidation would greatly harm the normal development of our ideology. But can this view be extended to the *totality* of Marxist philosophy, in particular as this philosophy is not just another academic discipline, not only one clearly defined theoretical system, but the conscious Weltanschauung of a practical, revolutionary movement?

The question: "Can we talk about trends in Marxist philosophy?" really touches on two problems. Are there today more or less crystallized, distinct tendencies within Marxist philosophy? And, if so, can this phenomenon be considered normal; generally speaking, what should be our view of it, bearing in mind the optimum theoretical development of our philosophy and its ideological and social impact? To answer these questions, first of all we have to clarify, what do we understand by a "trend" in Marxist philosophy. In the following discussion, I am going to use this concept in a very clearcut manner, as befits the current situation in my view. I shall only speak of trends where they involve *different approaches towards the task and "object"* of Marxist philosophy, and where the relevant views engender a clearly defined "research program," to specify certain philosophical problems and a suitable methodology, leading to a coherent, well-established distinctiveness both in content and in point of view—at least in the solution of specific problems. (Naturally we can only speak of a "trend" where the program reflects not only the views of one single philosopher, however eminent, but those of a group; and where it has passed beyond mere pronouncements and has led to some actual results.)

So if, within the scope of this definition, we now ask the first question: *Are there* different trends in Marxist philosophy today? I think any objective survey of international Marxist literature clearly compels us to answer: *Yes.* I cannot even attempt to give a sketchy overview of all the directions in Marxist philosophy today, largely because I do not have the necessary comprehensive knowledge of international Marxist literature. Thus, we have to limit ourselves to an outline of some schools of thought perhaps selected in a somewhat subjective manner.

Of all these trends, in view of its wide acceptance and effect, the most important is the one characterized by the definition of *extent* in Marxist philosophy (I will restrict myself to brief, shorthand descriptions of the standpoints in question). This concept—going back, undoubtedly, to certain philosophical works of Engels and

Lenin (most directly to *Anti-Dühring* [in which Engels first formulated his theory of dialectical materialism] and *Materialism and Empiriocriticism* [in which Lenin updated the theory of the inevitability of revolution]) is so well known that its more detailed analysis is superfluous. I trust it will suffice to mention that, according to this view, Marxist philosophy is the science of all *general* laws of reality, i.e., of nature, society, and thought, in contrast to *special* scientific disciplines confined to specific laws of natural phenomena and systems. Philosophy is seen to *generalize* and thereby *synthesize* the results of specialist sciences into a uniform worldview and ideology; at the same time it also gives them a set of methodological directives. Besides dialectical materialism conceived in this manner, if we add another organic constituent of a unitary Marxism, our definition is complete: the science aimed at establishing the characteristic general laws of the development of *society*—historical materialism.

Perhaps because this view is so well established in common knowledge, and thus often identified with Marxist philosophy as such, it might be desirable to outline the history of its evolution; in its crystallized form it only became dominant in the thirties, although, as I have noted, not without antecedents and traditions.

It is not well known that the idea of *"Marxist philosophy"* (apart from the founders of Marxism) is relatively novel. This idea sounded strange, indeed paradoxical, to the leading theoreticians of the Second International. For them, Marxism was *not* a philosophy but a definitive *social* concept, similar to the natural sciences: a "positive" science—independent of value-judgments and ideological standpoints—capable of describing and explaining the inception, development, and extinction not only of capitalism but of *every* social structure. According to the views of certain leading theoreticians of German social democracy (e.g., of Mehring), Marxism finally extinguishes, indeed denies, philosophy as a speculative fantasy; others attempted to "complete" the social theory of Marxism with certain cultural and ethical views borrowed from the philosophy of various bourgeois thinkers (for instance, from Kant; from Bernstein and Max Adler; or, from biological evolutionism influenced by early philosophical positivism as regards Kautsky). These philosophical differences were considered unimportant for the socialist movement and its theory: Kautsky once explicitly declared that philosophical views are a purely "private" matter.

In these circumstances, the question of the existence of a Marxist *philosophy* was not at all natural, and its pronouncement became identical with the struggle for the *universality* of Marxist ideology, with the fight against the opportunism of the Second International, against interpreting proletarian ideology in the spirit, and within the framework, of bourgeois ideology. Therefore it is no odd chance that this idea was, almost exclusively, propounded by revolutionary Russian social democracy, first and foremost by Lenin, but also partly by Plechanov. Similarly, it was no coincidence that this idea gained international recognition through the impact of the October Revolution. In this, the struggle for establishing the ideological universality of Marxism gained a decisive practical importance, creating the preconditions for the *cultural hegemony* of the proletariat (to use Gramsci's expression), without which, in the final analysis, the building of socialism is impossible.

In the twenties two quite distinct views emerged within the international Communist movement, concerning the essence and function of Marxist philosophy. One of these can be best characterized by the names of Gramsci, Lukács, and K. Korsch. Whilst they did not create a recognizable grouping as such, in their theoretical investigations they went back to the known works of Marx and, inspired by his statements, *fundamentally* rejected the ideology of the Second International. In their view, the social and historical theory of Marxism is basically philosophical and ideological and thus cannot be interpreted on the analogy of the natural sciences, by stating laws *independent* of human activities and intentions and thereby forecasting a deterministic march of events. The philosophy of Marxism is the "philosophy of practice," indeed in a dual sense. It is partly in the sense that—according to the basic ideas of this philosophy—Man creates himself and his history through his own activities and *by* these activities: his evolution therefore cannot be deduced from some abstract, generalized law or necessity; every turning point in his history depends on the conflict of social forces, the actual revolutionary class struggle, which arises from objective social conditions nurtured by previous human actions. And again, it is the "philosophy of practice" insofar as it consists in the theoretical ascertainment of the objective conditions, opportunities, and goals of present social struggles—and as such, it is an active factor in the fight of the proletariat for the realization of Communism.

Of course we have no possibility even to try to characterize the basic constituents of this view. I am convinced that these thinkers of the twenties and thirties could not always give satisfactory answers to the problems arising from their views. It seems that they had the greatest difficulty in clarifying the relationship between the objectivity of nature and human activities. In the case of Lukács and Korsch, this has sometimes led to illogical, indeed idealistic explanations of certain problems.* At the same time, I believe it would be unfair to evaluate these works strictly in terms of these mistakes, however serious their historical consequences (as pointed out by István Hermann, in his recent essay on "History and Class Consciousness," by Lukács). Not only because, in the first place, these works did contain some deep and fruitful problem-definitions and solutions, apart from some "erroneous" ideas, but also because the general approach of this trend in Marxist philosophy, emerging both explicitly and implicitly from these works, represents a fertile tradition. Many present tendencies in Marxism turn back to this source, albeit with significant critical qualifications.

This trend, however, was suppressed and, indeed, disappeared from Marxist philosophy in the early thirties. At that time the "standard" conception of Marxist philosophy became dominant, as indicated earlier on. Although the definitive "codification" of this concept (nowadays generally considered as a vulgarization or rather a deformation of Marxism) was completed by Stalin in "Dialectical and Historical Materialism" (1939), its formulation had begun earlier, in the disputes of Soviet philosophers in the twenties and early thirties, following the gradual reinterpretation and systematization of the philosophical works of the classics.

These debates started with an attack on the representatives of the ProletKult† movement who denied all philosophy (e.g., Yenchmen and Minyin): they were succeeded by the polemics between the

---

*Lukács himself underlined this most sharply—in some ways perhaps a bit one-sidedly—in a recent treatise critically assessing his own work of that period. The treatise was published as Preface to Volume II of his works published in German (Luchterhand Verlag, 1968).

†*ProletKult:* the cultural arm of the Communist movement, started by Gorky and others in 1909. Its aim was to represent the life and aspirations of the proletariat, with performers drawn from among the workers. It tried to develop new forms of expression, the mass prose chorus being an example. The movement declined in the twenties and became extinct under Stalin. German Communists tried to revive it in the early thirties (Brecht, Piscator). (J.S.).

mechanicists (Stepanov, Timiryazev, Varjas) and the dialecticians*
(Dyeborin, Luppol, Larayev, et al.). Already, the basic features of
this longstanding, "standard" concept were clearly visible in the
views of Dyeborin and his group, following the footsteps of Plechanov. Expelled from philosophical life in 1931 (largely for political reasons), the ideas of this group were nevertheless elaborated
—with certain important corrections—in a series of textbooks, treatises, etc., though now completely forgotten. The work of Stalin
essentially concluded this trend.

Stalin's conception of "extent" (or rather his formulation) also
completely rejects the nonphilosophical or antiphilosophical views
of the Second International theoreticians and emphasizes the philosophical and ideological character of Marxist social and historical
theory. At the same time, in regard to social theory, it retains,
indeed extends the precedent characterization. The basis and essence of historical materialism is, for Stalin too, the analysis of
developmental laws of history, similar to natural laws. These can be
recognized by humans (according to one of his last works) and can
be applied by them, either limiting or promoting their action by the
creation of suitable conditions, but these laws cannot be changed or
repealed by their activities. These general laws of social development are of a philosophical nature because in a certain sense they
are the *consequences* of the general laws of reality, as defined by
dialectical materialism: that is, historical materialism is the "extension" and "application" of the tenets of dialectical materialism to
the phenomena of social life.

How are we to assess the real social and theoretical consequences
of this philosophical standpoint? This depends, to a large extent, on
how we view the fundamental disputes going on in Marxism nowadays. Perhaps we can point out here that, in fact—and in general
opinion—this particular interpretation of Marxist philosophy has
achieved recognition and acceptance throughout the world. It is
also a fact that for many decades this concept has offered a conceptual apparatus and a schema to practically all forms of Marxist social
analysis and thus without question has served as a functional methodology—with what results, of course, can well be debated. (In the

---

* *Mechanicists* and *dialecticians:* obscure schools of thought in Russia during the rule of Lenin. Mechanicists emphasized the importance of industry and technology to Marxism; dialecticians attempted to apply the philosophical theory of dialectics to everyday life. (J.S.)

natural sciences, we can hardly speak of a similar functional methodology in practical terms.)

At the same time, some profoundly harmful consequences of the actual *realization* of this concept are only too well known. In the philosophical practice of the "cult of personality," the generalized rules of reality consisted of giving constant "theoretical" justification (or rather final validation) to previously made political decisions, thereby acting as ideological rationalization to current politics. The concept also offered, if not a theoretical basis, at least theoretical clothing to coarse "administrative" intervention into the problems and debates of certain special scientific disciplines. All this had a serious effect on the content of this philosophical attitude. The fact that in these "applications" the relevant philosophical theses were used artificially, often in a meaningless or contradictory manner, made them completely "fluid." The philosophical debates of the last decade, if nothing else, have exposed the logical and conceptual muddle, obscurity and indeed often metaphorical character of the philosophical categories and statements current in that period. This practice of ideological treatment at the same time forbade every independent, creative theoretical thinking and reduced all Marxist philosophers, with one exception, to the role of propagandists. In consequence, the investigation of new problems thrown up by social or cultural development ceased almost completely, the conceptual apparatus of Marxist philosophy became incredibly impoverished and vulgarized, the field of permitted problems was severely limited and its debating capacity against modern bourgeois tendencies reduced.

All these deformations and shortcomings have been known and recognized as such for some time. The majority of Marxist philosophers directed their activity in the last decade to weeding out these negative features, these theoretical deformations created by Stalin, while fundamentally maintaining the concept of "extent" in Marxist philosophy. Many attempts have been made to enrich the conceptual content of Marxist philosophy evolved in the period of the "personality cult," to make it more flexible as well as precise. This went hand in hand with the scrutiny of the actual meaning of several statements. The greater part of philosophical debates in our day is related to these tasks. I have no opportunity to digress on the results of this activity, nor on the difficulties and problems encountered. From our point of view, the important thing is that in the course of this reappraisal, one particular group of Marxist philosophers (not insignificant in numbers) has raised some general critical comments not only pinpointing the faults in *realization* of the Stalinist concept, but also questioning the whole justification of the concept of "extent" in Marxist philosophy.* This criticism, although it reflected differing ideas, occupied the same basis for its main lines of approach. (To make things quite clear, I must state that I myself share their views.)

First of all it has been contested whether the concept of "generalized laws" is capable of delimiting the specific field of philosophical investigations from that of the specialist scientific disciplines. On the one hand, there are certain scientific statements (like some very general physical laws) that are valid for all phenomena without exception, but do not belong to philosophy; on the other hand, Marxist philosophy has certain branches, of particular importance to us today (ethics, aesthetics, theory of knowledge, etc.), which do not fit at all into these general philosophical definitions. Even the philosophical nature of historical materialism is difficult to explain on a generalized basis: it is no coincidence that serious arguments developed around this question in the middle fifties. The majority of philosophers representing this critical attitude—following Marx —call attention to the "man-centeredness" of philosophical questions, completely left out of the concept of "extent." The philosophical importance of a phenomenon or problem is defined not by how far it is general, but by how far its recognition can influence the formation of a conscious and rational social attitude in people. As the set of such problems itself necessarily changes in a historical context, along with the evolution of society and culture, any definitive staking out of the area of philosophy—whether of "extent" or any other definition—becomes a very doubtful enterprise.

Another related view contests that Marxist philosophy is an ideology and one of an historical movement whose purpose is the radical transformation of societal life. The question is, does this ideology command enough content to satisfy the functions of comprehensiveness? The historical approach of the concept of "ex-

---

*This necessarily included the scrutiny of certain philosophical statements by Engels and Lenin, at least in their customary interpretation. Generally speaking it must be emphasized that all trends of Marxist philosophy dealt with here involve a reappraisal of the philosophical tradition embodied in the classics. For obvious reasons, I cannot go into the details of this in the scope of these short descriptions.

tent," represented by Stalin, gave an unqualified "Yes" to this question; and it was justified in this at least to the extent that it attempted to deduce the general characteristics and laws of social development (indeed, in practice, going beyond this, by applying these deductions to political decisions) from these laws which have a universal application. But how far can we accept this "deduction," how far can we make it congruent with the fundamental ideas of Marx on history and society, namely with the thesis that Man *himself* creates his history and therefore it can only be understood through the analysis of actual practice, carried out by people acting within given conditions? How far can we accept the deduction of the basic features of historical development from laws having cosmic validity in the light of Marx's always heavily emphasized thesis that no philosophical "schema" or "recipe" *can* give an explanation of the true history of society, whether these are based on natural necessities or supernatural goals.

On the other hand, if we reject this "deduction" (as this happens even with Marxist philosophers who do accept the "standard" concept of "extent"), what is the *ideological* content of these "general laws"? In our standard philosophical literature there are quite a few theses (e.g., those of the universal correlations and interactions of phenomena or that of the universality of movement and change, etc.) which are without doubt true: but they seem to be rather distant from the current debates and problems of modern science, as well as from the ideological questions relevant to people today, insofar as they have a bearing on their social behavior. These distant problems may have played a serious role in the history of ideological struggles, but today they have become rather trivial truths; there is, therefore, little reason to attribute central importance to them, when we are considering their social functions of philosophy.

At the same time, "standard" literature suffers from the reverse problem in respect to various philosophical categories (such as dialectical contradiction, negation, etc.). In Marx, these ideas had a primarily social dimension. However, beginning with Engels, they were generalized and extended to natural phenomena and without conceptual clarification, thus resulting in not a few contradictions. The demand for conceptual/logical clarification, for the sharpening up of ideas is therefore fully justified today. However, given recent experience it is also justified to ask whether the consistent "extension" of these categories does not lead to loss of content, most important and most essential from the point of view of ideology? If the category of contradiction can be equally applied to atomic particles, biological evolution, and, say, the relationship between induction and deduction in logic, then can it be said that the idea of the "*struggle* of contradictions" (according to Lenin, the central idea of dialectics) is anything more than simply a misleading and unusable metaphor?*

I believe it is not unjustified—in the light of the debates in philosophy over the last decade—to ask the question: does not our philosophy, based on the concept of "extent," run certain risks? While it may offer a valid opposition to the traditional forms of quasi-religious ideology, it might become removed from the most important ideological problems of today. It risks being transformed into an ideologically *neutral* "world view," largely inspired by the natural sciences; and the risk of merely *summarizing* the results of science (thereby even distancing itself from current problems in science and becoming methodologically barren as well).

One pole of this concept is perhaps represented by the "scientist" interpretation of Marxist philosophy. The proponents of this concept emphasize the use of Marxian *methodology* in various scientific disciplines—in the field of empirical natural sciences in particular. Although this concept touches at certain points on the "traditionalist" concept, its *content* is rather different. According to its champions, this lies in its dual function: on the one hand, it should be a critical analysis of current methods in science and a scrutiny of how far they are applicable in practice. On the other hand, it should investigate ontological problems. Ontology has *heuristic* functions in science; any ontological theory or system can only have a meaning if it has definite implications concerning the *future evolution* of science: can it contribute to a general impulse to progress; can it solve current fundamental problems? Different ontologies put forward varying programs for the evolution of science; more precisely,

---

*Although the following example is more anecdotal than typical, it does indicate the tendency. A not insignificant representative of the standard concept of "extent," the Polish W. Krajewski, has attempted in one of his essays to give a strict, scientifically provable definition of the law concerning the unity and struggle of contradictions. At the end of his analysis, the law was expressed in the following form: "Within each system there are some elements that mutually affect one another by exerting a definite force." I would not wish to call in question the truth of this statement, but what has it got to do with dialectics?

they try to clarify which program is more acceptable (in light of perceived reality and the actual state of human knowledge). Further, they assess the relative efficacy of partial programs in comparison to the state of the art in the respective sciences. This, however, means that: 1. the problem areas of ontology cannot be definitively staked out, only related to the actual state and nature of each science —alternatives of development change with scientific evolution; 2. the statements of philosophical ontology are *not* generalizations of accepted scientific theories, but program-forecasts in regard to the general direction and characteristics of scientific evolution; they are hypotheses, in the nature of "regulatory ideas," but are confirmed by the "learning process" of people in a longer historical context; 3. the scientific value of any ontology requires that it should not remain at a generalized level, as far as its orientation is concerned (e.g., materialism, determinism, dynamism, etc.). It should give concrete shape to the problems under debate in each science, in every period, replenishing them with new meaning and content. In this sense, Marxist philosophy is nothing but an ontology, representing, in a renewed form, materialism, determinism, the synthesis of dynamic and structuralist approaches, in short, a general philosophical "orientation," both in respect of their problems and the solutions thereof. Furthermore, it is a closely linked realist, historical-dialectical epistemology.*

This concept, in this particular form, is mainly represented by a group of Polish Marxists (H. Eilstein, St. Amsterdamski, W. Mejbaum, Z. Augustynek, etc.), but, it seems, it is also not quite alien to some representatives of the younger Soviet philosopher generation. This approach has so far been mostly realized in some works about the methodological and epistemological problems of natural science, to a lesser extent in attempts to solve certain ontological problems (determinism, psycho-physics, etc.). There have also been a number of initiatives to sketch out the consequences of the foregoing for the theory of society, distinguishing these attempts from other currents within Marxist philosophy.

In contrast to this tendency stands another that may be called the

---

*If the reader is interested in a more authentic exposition than this necessarily short and compressed description, I suggest H. Eilstein, "Ontological Hypotheses and Ontological Orientation," in *Teoria i doswiadczenie* (Warsaw, 1966); also see the monograph on Engels by St. Amsterdamski (Warsaw, 1965).

"ideological-critical" concept. Its representatives go back to Marx's criticism of ideologies (as examples of false consciousness). They emphasize that philosophy, in its essense, is *"ideology"* proper: a system of views that has an influence on our attitudes to reality insofar as this is not merely technical but supposes a choice between *values*. Every traditional philosophy is but the ratification of a hierarchy of values accepted by a particular class, and thus has no independent existence, regardless of whether these values are deduced from the structure of the cosmos, the nature of the human mind, or the iron laws of historical development. As such, it reinforces acceptance of certain clearly defined forms of individual and social behavior over against the already-existing institutions of a community. Therefore, philosophy *is* "ideology" in the Marxian sense of the word, an invention of the false consciousness, serving the interests and needs of antagonistic social groupings. (In some extreme and uncommon interpretations of this concept, these views are extended to the natural sciences: the descriptions of natural phenomena are but the expressions or reflections of the technical needs of mankind throughout history; in other words, of its practical/technical relationship to nature.)

What should be the task of Marxist philosophy in such circumstances, if it is to refrain from being a new tool of ideological mystification? It can be nothing else but to be *critical,* approaching the historical development of ideologies in terms of their actual human and social essence in the panorama of societal life as a whole and the role ideologies play in the immanent movement of history. Philosophy in this way plays not only the part of criticism and demystification but can also "reunify" the increasingly differentiated and too-highly specialized humanistic sciences as well, guiding them back—in the spirit of a historical materialist dialectic—to their creator: man, who lives and transforms the world.*

The concept described here (to some extent going back to certain ideas of a number of Marxists in the twenties) is largely represented by Polish philosophers and sociologists (L. Kolakowski, B. Baczko, Z. Bauman, K. Pomian, etc.). Their ideas have, understandably,

---

*The articles of L. Kolakowski ("How Do Philosophers Make a Living?" "The Concept of Extent and Function in Philosophy," "Ist der verstehende Materialismus möglich?" etc.) deal in more detail with this; also see B. Baczko: "Marxism Today and the Horizons of Philosophy," etc.

materialized mostly in works on the history of philosophy and culture, or the theory of culture. However, we find similar viewpoints among Czech and Yugoslav Marxists.

Another concept of Marxist philosophy that may perhaps be best called the concept of "social ontology," has also some crucial links with the traditions of the twenties (although in a rather different manner from the one indicated above). This concept was mostly worked out in the later writings of György Lukács.* The starting point of this concept came with the new understanding by man of his relations to surrounding reality. This turning-point in philosophy was elaborated by Marx, who fashioned a key for the resolution of the basic contradictions of those bourgeois ontologies that replaced religious ideology: the antinomies of object and subject, causality and teleology, necessity and freedom. According to Marx, the fundamental, primary relationship of man to reality, the basic "cell" of the real movement of social life, all derive from *work:* the activity that gives objective shape to subjective human capabilities, needs, and goals. However, this activity can be truly effective only if man is able to progress from the subjective and enter into a *causal* relationship with nature, being himself capable of going beyond the biologically given. Work, as the dialectic of learning and "objectification," creates the basis of social life as a specific sphere of existence; higher forms of the conquest of reality grow out and become independent only from these beginnings. This ever-widening, increasingly complex and indirect activity of "man the working being" is history itself. Man is both the subject and object of history: his environment and human nature change together. This aspect of history is what Marx described as the "overcoming of natural limitations," in the course of which human capabilities, needs, etc. take on an increasingly social character, i.e., they are recreated by man in an historical framework.

Every generation works away "within given conditions," in terms of productive forces, relationships, and ideas partly inherited from

---

*Considering that this is also my own personal point of view, naturally I am going to describe these views as I learned and understood them myself. The reader can get acquainted with the views of György Lukács in the publication "Gesprache mit Georg Lukács" ("Talks with György Lukács") (Hamburg, 1967). Mihály Vajda has a similar treatment of these problems in his article, "An Objective View of Nature and Social Practice," *Hungarian Review of Philosophy,* 1967; also see the essay by Agnes Heller, ("The Position of Ethics in Marxism") (Praxis, 1967). It may be mentioned that several Yugoslav Marxists share these views, e.g., M. Markovic, P. Vranicki, etc.

past generations, partly learned from experience. But through its own activities, it also modifies and changes these circumstances. This means that for the individual there exists an "objective" area of activity, circumscribed by given conditions, an area of *alternatives* and of *potential* development (narrower or broader, depending on the historical period). In practice, Man can *choose* from among these possibilities, and their realization would depend on the totality of human actions, which would become integrated (consciously or unconsciously), often influenced by the seemingly accidental occurrence of manifold external factors. Man, according to Lukács, is a "responding creature" who reacts to the alternatives offered by social developments; he is capable of transforming the (partly spontaneous, partly contradictory) tendencies of such developments into *questions* to which he tries to find conscious answers. The creation of communist society demands the advent of objective conditions within which the individual, as well as mankind as a whole, can consciously and *genuinely* choose from the ever-expanding circle of developmental possibilities. In other words, he can become master of the incessant flow by which he recreates and reshapes himself.

According to this concept, one can only understand the tasks of Marxist philosophy if one starts from these fundamental tenets of Marx's philosophy. Philosophy is one of those spiritual forms in which mankind "becomes pregnant with its own conflicts" (Marx). The task of philosophy is to elevate to conscious questions (and answers) the alternatives of the present, by pinpointing the place of *today's* basic conflicts in the general development of mankind—i.e., in terms of historically created human values—thus clarifying their significance and "meaning" for Man's development. In this sense, philosophy is a "summing up" (constantly revising itself, always growing out of the present) of those "general results that can be deduced from the analysis of the historical development of mankind" (Marx). This is the real ontology of Man's history, indeed history itself, viewed from the standpoint of unfolding "human essence."

Given that as we can define the task of Marxist social science—in very general terms—as directed towards analyzing current human conditions, movements, etc. and thereby supporting and preparing their transformation in a revolutionary, communist sense, it is obvious that (according to this concept) it is impossible to draw a sharp and clear-cut boundary between philosophy and social science. Of course, this cannot mean that, from the point of view of Marxism, philosophy and social science are one and the same thing. It merely means that the differences between them (in contrast to philosophy and natural science) are not those of subject matter and basic approach, but those of the level of abstraction, of categories and methodology. Therefore, in normal circumstances, they mutually support and condition one another, as far as their content is concerned. Philosophy, divorced from practical social investigations and actual social practice. inevitably becomes a collection of empty schemata or ideological formulae. Likewise, Marxist social science, consisting of specialist disciplines, must become "philosophical" in character. According to Marx, there are no "value-free" social sciences, genuinely independent of ideology. Even the strictly practical and impartial investigations of society postulate (through the choice of questions to be answered, as much as through the answers given to these) a conscious or instinctive point of view about society as a whole. And this means a definite stand, a choice between alternative tendencies of social development—whether correctly or mistakenly assumed.

The demand for commitment, for "partisanship" in Marxist social science does not require any "retouching" of facts in aid of a given political line or abstract ideals (social science would consequently cease to be a "science"). It requires that the questions to be analyzed be chosen from a consciously accepted, socialist perspective. The analysis of every detailed problem as well as every result of strictly objective methodology should be correlated with the trends in the whole of society and the possibilities for its revolutionary transformation in the spirit of socialism. Just as no social theory claiming to be Marxist can renounce the linkage between its specific area of scrutiny and the totality of social practice, nor can it become independent of philosophy: their relationship is characterized by their mutual need for one another, indeed by a transition from one to the other.

According to this concept, the relationship of philosophy and natural science is different in principle, not because the spokesmen of the concept deny the existence of nature, independent of man and based on objective facts (the act of work is defined by natural causation). The task of natural science, as it pertains to human experience conditioned by historical trends in production, is—as a matter of fact—to create a *nonanthropomorphic* picture of natural reality. The laws of this reality can be recognized by mankind, indeed utilized, but they are not created by man. For this reason. the subjects and attitudes of natural science and philosophy must be different: the starting point of philosophy is always "homocentric," it continuously researches the place and possibilities of man within a reality more and more conditioned by humanity, throughout the flow of history; natural science dispels the naive view of Nature as ephemeral and spontaneous, rooted in anthropomorphism and anthropocentrism; it explores the structure and correlations of nature, which are independent of human aims, needs, or qualities that are purely grounded in biology.

However, the interplay of philosophy and natural science cannot cease; after all, the latter has only gradually been divorced from the former and become independent in its own right. Not only because a philosophy that treats man not as a spiritual being confronting nature but as a material entity must strive towards the repeated codification of relationships between man and nature, between social and physical spheres of action, at every stage of the development of these very natural sciences, but also because philosophy cannot exclude from its investigations such an important part of social activity as natural science per sé. This, therefore, means not only the logical and epistemological scrutiny of natural science but also the critique of the "human significance" of scientific development, i.e., the analysis of those constantly changing relationships (together with their contradictions, perspectives, and actual possibilities) that link natural science, a historically evolved mode of grasping reality, with other forms of social activity. This demands a critical confrontation between the scientific "world view" and the spontaneous and ephemeral "ontological beliefs" of the trifling, common outlook. Therefore the task of the philosophy in respect of natural sciences is not to offer solutions to problems in its stead, not even to supply methodological tools for such solutions, but first of all to *reintegrate* natural science into a universal human culture, against increasing specialization. This is the meaning of revolutionary, materialist dialectics for man, the sole creator not only of culture but also of himself.

In the above, I have attempted to prove, through short descriptions, the evidence of actually developing philosophical tendencies within Marxism today.* The fact of their existence cannot be doubted; but it must be pointed out that their recognition, even more their acceptance (in Hungary as well as elsewhere), has met with reluctance, often with strong resistance. No doubt one reason for hostility towards these tendencies is laziness grown out of routine thinking. This fundamentalism—while proclaiming the creative nature of Marxism—can only imagine its essence as a closed system of thought, every important aspect of which being settled and unchangeable. It is an attitude that was very much influenced by the abnormal conditions rooted in the "cult of personality." But I do not think it sufficient—or just—to explain the current situation purely as a consequence of this state of affairs. We, therefore, are compelled to ask the following blunt question: can this phenomenon—i.e., the evolution of various currents in Marxist philosophy—be considered "normal"? Further, what are the implications of such an evolution, and what should be our attitude towards the whole affair?

In a certain sense we may say that nothing could be more normal than the evolution of such trends. It is easy to see that the differences between the various trends are, to a great extent, *thematic:* each of them emphasizes a different philosophical *problem-area.* Other differences, to some extent, follow from this fact. A truly universal philosophy—by the fact of being *universal*—must always offer different approaches, different thematic problems. Marxism can attract people *because* it has several aspects, different features: either as a scientific ideology that excludes everything supernatural; as the theory of the revolutionary transformation of society; as a new, modern form of humanism, etc. However much these features may constitute a unity within the whole theory, they offer different possibilities for individual approach and learning; by stressing different problems and manifesting itself in different philosophical "styles," Marxism promotes the attainment of its own universality, the broadening of its ideological influence.

This explanation, while it may point up certain factual aspects of

---

*I should like to reemphasize that this survey cannot claim to deal with every important current. For example, I have not mentioned the views of the well-known French Marxist, L. Althusser. According to him, Marxist philosophy is essentially a theory of knowledge (epistemology) developing in a given historical setting; to this, he attempts to apply his own "structuralist" ideas. Ideas, similar to Althusser's, have also emerged in the mid-fifties in the Soviet Union (e.g., E. V. Ilyenkov).

the case, cannot be sufficient. It would be self-delusion to say that current trends "complement" one another: largely they represent different approaches to the same philosophical position. Their differences are more than a question of theme. There are considerable divergencies of an ideological nature between these trends, not only in terms of perhaps unimportant detail, but also in respect of certain questions essential to Marxism (e.g., in the interpretation of dialectics or historical determinism). As the debate and confrontation between these tendencies has only just started, it is possible that some quite sharp differences of opinion will prove to be only stylistic misunderstandings or lack of precision. But the experience of some debates about essential problems here in Hungary (e.g., the debate about alienation, anthropology, or historical materialism, which is taking place in rather specialized circles) proves that—while there is some convergence among contrasting views in the course of debate, mainly owing to the elimination of untenable ideas and clarification of misunderstandings—the real differences do not disappear, indeed they tend to crystallize. Of course everybody approves of a unified Marxist synthesis, at least in principle. Still it seems we are at the beginning of the road and shall only reach our goal by the clear and sharp confrontation of contrasting views.

All these various movements, however unusual they seem after a long period of quite contrary practice, do not constitute a historical anomaly, nor something to be concerned about. From a historical perspective, the evolution of such tendencies is quite understandable, indeed natural. Every system of philosophy that confronts questions raised by a new stage of historical development—involving new social and cultural developments, new contradictions—must face the need for adaptation in regard to concepts rendered obsolete in the light of new experience, but also in regard to the very act of posing new questions. Further, as it renews its own structures, it reinterprets its own theories from the point of view of new problems. The vitality and continuity of thinking can only be realized through this theoretical "reorientation," which can be ongoing or intermittent. This notion is particularly relevant to Marxist philosophy by consciously putting historical reality in the center of its theoretical investigations—its creator, Marx, always emphasized the demand for a *historical self-criticism* of the theory. It goes without saying that, in present times, many social, cultural, or scientific problems have arisen that were unknown in the twenties or thirties.

For this reason, the "renaissance" of Marxism, our common aim, should be identical with carrying out the "reorientation" of Marxism.

However, it would be a near miracle if such a task could be resolved straightaway, to everybody's satisfaction. Although these attempts grow out of the same ideological tradition, in fact, from the same social conformation—thereby sharing many elements—it is impossible for them not to also contain *different, divergent* elements in the process of "reorientation." A renewed aspect of theory that fits the problems of a new historical period can only be attained by a clear confrontation of different attempts, either in direct debates or in works realizing given programs. This is the only way in which the ideological consequences, the scientific foundations, and the validity of these new concepts can, in the last resort, be measured.

If there is anything extraordinary in the present state of affairs, it is perhaps the fact that the urge to confront new problems has arisen not only following a long period of theoretical stagnation and dogmatism (overlong, in the accelerated history of our times), but also after a period that represented a deformation of the basic principles of Marxist philosophy: its revision occurred without being conscious that a revision had taken place, without any theoretical foundation. Therefore, in our current arguments about fundamentals, the question, "What is the meaning of Marxism today?" is inextricably tied up with another: "What is the original, *authentic* Marxism?" This circumstance no doubt augments and broadens all differences of opinion. But at the same time, it has an important positive consequence: it keeps in the forefront the problem relating to the real, historical continuity of theory. This is accomplished especially by the ongoing relevance of the second question, which acts, to a certain extent, as an antidote to those, often very authoritative, efforts at completing the task of Marxism's "reorientation" by simply—and eclectically—merging some alien fashions of thought into our philosophy.

From the point of view of "pure" theory, therefore, the emergence of different, often conflicting philosophical trends within Marxism are understandable and a sign of good health, proving the vitality of Marxist philosophy, its will for self-renewal. But again, Marxist philosophy—according to its own goals and intentions—cannot be considered as just one among many philosophical systems concerned with explaining the world. It is not one ideology among many, but *the* theory aimed at changing the world, shifting it in a well defined direction: the ideology of a clearly recognized social and historical movement. This consciously accepted function, however, puts certain justified claims and demands on Marxist philosophy that would be meaningless in the majority of philosophical ideologies. Does not the appearance of several philosophical trends within Marxism endanger the practical-political unity of the movement? Without a certain strength of this unity, conscious political and organizational action would be impossible. Would not the development of philosophical tendencies, proclaiming different points of view on important philosophical questions—even if only for a time—create favorable opportunities for the intrusion of bourgeois ideologies into the workers' movement, leading to a loss of its theoretical and ideological independence? Would the emphasis on confrontation between these trends not lead to weakening the fight against bourgeois ideologies? Would not Marxist philosophy, appearing in contrasted tendencies, become "boundless"? Would it not, therefore, be necessary to: reduce differences in opinion by whatever means; define our actual task in creating a consonance and not indulge ourselves in disputes and confrontations; and—to begin with—draw a very clear demarcation line between theoretical differences of view that are *inside* Marxism and those *outside* its boundaries? I feel, these are the reservations lurking behind the strong hostility towards these tendencies; these are the grounds for the frequently declared principle: "Debates—yes, tendencies—no."

Let us add that these are *real* problems. And any philosopher for whom these are merely "political" problems, irrelevant to theory, cannot call himself Marxist. One cannot call a philosopher Marxist unless he considers his activity (at whatever remove) as part and parcel of the struggle fought for the creation of a humanistic society, free from exploitation, abolishing alienation, and he is willing to link this abstract commitment with an active partisan share in the social movements of our day. (Maybe this, no doubt rather broad, demarcation can serve as a partial answer to the problem of "boundlessness" in Marxism.)

But the above problems are real in another sense too: they cannot be resolved by a unified, final, comforting formula. The evolution, crystallization and confrontation of trends within Marxist philosophy *may* bring negative symptoms, *may* create new dangers and *may* (in certain, though indefinite, circumstances) give credence to the accusation of "watering down" ideology. But, I think this is the most one can honestly say about these dangers: they are possible but not at all inevitable. Those who have these reservations usually exaggerate them; furthermore, in my opinion, it would lead to a greater damage, not a smaller one, if we tried to avoid confrontation between these tendencies.

"Confrontation" creates more favorable conditions in every respect as long as we can properly handle this new aspect of ideological development. No doubt, all those who demand an unequivocal elaboration of these theoretical and philosophical differences in the making, up to and including their ultimate consequences, and who are actively engaged in the debates raging around these problems, must bear a clear-cut ideological, indeed political, responsibility for whatever those consequences turn out to be. But, equally, those who wish to maintain the appearance of a monolithic Marxist philosophy grounded in the past period—in spite of the changing situation—must bear a similar responsibility.

Could we not avoid the peculiar dangers arising from the debates within and between these tendencies by clearly defining their boundaries, by laying down those basic principles about which there can be no debate among Marxist philosophers? I believe that no one has successfully defined this philosophical "minimum" in Marxism, although many share the belief in the desirability of this idea. To be quite frank, I am firmly convinced that there is only one answer to this conundrum: such a solution is *not* possible.

May I suggest that there are, or there can be, situations when the abstract debate about theoretical, philosophical questions is closely interwoven with the choice between practical, political alternatives: the Movement, the Party *must* decide *now,* regardless whether the theoretical debate about such problems had been concluded or not. Such decisions, in certain respects, could put a limit to theoretical arguments; and, we may add, *this* in itself may have a negative effect on the development of theory. But the theoretician, in our case the philosopher, must be clear in his own mind that this is the price he has to pay for not being a philosopher of the ivory tower but rather the theoretician of a Movement, to which he contributes through his own detailed efforts, even though these may act indirectly; just as a politician engaged in cultural policy or ideology must be clear in his own mind that his involvement is a necessary *exception,* only justified because it is necessary.

Beyond this question, there are of course some philosophical statements agreed upon by all Marxists, and which one could not deny and still call himself Marxist. Still, the compilation of a "list" of such theses, indisputable for Marxists, could not and would not solve the problem of delimitation between Marxism and non-Marxism; besides the fact that it could not be done.

In the first place, all philosophy is a *system* of thought, not just a collection of theses. Some, indeed many, statements of abstract philosophy are very simple, but their sum does not exhaust, nor does it delimit, a certain philosophy. Whoever tried to compress great philosophical systems into such fundamentals usually found that such an "extract" could be claimed by many another philosophy, often quite different in content and ideology from the one so "condensed." Another point to bear in mind is that the stress on such theses—their actual meaning within such systems—is often quite different. The student of philosophy knows very well that often the most sharply contrasting philosophical ideologies of a given period may assume a superficial propinquity owing to certain identical *sounding* philosophical "slogans," but their actual content, their interpretation, is widely different. Philosophical arguments, due to their abstract nature in most cases, only gain their clear meaning in the context of their own systems. A list of "Marxist axioms" viewed in abstract could not offer a suitable distinction from certain types of bourgeois ideology. Actually, it would create a dangerously misleading appearance of congruence in respect of certain theses differently understood or interpreted by Marxists; which is why they must be clarified.

This leads us to the second problem. In certain cases the debate is raging concerning "theses" that are fundamental to *all* Marxist attitudes. What can be done in such cases? Should we decide *now* between conflicting opinions when the theoretical argument is far from finished?* But on what basis? Should we perhaps use the

---

*To prevent any misunderstanding: what I mean by the conclusion of a philosophical debate is not the complete disappearance of a contrary opinion, nor the birth of a document signed by all participants. Philosophical arguments, deplorably, hardly ever conclude by convincing the opposite number: a philosopher wants to convince *others,* not *an other.* A debate is only concluded in an objective manner if one party can no longer rebut contrary arguments, cannot bring up coherent, well-founded counter-arguments. In normal conditions of a public debate, effective argument consequently ceases, even if the losers still maintain their opinions.

Marxist classics as our criterion? Quite apart from the fact that Marxism is no biblical exegesis—and we cannot exclude the possibility that even the founders' statements, often essential ones, would have to be modified owing to new facts and experience—the polemics in these debates mostly concern the interpretation of certain of the founders' theses in the framework of their whole theoretical system. Should we accept the verdict of the majority? This would be a very unreliable criterion in scientific questions, especially dangerous in a period when, in consequence of the spiritual atmosphere of the recent past, strong conservatism still rules the roost. Should we accept a compromise of interpretation, encompassing the major views of today to the exclusion of others? By what right could we consider the currently appearing tendencies as the only ones entitled to settle limits and set norms for the future?

In contrast, we may run the risk of accepting "boundless" Marxism. Once we accept the existence of different philosophical tendencies within Marxism, should this mean that we have given up the clear, independent *ideological-theoretical* character of our philosophy? I do not believe so. What we have given up are not the "boundaries" but the naive dogmatic idea that these are staked out once and for all. And if our conviction about the creative nature of Marxist philosophy means anything, it means that these concrete "boundaries" are always being created, modified, and changed by Marxist theory and practice itself.

To turn from this shaky "poetical philosophizing" to the pragmatic: as we have indicated before, Marxist philosophy ceases to exist when the fundamental goals of Marxism as a *social movement* are discarded, when its theoretical traditions are considered irrelevant, when a philosophical system becomes incapable of *factually* answering theoretical and ideological problems arising from the practice of the movement, when it can no longer promote the realization of its goals. In the last analysis—historically speaking—it is on the basis of this criterion that one can distinguish what is Marxism from what is not; even when at a given point in time different, sometimes conflicting views may emerge as to how one can accomplish this consciously undertaken theoretical task. In such cases as a rule, the genuine Marxist version is expressed in the historical evolution, in which the conflict, i.e., debate, between different theoretical trends represents the various real needs of social development and, in consequence, suffer modification and change. Therefore, I have spoken deliberately about the *confrontation* of these trends, not just about their *existence*. Considering the chasm between these opinions, the mere ossified existence of different philosophical tendencies within Marxism, isolated from one another—side by side, so to speak—would really mean the beginning of a process of dissolution in ideology; and we have to recognize this.

What can strangle at birth such germs is *debate,* the constant, active confrontation of these tendencies in terms of their consistency with the practice of the Movement. Because this confrontation means that every single trend is constantly challenged by all others to clarify its own relationship to the fundamental problems of the socialist movement—to spell out its interpretation of Marxist traditions—they must give logical reasons in every instance: why, on the basis of what experiences and through what thought processes have they revised or modified certain, previously accepted, philosophical ideas of Marxism. They are asked to pinpoint their own links with bourgeois ideas, if any such exists, etc.

This polemic question-and-answer process among philosophical trends coming from various directions ensures real continuity of new approaches with tradition and prevents the ossification of "schools." The boundary between Marxism and non-Marxism takes shape through this struggle (fought exclusively, it goes without saying, with words) of conflicting conceptual and theoretical propositions and ensures that the struggle never gets divorced from social action. This is how a common physiognomy of our philosophy is formed, by aiming towards synthesis. In this sense, confrontation among major philosophical trends within Marxism can and should mean the most favorable aspect of our theoretical and ideological development, at least for the time being. Doubtlessly, several conditions must be created to ensure development in this manner. We must establish an atmosphere of debate that corresponds to the need for scientific ethics and scientific courtesies (though, in all candor, even these simple conditions do not always prevail). We must thwart any attempt at a monopolistic stand, which would not be duty-bound to answer questions put to it (or—what's worse— could not even be questioned). I am sure many another condition could be formulated; certainly, even the above mentioned ones leave much to be desired. On the whole, however, it is not illusory to demand such a practice of confrontation today; in the more important recent debates (some of which have already been mentioned) just this sort of questioning between contrary views led to the undoubted success of these debates, in no mean fashion.

Would not this sharpening of conflict between Marxist philosophers lead, in a way, to a relegation of the fight against bourgeois ideologies, blunting the edge of their struggle? One cannot give a more telling answer to this question than the reply of a prominent Yugoslav Marxist, Gayo Petrovic, at a similar occasion: "Why should a living Marxism be less effective than a dead one?"

This reply not only sounds good, it conforms to our recent experience. As we have emphasized before, the relationship to certain trends of bourgeois philosophy, the demand for clarification of such relationships, is necessarily an integral part of the confrontation between Marxist schools of thought. This has proved particularly true of those debates that were not limited to the discussion of isolated details—i.e., were not a matter of differences in formulation but of broader relationships; the connection of one particular problem with the *general conception* of Marxist philosophy. It is no coincidence that the considerable enrichment and deepening of the Marxist criticism of existentialist theory of alienation, indeed of the whole existentialist philosophy, paralleled the debate about alienation among Marxists. The same can be said about the debate on anthropology going on throughout the world: the previously neglected Marxist criticism of the—otherwise quite influential—bourgeois philosophical anthropology now owes much to the attention paid to it by these various tendencies. Further, it can be seen that the Marxist assessment of structuralism (in many ways still far from satisfactory) is closely connected with polemics among our philosophers about the meaning of Marxian historical determinism.

I may add to all this another, perhaps somewhat debatable, point. It seems that the infiltration of bourgeois ideology into our philosophy does present a real threat but on another front; namely, insofar as the impoverished philosophical concepts of the Stalinist period are left untouched and uncriticized and become "modern" by being quickly and eclectically "complemented" with a little bit of Freudian personality theory, some existentialist ethics, and a pinch of neopositivist philosophy. It is incontestable that—in consequence of the dogmatism of the earlier period—our philosophy is quite backward in certain problem areas in which bourgeois philosophy has been concentrating and excelling. This failure, though, cannot be corrected simply by adapting the solutions of bourgeois philosophy to a "materialist" framework, or by embracing their methodology and formulation of problems. The innermost unity of a philosophy usually lies in the particular approach it has to a given phenomenon; *what* it will find is, to some extent, determined by *how* it is looked for. No "theory of science" will become Marxist simply by making an addition to the usual statements of neopositivism: science, in the last resort, reflects the essential correlations of the material reality that is not directly visible to man. We can only speak of a "Marxist theory of science" where—in contrast to viewing science as an independent, closed sphere concerned exclusively with logical functioning in positivist terms—we scrutinize science as one particular aspect of social activity and analyze its historical relationships. (I should add: only through this conceptually different approach and method can Marxist philosophy utilize some indisputable logical and methodological discoveries and observations reached by some logical positivists.) It is striking that most frequently, those people declare and practice the principle of "complementing Marxism" by borrowing bourgeois philosophical methods and practices, who reject out of hand any question about the exclusive truth of the traditional concept of "extent." Personally, I believe this curious "coincidence" cannot be explained by individual attitudes or indeed by the "bandwagon" concept: it is profoundly interwoven with the notion that Marxist philosophy—in the form it is laid down in our "standard" textbooks—cannot answer new problems as they arise. Thus, to become contemporary, it requires a "complement" of alien matter.

To pose this question leads us immediately back to a problem already mentioned: the maintenance of the current position, embodied in the slogan, "debates—yes, tendencies—no," involves a number of negative aspects, seriously harmful to the healthy development of our philosophy and ideology.

In the last decade, any number of debates have been conducted within Marxist philosophy throughout the world. A good part of these debates, however (save for a few exceptions already mentioned), limited itself to the *isolated* discussion of some detail, without linking this to other questions debated elsewhere at the same time.* In a historical context it is perfectly understandable that a critical reappraisal of Stalin's philosophical views could only emerge through looking at certain details. But the situation today—when any number of questions, often closely connected, are debated in groups divorced from one another, and thus the natural points of contact are disregarded and the theoretical differences are never clarified—is far from natural and, what is more, is liable to create an unhealthy state of affairs. Undoubtedly, it is the philosophers themselves who are largely to blame for this situation, insofar as, influenced by a distinct "atmosphere," they feel no compulsion to really sharpen their debates and carry them through to their logical conclusions. The tone of the polemics, often resembling theological controversies, cannot compensate for this.

This situation has a serious effect, first and foremost, on the *scientific* results of our debates. It can quite often be observed, in some disputes over a given detail, that the protagonists refer in their arguments to certain theses or statements as indisputable or self-evident proof, while—sometimes in the very same periodical—a sharp debate is going on concerning the truth, or at least the interpretation, of these very statements. The debates merely go round in circles; their results do not add up—indeed, they mutually detract from one another—and those debates treating essential problems often degenerate into verbal bickering.

The broader, more ideological consequences of this situation are no less serious. As the debates about detailed problems continue independent of one another, their relationships never emerge and thus the consequences of a given approach for the fundamental problems of Marxist philosophy are never realized; although, in the

---

*To give one example: within the problem-area of dialectics, several debates were in process at the same time—on the nature of "dialectical logic," on logical contradictions, on the law of "the negation of the negation," on the relationship of necessity and chance, etc. Even a superficial survey of these matters suggests a clear affinity even though the subjects are different (as there is a close affinity in content among different questions). Unmistakably, various Marxist philosophers disagree on the question of materialist dialectics itself, arguing about its place in the whole of Marxist philosophy; this is at least one ground for different views on actual questions. In spite of all this, the debates were not conducted on a rigorous theoretical level, and it is, therefore, very difficult, if not impossible, to gauge the depth of the differences, to assess the true content and character of these contrasting attitudes. I think that, apart from the first two, closely related, debates about the fundamental questions of logic, the others yielded very meager results, not even a selection of views more worthy of international discussion.

majority of cases, this is what it is all about. Thus their general survey, or a well-founded individual choice among various views on the agenda, becomes impossible. No philosopher can master every detailed aspect of philosophy. The multiplicity of debates alone calls into question the "textbook" views at several points; but no proper alternative is offered, nor a yardstick against which to measure the positive and negative aspects of the traditional views. In consequence of all this, an atmosphere of theoretical uncertainty has emerged; and this, though it may have some merits, has a definitely negative effect.

This feeling of uncertainty is reflected in certain attempts to resolve disputed questions by a compromise formula, or by resorting to such terminology as: "on the one hand"—"on the other hand." Alas, in philosophy (in most cases) a "middle road" is hardly ever the most judicious, best substantiated position: usually this contains the most eclectic, least supportable view. Such a tendency may probably lead to a blurred face of Marxist ideology, reducing the value of its philosophical or scientific results. The emergence of this tendency is even more striking since certain points of view—currently appearing in the social sciences of our countries—that do reflect the features of bourgeois ideology hardly ever try to criticize the general philosophy and social theory of Marxism; what they do emphasize is the *irrelevance* of all philosophy in specific scientific investigations. (Obviously, this phenomenon is more complex and cannot be dealt with in one sentence.)

The appearance of "rubber" formulae of compromise in our philosophy gives cause for concern precisely because, instead of treating the main problems of the day in the social sciences (as a contest between *philosophical* views would do) it attempts to "transcend" these problems, tolerating a multitude of interpretations and running the risk of becoming truly irrelevant to the scientific development of our age.

At the same time, this theoretical uncertainty appears in an inconsistent manner in the teaching of philosophy—though, of course, we cannot deal with this problem in any depth here. The cancer of our education in philosophy does not reside mainly in a too-literal dogmatism. The traditional concept of "extent" in Marxist philosophy and the structures based on this are accepted uncritically as perfectly natural, being beyond debate; at the same time, one can notice some quite astoundingly "individual" ideas in happy confusion, never publicly debated, hardly sustainable even against elementary criticism.

A last comment: although one can see the emergence of divergent trends in Marxist philosophy, their critique and confrontation are not in the forefront of our philosophical life. The fact that these fundamental disagreements, more often than not, are not spelled out and made public carries another dangerous consequence: the "Balkanization" of our philosophical theory. We have reached the point where quite differerent philosophical concepts are not only the accepted but the ruling ones among Marxists in different countries. This is a natural consequence of the differences in the historical and ideological developments in these countries and as such quite normal. But the lack of confrontation between tendencies may lead to the paradoxical situation where something might be a fully acceptable Marxist viewpoint in one country, but will be considered untenable, indeed anti-Marxist, in another country; without any debate conducted in the normal manner between the representatives of the two viewpoints. If there is one feature of Marxist theory that threatens the unity and international universality of our philosophy, it is this countrywise division, this "provincialization" of Marxist theory.

It is a stony path strewn with stumbling blocks that leads from the monolithic philosophy of the "personality cult," with its impoverishment and vulgarization, to a true renaissance of Marxist philosophy, to a harmonious system of vital, creative theory, capable of answering the fundamental questions of our time. The difficulties mentioned in the latter part of this essay are but the "infantile disorders" of this development. To overcome these disorders, it is necessary to treat emerging trends in depth, on the basis of principles; to confront the different concepts clearly and not to attempt their reconciliation on the sly. It is my belief that by doing all this, we can create the most favorable conditions for the emergence of a Marxist philosophy, in detail and as a whole, that can profess to realize, in the conditions of the second half of our century, with unshakable faith, the one-hundred-year-old demand: "We don't say to the world: abandon your fight, it is only foolishness. We give you the battle cry. We shall show you, what you are fighting for. Consciousness is something to be achieved, willy-nilly."

AFTER THE BREAK
GYORGY BENCE AND JANOS KIS

In the confrontation with the official ideology, the various trends appearing in the name of "true Marxism" strove for a renewed, "constructive" Marxism, capable of affecting political decisions. However, even though the most abstruse debate had a political significance, it was not politics but abstract, philosophical disputes that the neo-Marxist camp focused on. For this reason, when it became clear around 1968, with the discontinuance of these debates by "administrative methods," that those in political power reject the advice of Marxists, these neo-Marxist trends lost not only the practical means for publicizing their views but also any justification they may have had in principle. Following their suppression, the whole movement was rather quickly forgotten.

The majority of its followers openly or tacitly renounced Marxism. A minority among them joined the specialists of official ideology. An insignificant minority retired from official cultural life and became "marginalized."

However, since the second half of the sixties, official culture has not been the only medium of self-expression in Eastern Europe. In several countries nonofficial forms of communication have appeared—sometimes an entire system has resulted from the exchange of manuscript literature—and they have been spreading elsewhere. Quite a number of political ideas, practical programs, tactical plans have been hatched in this medium; even embryonic movements can be discerned. Thus, those Marxists who remained in opposition are not condemned to silence. They can join the debates flaring up outside the official communications system. They can express their changing views publicly; they can define their

---

György Bence (1941–), *János Kis* (1943–)— philosophers. Their book, co-authored with György Márkus, *Is a Critical Economic Theory Possible?* was suppressed. In 1973, they were dismissed from their jobs and forbidden to work in their profession.

position among others representing different opposing ideologies. Surely, it would seem that if anybody is in a position to recreate Marxist traditions, they are.

However, it is not a simple matter. Indeed, the political kernel of tradition is still alive for these "marginalized" Marxists, but it is not at all certain that it can engender an independent tradition of thought. Let us examine the reasons why.

The sixties passed in the heady rapture of the "renaissance" in Marxism. More and more new items of Marx's original thinking emerged, once the fragments of disintegrating Stalinism were cleared away. Communist thinkers of the twenties gained new recognition and "Western Marxism" was rediscovered. For a while it seemed that Marxist tradition had never been so complete and alive than in that period. If, however, we scrutinize the vast material constituting the "renaissance" of Marxism, the picture looks much more uneven. Some elements in the tradition were fully advanced; in other areas yawning gaps remained.

These trends within "true" Marxism were unified by a practical program, the main outlines of which were quite clear, even though its details were not. It demanded the democratization of the institutional system and within the context of the detailed philosophical theory of praxis.* This was the most consistent aspect of "renaissance" Marxism. It held out the promise of organic development—involving interest in anthropology, philosophy of history, theory of knowledge—beyond the explicit social criticism in the whole philosophical system of "praxis."

No similar Marxist theory was generated in economics. One group of Marxist economists merely attempted to work out formal models of growth, in order to improve economic planning. Others did analyze certain features of bureaucratic planning, but their critique never achieved a truly theoretical description and explanation of Soviet-type economics. Such a "theory" remained the privilege of official economics.

Marxist sociology was even less noteworthy. It succeeded in demonstrating that the stratification of Soviet-type societies cannot be explained on the basis of ownership relations alone. But these investigations were mostly limited to the establishment of categories in

---

*A concept originated by György Lukács, according to which Marxists should constantly check the validity of theory against the reality of day-to-day events.

social statistics. No one has yet tried to identify (and analyze by sociological methods) the real class relationships underlying these statistical categories—the interaction of those large functional groups in society that represent different social and economic interests throughout the changes in macro-economics and macro-society.

The weakest, critically weak, point of this whole "renaissance" was the fact that it never pinpointed the real social embodiment of "true" Marxism. To be more precise, not even the task itself was ever formulated. The majority, without further scrutiny, accepted from Marxist tradition the preeminent relationship with the working class—then substituted the present political leadership for the working class. This subconscious identification was made even by those who sought to orient themselves towards groups largely, or totally, different from the working class. When the leadership made short shrift of this dialogue, the whole construction of ideas collapsed. Without a forceful socio-economic theory it was impossible to say which social forces could be enlisted to support the desired reforms, at least in the long run. The program became irrelevant. It became immediately apparent that the philosophy supporting this program had not become a leading or sustaining element in the "renaissance" of Marxism predominantly owing to the fact that it had been able to tell us *more* about Soviet-type societies than the economic or sociological constituents of the program. The efforts of economists and sociologists were brought up short before the actual functioning of the system, while philosophy merely disregarded it. It deduced what the "Good Society" should be like from general definitions of "human essence." Such generalized postulates may fit any and every society, or none at all.

The "renaissance" of Marxism did not pass on a live tradition to Marxists who were in opposition to the official institutional system; at most it conveyed fragments of a tradition. This in itself may not be fatal. The boundaries of Marxist tradition may well be established, even without a detailed theoretical system, if at least some of the other opposing ideologies could lay claim to a grand tradition in contrast. If, for instance, liberalism could strike roots in a tradition, a few simple statements could decide who is acting within the Marxist tradition, who within liberalism. Although there are some liberals within the Soviet and East European opposition, their liberalism hardly represents more than a political program. Only certain

Russian ideologies from the conservative-romantic mold represent a characteristic philosophy and a set view of society. Their aggressive idealism and social traditionalism is of course quite incompatible with Marxism, but it is also incompatible with liberalism. It is not Marxism alone but any modern, secular ideology that the conservative ideologies reject.

It is true that Russian conservatives conduct their polemics mostly with Marxism. But, in actual fact, even the dividing line between conservatism and Marxism is not continuous.

The area of conflict between the ruling system and the opposition has a bottom and a top line. The bottom line is defined by the fact of being in opposition. The exposition of opposing ideas inevitably depends on some minimal group activity. The technical means and institutional preconditions of communication are not made available; channels of public communications must be created, at the same time as such ideologies strive to become public. This assumes some cooperation and solidarity among people; a very loose cooperation, a rather abstract solidarity, but still real ones. Nobody can shy away from the defense of legal freedoms in communications. No opposition ideology can assert itself without including freedom of expression in its practical program. The demand for legality, for a system of rights, is common to all tendencies.

The top line of ideological differentiation is delineated by how much leeway these tendencies have in creating nonofficial methods of contact and communication. Even the best organized groupings are very fragile. They decide on their practical tasks on the basis of what opportunities permit; they have no long-term strategies coupled with an exclusive ideology, which would pinpoint that part of the population, that particular class or group, having a special interest in the realization of their goals. The Polish Committee for the Defense of Workers (KOR, formed in 1976) is the first opposition organization formed for the defense of one particular social class.

It is almost impossible to forecast the future of opposition movements in the Soviet Union and Eastern Europe (What trends would appear may very well depend on the particular country). But, unless a sociological and ideological differentiation takes place, the various programs and social groups embodied in these movements cannot be distinguished.

Given the current state of Marxism, no distinct Marxist tradition can be recreated. Contemporary Marxism does not offer a specific description of East European economic or social life; it does not specify one social class capable of implementing its program; indeed, today there is no quintessentially Marxist program. Therefore, we must put the question quite bluntly: how useful is the language of Marxism to those social groupings whose aim is to find self-expression outside the framework of official institutions?

To answer this question, we must examine the various movements compatible with Marxism, which can be simplified under a few broad headings. Their types can be best characterized according to two basic points of view. The first includes the legalists, who want to put the existing political structure on a more properly constitutional basis, and the liberals, who want to transform this political structure. And the second is the radical reformers. The first grouping has long-term aims that they consider valid in themselves. The latter concentrate on the political and social preconditions that favor the setting of such aims.

Legalism developed, first and foremost, in the Russian underground movements. Liberalism has appeared in every East European country that has opposition movements. Radical reformism is a Polish phenomenon.

We cannot consider everyone a legalist who attempts to strengthen and extend human rights, in which case every opposition ideology could be called legalist. We specify under this title those ideologies that stop at the demand of such a common minimum. The representatives of this group always point at the shortcomings of Western parliamentary democracy.

The most typical legalist ideologists—Russian conservative nationalists—claim that the parliamentary system is *too* democratic: it gives primacy to the material interests of the masses over and above moral values of universal validity. Those Marxists who sympathize with legalism also reject Western representative systems, but for the reason that they are *not* democratic enough. Like most socialists, they see in the parliamentary system only a "formal" democracy. They believe the institutional structure, as is, of Soviet-type societies is capable of accomplishing democracy of a higher order.

This is, of course, the old ideal of "democratic socialism," with one important difference. The original spokesmen of "democratic socialism" were not at all legalists: they did not suppose that democratization would depend on the creation of a formalistic legal system. The concept of legality appeared in their political thinking roughly in parallel with their "marginalization," and it gradually gained an increasing measure of importance—there was less and less talk about "the restoration of Leninistic norms in party life" and more and more about the repeal of laws restricting human rights, about the freedom of the press, about an independent judiciary, and so on. However, the transformation of "democratic socialism" into "legalistic socialism" brought with it unexpected consequences. The previously quite sharp dividing line between opposition Marxism and liberalism becomes blurred. If and when "democratic socialism" adopts the call for a formal Bill of Rights, why would it stop there?

"Democratic socialism" is today tottering in the no-man's-land between legalism and liberalism. It may turn in either direction, but in neither of them can it take the last, logical step: it goes too far for the legalists, not far enough for the liberals. It is therefore clear that Marxism cannot provide either rival trend with a political system.

As far as radical reformism is concerned, the possibilities and limitations of Marxism are quite different. Radical reformism, strictly speaking, does not offer a program. The question of what kind of social system should replace the present one does not figure in their tactical thinking. According to the spokesmen of radical reformism, only such aims are worth pursuing in Eastern Europe as can be achieved without a crisis of political power; any other aim would lead either to utopias or to catastrophe. Reform or revolution are no meaningful alternatives: one can only sensibly choose between two kinds of reformism.

The reformists of the fifties and sixties—the "old evolutionists" —wanted to introduce reforms "from the inside," by enlightenment and persuasion of the political leadership. The "new evolutionists" (following the terminology of Adam Michnik, the Polish historian, used in an address given by him in Paris, in September 1976*) draw the conclusions from the failure of those tactics. Internal criticism, according to Michnik, cannot effectively influence the leadership; any such criticism is vulnerable to the vicissitudes of power politics. In the long run, it will be compelled to silence or the surrender of its critical stance. Only the external pressure of independent social

---

*Published in *Esprit*, January 1977.

movements can exert a serious, lasting effect on the government. The logic of this political realism says that it is not enough for such aims to be compatible with the continuity of power. Only those aims can be attained that have the backing of a social force, with a strength proportional to the scale of the demand. The evolution of independent social movements is not merely a tactical means for radical reformism. Organizational autonomy of society is a goal in itself. The better organized a society, the smaller the overweening power of the political leadership, the nearer the point in time when a transformation of the power system may be attempted.

Many known Marxists have joined the radical reformists, as well as the legalists and the liberals. (See, for example, the interview with Jacek Kuron, a leading member of the Polish Committee for the Defense of Workers, in *Le Monde,* 29 January 1977.) However, so far we only know of individual cases—Marxism as a theory is not responsible for these ties. "Democratic socialism" or the philosophy of praxis have nothing to offer to radical reformism, as it does not stake out final aims; its program is not based on an ideological apparatus, nor is a philosophical value system necessary for its justification. On the other hand, it may need a dynamic socio-economic theory. More precisely, this depends on its temporal outlook. If radical reformism only encompasses short-term tactics, then it does not presuppose more knowledge about the behavior of social classes than what can be learned from everyday experience. If, however, it is really in the nature of "evolutionism," if the movement frames reforms that can only be accomplished over a very long period, then it is desirable to foresee the likely development of class relationships, at least insofar as social science can forecast anything at all.

This task is not alien to Marxism. Marx himself did something of this nature in *Capital,* Rosa Luxemburg in *The Accumulation of Capital,* the Russian Marxists of the 1890s—Struve, Lenin, Tugan-Baranovski—in their polemics against the populists, Trotsky in his analysis of the economic and social preconditions of the first Russian revolution in 1905 . . .

A vast number of analogies and heuristic principles can be extracted from this tradition. There is also much that must be swept aside in applying these fertile analogies and principles. Marxism has not developed a useful theory of Soviet-type societies; nor of those tendencies that led to Stalinism, those in conflict with it, or those that emerged with its disintegration. This, however, is a less insurmountable shortcoming than the fact that in the generalized explanation of history offered by Marxism, there are many things quite incompatible with such an undertaking. For instance, the threefold typology of historical societies (traditional societies, capitalism, socialism); the opposing systems of capitalist market economy and socialist planned economy; the definition of social classes through property relationships, and so on.

Radical reformism offers a sensible research program to Marxists; however, if they think through their tasks properly, they must realize that practically nothing can be utilized directly from this Marxist tradition. They cannot even assume that they have any advantage over social scientists coming from a different background. The case of Marxists favoring either legalism or liberalism is somewhat simpler. They can continue what's left of the Marxist tradition in Eastern Europe. However, the question arises, why bother? It seems the answer lies in the fact that Marxism is at least politically expedient, if nothing else.

WHAT IS MY POSITION ON MARXISM TODAY

ZOLTAN ENDREFFY

First of all, what do I understand by "Marxism"?
Marxism is first a philosophy—most importantly, a philosophy of history—and then a political movement built on this philosophy. The central motif in Marxian philosophy of history is alienation. This means that in the history of mankind up till now—i.e., its "prehistory" (according to Marx)—the productive forces, which determine social relations, become alienated from the individual, turn against him, subjugate him . . .

At a definite point of historical development, however, alienation can be abolished. The growing dominance of machine-based mass production in industry, and the emergence of social consciousness among the proletariat, creates the preconditions for emancipation . . . Thus, the true history of mankind could begin, a history characterized by the rational control of production, domination over nature, and, on this basis, the free development of every individual human being.

Now, in regard to determining my position on Marxism, I must first of all voice my doubts concerning this whole set of statements.

Not that I object to the abolition of alienation. I do not approve of the misery, the class conflicts, economic crises, and the like, all related to alienation. But this is not enough. Surely Communism aims at raising the standard of living of every individual to what was only available to the ruling classes throughout "prehistory." Yet, the example of all ruling classes so far shows that this, in itself, will not solve the true life problems of man. However enviable may be the material conditions of someone, he may still suffer from a sense of emptiness, even absurdly so; he can still live a meaningless, undignified life. He can rot from boredom, like the Russian land-

---
Zoltán Endreffy (1944–   ), philosopher. In 1974, he resigned his chair at the Technical University of Budapest; has been working as a factory worker since. From 1975, he has been studying at the Catholic Theological Academy.

owners in the nineteenth century; he can waste his life in the baths, orgies, or circuses of the late Roman empire; he can try to escape from an absurd life through drink, drugs, or suicide—as many are doing in today's welfare state.

Of course, one can always reply that all these are consequences of alienation, and they would cease with its abolition. Well, that's possible. But so far this is only a hope, not reality proven by experience; therefore no more defensible than my reservations.

One can argue further that it is not the duty of Marxism to solve life problems for individual people; rather it should be left to the individuals themselves what they should do with their freedom. I, however, as a person struggling with such life problems, am entitled to take issue with Marxism: why doesn't Marxism consider it its duty to deal with the most important questions in life—all of these begin where Marxism ends.

In other words, what I am afraid of is that communism will become one huge Sweden, with a very high standard of living, perfect hygiene, and splendidly organized social relations—and the people will resemble the characters of a Bergman film.

Of course, all of the foregoing assumes that the social program of Marxism is, in the first place, feasible. But, as far as the unlimited wealth of material goods is concerned—a fundamental precondition for the abolition of alienation—I doubt whether this is possible. More precisely, it is questionable whether such a high living standard (and the necessary industrial and technological level) could be achieved for all of the four billion inhabitants of earth, increasing all the time. Without these standards, communism, as conceived by Marx, cannot be accomplished. It is my belief that the amount of raw materials in the earth are insufficient to meet the requirements of world communism; nor could the ecosystem absorb the pollution created by such an economy.

Furthermore, why should conflicts between people cease in communism, why should every kind of oppression or exploitation disappear? According to Marx, the preconditions for this are the wealth of material goods, a certain level of production technology, and the political rule of the working class. In other words, Marx states that the satisfaction of general interests are the consequence of certain objective factors developing in society. The spiritual or moral improvement of individuals is not decisive, only the objective structure of society. As Marx says: "communists don't preach morals . . . They don't exhort the people to love one another, and not to be selfish ... As enlightened as self-interest is at the heart of every system of morality, our task is to ensure that the private interests of the individual should coincide with general human interests."

I, however, believe that any kind of transformation in objective structures is in vain if it is not parallel with an internal improvement in people. As long as people remain selfish, violent, and so on, they will find ways of oppressing and exploiting one another.

These are, therefore, my doubts and reservations about Marxism today. In fact, I have no quarrel with what Marxism *says* but only with what it does *not* say. I object to its silence about the destiny of man, from the anthropological point of view. Without this, one can hardly confront the life problems I indicated above. Furthermore, I blame it for its indifference to the improvement of man: his spiritual and moral perfectibility. Though I admit it's foolish to blame a theory about berries for not talking about bears (who eat them), at the moment I'm more interested in the bear.

THE SCIENCE OF ECONOMICS AND THE EAST EUROPEAN SYSTEMS

TAMAS BAUER

Scientific investigation of the state of affairs in Eastern Europe is dominated by two trends of thinking. One extends from the official political economics to "internal criticism" and is, in effect, an apology for "realistic socialism." This trend deduces from legal, political, and ideological phenomena (e.g., state ownership of the means of production, the rule of the Communist party) *either* (in accordance with official political economics) that all ownership is now collective and that social equality has been realized *or* (in accordance with "internal critics") that objective conditions do exist for the realization of these goals but, owing to mistakes, to more-or-less subjective shortcomings, reality lags behind potentialities. In neither case do they attempt to analyze the real institutional power structure that characterizes the East European economic system; e.g., what the actual property relationships are; what the true situation of direct producers within this structure is; what kinds of interest groups are created by this institutional structure; what the genuine rules of redistribution are, etc., etc. The ideological implications of specific economic and social relationships of the system are disavowed by reference to extraneous influences (the heritage of the past, Western propaganda, etc.); many economic abuses are likewise explained with reference to such influences.

The apologetics of political economics monopolized economic thinking throughout the fifties. Those economists who sought an alterative, turned mostly to the purely technical aspects of economic problems (management and organizational theory); they, more-or-less consciously, swept the social significance of economic problems under the rug. This is quite characteristic of the Soviet mathematical

---

Tamás Bauer (1946–   ), economist. Works at the Institute of Economics of the Hungarian Academy of Sciences. His special areas of interest are the economic reforms and investment cycles of East European countries.

school and its adherents in Bulgaria and Czechoslovakia, or of the efforts towards an economic "praxeology" in Poland or East Germany. As a matter of fact, this is also characteristic of those economic reformers (Hungarian, Soviet, Czechoslovak, and Polish) who simply ignore that there is a problem with self-management. This trend tacitly assumes (and is sometimes openly proclaimed) that state ownership and the leading role of the party, etc., facilitate the Common Good, contingent only on attaining better insight into the laws of economics for its realization. Even in the writings of the most enlightened authors, the cause of all faults is sought in the economic policies, not in the power-relationships emerging from the institutional structure of the economy. Although this trend pays more attention to actual economic relationships, interests, and counter-interests, they are treated as a question of management, organization, and managerial competence. Therefore it assumes that poorly working mechanisms can be changed at will, as if it were only really a matter of detection. The only barrier to action, in this view, is the actual level of technical and economic development.

These trends in economic thinking are unable to explain the fundamental traits of East European economies. They cannot explain economic slowdowns, the repeated troubles of economic imbalance, the peculiar difficulties of coordination, etc. Or, seen from a broader historical perspective, they cannot sensibly explain the necessity for economic reforms; nor why these get on the rocks once launched.

A scientific approach to the economic phenomena of Eastern Europe presupposes the satisfaction of several methodological requirements, all of which are disregarded by the trends indicated above. Without claiming completeness, I quote a few.

1. The interests and actual situation of the participants in production must not be deduced from formal, legal relationships. Their interests, their consciousness, their ideology must be explained by their effective place in the system of production.

2. The efforts and actions of participants in economic life—including the central organs of power—should not be deduced from the interests consistent with the official state ideology but, on the contrary, by those generated by the institutional structure of the economy.

3. If a clearly stated goal is repeatedly frustrated, one should not

assume that unique, chance circumstances are responsible but should try to establish organic reasons; such problems arise not from insufficient knowledge but from a clash of existing interests.

4. Failings in economic life should not be automatically dismissed as necessary, universal economic evils, attributable to the complexity of economic structures, uncoordinated management hierarchy, poor decision making. It is also worth analyzing which "eternal verities" are made recourse to by a given social-economic order; in what manner are these unfavorable tendencies being generated by the interests characteristic of a given system.

No doubt many other requirements could be listed over and above the few quoted above. But, I believe, the basic recommendation would be the same: I am claiming the same methodology, the same approach to facts as applied by Marx in the analysis of nineteenth century capitalism. I believe it would be fruitful to any investigation in—and about—Eastern Europe if it revolved around the analysis of social relations in production; if social and economic processes were explained in terms of productive relationships, thereby also vindicating the historical view.

I mention the historical view to call attention to the fact that the present social and economic order in Eastern Europe is a historical phenomenon and should be analyzed and explained as such. We cannot present it, a priori, as—even if only as in part—the Marxian vision come true. This may only be the end result of the inquiry.

Those scientific and methodological requirements for an analysis of East European economic relations are—to the best of my knowledge—essential features of the *oeuvre* of Marx and Engels, as well as of many Marxist economists in the nineteenth and twentieth centuries. Only in this sense can I view Marxism as a working proposition in Eastern Europe.

As I am unfamiliar with the history of knowledge, I do not know —although I may assume—that the above-mentioned requirements are not exclusive to Marxists. This, however, is beside the point.

There is another point I should raise concerning Marxism as a working proposition for understanding the East European planned economy. I have the feeling (nothing more) that it would be equally fruitful to utilize the categories of Marxian theory of value (private work, social work, concrete work, abstract work, etc.).

Finally, I have to reply to the inevitable rebuttal that Marxism miserably failed in Eastern Europe both as theory and practice. This argument is only partly true. Although I think it is a very important question for the history of knowledge how the current official ideology in Eastern Europe developed from classical Marxism through the mediation of German and Russian Social Democracy and resulted in the apology for "realistic Socialism," it is equally important to realize that this ideology contradicts (both explicitly and implicitly) classical Marxism at least as frequently as it upholds the hallowed tenets. Similarly, though I consider the role Marxism, or rather that of its Leninist version, in the development of the Russian and then East European social and economic systems to be an important problem of economic and social history, I firmly believe that—beginning with Lenin—pragmatic considerations have regularly overridden ideology. It is precisely for this reason that ideology had to change, in order to continue effectively as self-justification. Thus, precious little remained of the original Marxian vision. It is quite another question how realistic this vision has been. However, I suppose it is unnecessary to make a stand on this particular question, one way or the other, in order to explain the differences between the realities of Eastern Europe and Marx's vision of Communism.

WHAT IS MARXISM?

MIKLOS HARASZTI

Marxism is a historical plan. It has a public and a secret doctrine. The public doctrine simply proclaims liberation, and the secret doctrine proclaims liberation to be incumbent on Marxist planners taking power. I doubt whether there is any Marxist tendency not covered by this definition.

This duality simply signifies that Marxism is an ideology: the proper ideology of the planners. Its argumentation—emphasizing at one time the necessity, at another the inevitability, of power for the planners—is merely the handmaiden of the power shift.

Marxism remains insignificant in societies themselves evolving toward a planned society: an independent "revolutionary" ideology for planning would only disrupt the continuity. In the Eastern part of the globe, however, this intellectual Bonapartism is irresistible, while in the West the vitality of democracy renders it impotent.

Where Marxism does become victorious, it will mold the directing-planning-organizing intelligentsia into a ruling class—in effect, becoming the state—and its ideology will become meaningless. The concept of individual autonomy is subordinated to the autonomy of the whole. The party—originally the vanguard of organized intelligentsia—becomes the official guardian of the indivisibility of power, and it believes that Marxist "state religion" is necessary to ensure the rule of the planners. But it must notice, with increasing trepidation, that this guardianship is nearing its end. The liberated planners are ungrateful. There is no alternative to the rule of organized intelligentsia. The planners themselves desire the support of a public opinion instead of dogmas; but it is precisely to the destruction of individual autonomy in the Marxist transformation of society that

---

Miklós Haraszti (1945–   ), writer. In 1970 he was expelled from university, and he was a manual worker from 1970–71. In 1974, he was sentenced to eight months imprisonment, sentence suspended, for his sociographical essay, "Piece rate" (published in English as, *Workers in a Workers' State* [New York: Universe Books, 1978]).

the planners owe their power.* With the "unnecessary" terror, and then the "unnecessary" coordination, in the end it will be "unnecessary" holy text that will fall victim to this paradoxical success of Marxism. The new ideologies of the liberated planners may even include the demand for individual liberty—they need not fear its realization.

Marxism is, of course, not the ideology of the working class. This intellectual vanguard, which took over the leadership of the workers' movement, has been following goals favoring the totality of the modern intelligentsia—the elimination of the bourgeoisie, now dispensable in economic growth; the liquidation of crises and of the class struggle; the introduction of the rule of the whole over individuals—under the slogan of "reason-knowledge-expertise-planning." Once this has been achieved, it will become burdensome to attribute it to the working class. The linkage between socialism and the working class, the idea of liberation, indeed of "self-liberation," of the workers becomes a gesture of deliberate "false consciousness" (to use Marx's words) to ensure social dominance where the intelligentsia would otherwise be unable to gain the upper hand (e.g., in an evolutionary manner). Not even the intelligentsia could achieve the impossible; the liberation of the working class. The prophecy of Marx is becoming more and more cruelly true: the freedom of private property, the rule of the bourgeoisie, is only a transition, to be followed by the great negation—a new civilization.

Marx had enough foresight to perceive that this negation is forced through by the very development of the private-capitalist system. However he may have embellished it, he saw quite clearly where the growth of technology would lead: to a fusion of knowledge, and economic strength, resulting in a situation he describes as the reestablishment of the "umbilical chord" (characteristic of precapitalistic systems), that is, a state of full dependence between ruled and ruler, a complete "embeddedness" of the individual in the whole, the extinction of the autonomy of private interests. Once a Marxist gives up the ideological principle of liberation and merely bathes in the glory of acute foresight, he is no longer a "Marxist,"

---

*Marxist guardianship only assisted this destruction of individual autonomy—begun in late capitalism—though it did transform this process into a creed of redemption, in order to hasten it.

Has the working class been sold down the river? True, the workers have gained nothing—whether from socialism or any other historical movement—resembling an abolition of dependence, exploitation, or meaningless work, which were the promises fuelling their economic struggles. In spite of this, they cannot be considered fully dispossessed. The solution implied in Marx's famous critique —"organization inside the factory; anarchy outside the factory"— namely state ownership of labor, promised security to the workers and power to the organizers. Global direction of the labor force is the grand gift of socialism to the working class.

This class is tied so strongly to modern productive forces that it cannot escape from the dependent role of "executant" of the will of the ruling technology. By the same token, the directing intelligentsia—viewed as the other pole of technology—is compelled to eliminate private property, abolishing autonomy in the labor market, and ensure trouble-free performance by the workers in production.

Socialism, the concentration of all capital in the hands of the state, did not "release the working class from its chains" (again, to use Marx's words), but only from the capriciousness inherent in capitalist competition. Now, they can consider their chains as God-given and reassuring. Thus, the liberation of workers seems indistinguishable from a deprivation of their rights. However, if our indignation is fuelled by illusions that the working class *could* become free without the abolition of the factory—that is, without the disappearance of the working class itself as such—we are guilty of another form of intellectual hypocrisy. Freedom of association for the workers is, of course, a demand near to the heart of every worker—if only they dared to ask for it. However, if, in the future, socialism does show some permissiveness towards this demand, it would only prove that technology, planners, and organizers could make allowances for the ensuing dislocations.

We need not underscore the liberation of the intelligentsia. Nobody should be deceived by the strict hierarchical order, the professional differentiation, concerning the true power of the organized intelligentsia "downward," over the individual. Nobody believes that the assertion by the government leaders of such conceits as being of "working class origin," or similar liturgical stupidities, can deny the fact that they are the intelligentsia in power. It is also quite clear that the organized intelligentsia that has come to constitute the ruling class still needs a parallel "leading role" for a Marxist party, since a more barefaced expression of their various professional and group interests might shake belief in the cult of the "common good," behind which the experts, planners, organizers rule. This may lead to trouble for the bi-polar division of labor, encouraging the "selfish" or the "ignorant" to anarchy. The liberated intelligentsia will march under the banner of Marx-Engels-Lenin-Stalin and their party, for just so long as anything might endanger its rule—including greater freedom for its own members.

Marxism embodies the soul of technology: recognized and religiously adored necessity. Marx, however, was not the first ideologue of this new agent in history: he had been preceded by the "utopian" socialists (e.g., Fourier, Saint Simon, Owen, etc.). But it was Marx who managed to capture the spirit of the age. His critique and promise were so well founded, and his scientific insights such significant contributions, as to entice the intelligentsia away from the spell of individualistic values and urge them toward precipitating their rise—even without Marx—to power. It is almost incomprehensible today how anyone could have swallowed the idea of a classless society. The astonishing success of this specious promise proved that the social crisis was over-ripe. Furthermore, it proved the facility of Marxist socialism to offer self-justification to both of the modern social classes generated by technology, enabling future rulers and subjects to assault the bourgeoisie in a united front.

Marxism offered the world to the organized intelligentsia, a world that only Knowledge—more precisely, Science—could rule. The growth of capitalism—in which knowledge, information, and organization increasingly became the mainsprings of production and the source of power—was the first to offer a world-historical trump card to this ever-changing group—the hereditary suppliers of knowledge. This group is both midwife and child of modern production and management, of self-regenerating science and technology, of property growing into large organizations, of the overweening state: it is the intelligentsia, not the working class, that deserves the title of the "gravedigger of capitalism." The creation of an organized intelligentsia is the defense of society against capitalism, which tends to desecrate all the fundamental features of dignified life. In this revolution, it is individual freedom that the intelligentsia considers expendable. The life work of Marx is one potent argument in favor of the dominance of total planning (i.e., the role of the intelligentsia in the division of labor); and the intelligentsia are right in expecting this turn of the wheel.

One factor in the success of Marxism was the way in which it brought these real interests together in the quasi-religious ideology of liberation. Another, even more important factor, was the linkage of its vision of liberation and the most up-to-date trends of development. This was in consonance with the desire of people for an optimistic ideology preaching the identity of the good, will, and history. Marx put his money on centralization, monopolization, integration. He deduced the end of bourgeois rule from these inevitable consequences of bourgeois production. The world proclaimed by him is the final or permanent victory of these trends.

Who can deny that Marx was the winner with Marxism? The centralized whole cast off every subsidiary form of autonomy and ensured that the enterprise of each individual became subjected to the common good. A lucid society is the dream of every intellectual worth his salt, as it excludes "alienation" and where the place of each individual within society is organically determined. Individual existence can only become rational—according to the doctrine of Marx—if it becomes part of a rational whole, throwing off the shackles of false rationality rooted in autonomy. Though it is ironic, there are noticeable remnants of the idea of "classlessness" in this employee society "freed" from private property. Can this so-called "workers' state"—organized by the thoroughness of the intelligentsia, in which technical management, economic, administrative, and cultural activity, as well as corporate concerns, are united in one huge organization—be conceived as Marxism itself put into practice? It is a fact that the state, having expropriated all capital, became identical with the intelligentsia, the proprietors of all knowledge and all technology. Intellectual activities were organized and the state was structured on the level of the indissoluble, divine unity of anatomy, which, as a result, made the employees into natural underlings, the leaders into their natural representatives and spiritual guides. The coarse rule of money comes to an end. A new civilization rises up, forbidding everyone (not so much by law as by its intellectual power) to worry about the "original intentions" of Marxism—these are too difficult to disentangle anyway. So, the historic plan succeeded.

Those Marxists who would like to jettison the historic plan, who want to crawl out of the ideological straitjacket, are, in actual fact, the creatures of this consummation. Their efforts signal the victory, not the demise, of Marxism. The Marxist, straining against the leash, either challenges the validity of the plan in the evolution of society, or he attempts to change the plan. But he cannot ignore the fact that development and the good are, in reality, unrelated.

Marxists cease to be Marxists, once their belief in development crumbles. Some of them try to remain merely observers on the sidelines, without any constructive ideas; but, as long as they remain Marxists, in whatever manner, they are simply planners in reserve. It is easier for the camel to squeeze through the eye of a needle than for an intellectual (Marxist or not) to be a nonplanner.

This flight of some serious thinkers away from the historic plan signifies that it has lost its creative tension, it has come to represent the status quo and consequently has become empty. Even if we may consider a later "democratization" of the system, non-Marxists are as much the builders of the planners' society as the Marxists, though the non-Marxists may have been thrown out to the margins of this society.

Therefore, I believe that Marxism, being the property of various communist tendencies, will cease to exist with their victory. It has some future only where the grand wedding of state and economy is delayed; and even then it is only a matter of time before a crisis rekindles the fervor of "independent" intelligentsia for the traditional ideology, proclaiming the common interest of employees in corporate state power. And then they will harry the diminishing number of private proprietors, the eroding independence of certain social groups, the evermore meaningless fiction of individual autonomy. Should they be Eurocommunists or members of the New Left, old Marxists or neo-Marxists, their role is the same: following the example of "priests, soldiers, and burghers,"* they are pioneers for the rule of expert bodies most capable of achieving integration. The more radical they are as spokesmen of liberation (whether they are "populist," "democratic," "scientific," or "anti-intellectual"), the more unwitting pioneers they are. "Correct" knowledge of society means a right and duty to power; the individual has no right to refuse this power—this peculiarly Marxist conviction is their common heritage.

---

*A quotation from the Hungarian poet Attila Jozsef. (J. S.)

In spite of the betrayals of reality, this new civilization will always remain "Marxist" in a certain sense: it will follow the logic of its own productive forces, vested in the state, in subjecting society to the drug treatment of subsequent reorganizations. But individuals within it will cease to be Marxists, including the professional specialists of Marxism: they will all try to survive as they can. Even that pale image of the classic Marxist, the marginalized or oppositional Marxist, will die out; being, perhaps, the last to exercise autonomy in choosing to embrace Marxism. We may even think that there is something good in our new civilization inspired by Marxism, if it allows a kind of Taoist withdrawal—instead of prison—to its renegade eggheads. The workers, of course, are not so lucky.

However, in spite of everything being stacked against autonomy, what else can I advocate? I am constitutionally incapable of any other action. Once it becomes clear that socialism has not inaugurated freedom but the tyranny of the technological division of labor, the only remaining political recourse is to work toward enabling the people to free themselves if and when they get thoroughly fed up. One thing is certain: the way forward is not to "make use of" the scope permitted by the existing institutions—this would only strengthen the system's integration—but to realize a (as yet) nonexistent freedom. This is my purpose in this essay.

However, it seems that institutional pluralism or open actions can lead to nothing other than a new version of rule by the intelligentsia. I do not believe that the defeat of monolithic political power would abolish the embeddedness of the individual, the tendency towards an intertwined state and economy, the dictatorship of mass production—socialism is just a particularly brutal embodiment of these tendencies. Political freedom could not reverse these processes, prophesied by an optimistic Marx. Contradictions between various groups of the intelligentsia and the dictatorship they together created offer no guarantee that whatever "democratization" they may allow would be more than the rule of experts minus the ideology. The downfall of doctrinaire police states is not inevitable; but even if this long-awaited moment did arrive, it would not mean the complete liquidation of totalitarianism, only a rearrangement of managerial effectiveness.

Those who, on the other hand, cut loose from the system remain guilt-ridden for their complicity and look forward to an uncertain future. If a pluralism emerged from some sort of upheaval, a framework for the rebirth of a more efficient monolithic power would still remain. The survival of the marginalists (as opposed to their triumph!) depends on the strength they can exercise for the sake of the rebirth and survival—even if not yet a complete victory—of freedom.

Is there anything in our society—or in ourselves—that could offer a way out of the tyranny of planning? (Scientific salvation is out of the question.) The only way to know is to pierce the cell membrane of society. The end of Marxism may even mean recognizing that there can be no correct state of affairs, only correct attitudes. One should not set the fox to care for the geese. If a society of free individuals is at all possible, it can only be accomplished by free people, i.e., by people who are already free.

The question of what Marx actually intended and how far he has been misused is of little consequence. He may have created a surrogate religion, but it, nevertheless, does not contain a perennial message valid beyond its political victory—such a message may be distorted by time, but it will also be repurified by it, eternally realizable. He set his measure for the absolute too low. True religion is tied to the absolute of existence; Marx's absolute is only a rational projection based on social conditions. Its validity depends on its realization. In a genuine religion, we seek the timeless.

All Hungarian materials have been translated by Julian Schopflin

EAST GERMANY

PREFACE

THE SPECIAL CASE OF EAST GERMANY

From its inception in October 1949, the German Democratic Republic (GDR) was confronted with problems shared by no other East European country that fell under Soviet domination.

As a rump territory of the defeated German Reich converted into a "sovereign" state by the Soviet occupation power, the GDR was hard put to establish its legitimacy. It did not constitute a nation and, to this day, remains a land in search of national identity. Any national sentiment rising among its citizens inevitably looks outward—toward West Germany.

But the horrors of Nazism coupled with the promise of socialism furnished an ideological underpinning of the new state's legitimacy. It was to become the antifascist, truly socialist Germany, a "better Germany" and a "socialist nation" (as distinct from the "bourgeois nation" in the West), an embodiment of the ideas of the fathers of Marxism, who, although of German heritage, never saw them fully realized on German soil.

This self-portrayal of East Germany's legitimacy as a state continues to be official ideology. Erich Honecker, the GDR's party and state leader, put it as follows in an address before the East German Socialist Unity Party (SED) Central Committee on 24 May 1978:

> ... the GDR's existence is unique proof of the triumph of the ideas of Marx, Engels, and Lenin on German soil. It becomes clearer with each passing day that the GDR is truly a worker-peasant state representing the interests of all the people. In it, the working class and all other workers have—for the first time in German history—found a real fatherland.... We are thus converting into reality the world-changing ideas of Karl Marx, Engels, and Lenin.

The professed foundations of the new German state attracted to it many prominent intellectuals of the Weimar generation who had fled Hitler's Reich and spent the war in the West, mostly in the United States. Writers Arnold Zweig, Stefan Heym, playwright Bertolt Brecht, philosopher Ernst Bloch, and many others welcomed the creation of "a better Germany," which to them meant, first of all, a Germany thoroughly cleansed of Nazism. The GDR authorities, on their part, promised status and remuneration: they sorely needed this infusion of intellectual respectability or *Geist* to bolster the shaky legitimacy of their regime.

But most of the intellectuals came voluntarily and enthusiastically. By no means all Communists, they nevertheless shared an animus against the West and its bourgeois society. They did not find it incongruous (Brecht in particular) to enjoy the best bourgeois creature comforts in "socialist" East Germany.

Their dream of a Germany in which power *(Macht)* and intellect *(Geist)* would ultimately become reunited in a proletarian spirit was, however, in for a rude awakening. The men entrusted by Moscow to run the state, a group of party apparatchiks headed by the wily and ruthless Walter Ulbricht, were not destined to become builders of a German millennium. If anything, they were executors of Stalin's political will, which required the GDR to become a reliable bridgehead from which Moscow would some day "solve" the entire German question. And, as seasoned party apparatchiks, Ulbricht and his men had only contempt for the *Intelligenzler*—a contempt so well described by Arthur Koestler from his own experience in the German Communist Party.

So the "better Germany" rapidly became a Stalinist satellite, and its intellectuals were reduced to subservience. Those who had returned from exile to live in the "socialist" German nation, rather than in its bourgeois Western counterpart, felt there was no turning back. However disillusioned by the GDR regime, a new "exile" in the capitalist West was not considered a viable or honorable option (although Ernst Bloch, the late Marxist philosopher, did ultimately go back to the West to escape ideological harrassment).

Whatever remained of the myth of "the first truly worker-peasant state on German soil" was exploded on June 17, 1953. On that day, workers in East Berlin and throughout the GDR, angered by a high-handed increase in work norms that would have drastically cut their wages, rose in spontaneous demonstrations. The protest was put down by Soviet occupation troops. Some 400 workers were killed in the fighting, dozens were later condemned to death by GDR and Soviet military courts, and thousands were sentenced to long prison terms.

It was on this occasion that Bertolt Brecht wrote what was possibly his last poem:

> Following the June Seventeenth uprising
> the secretary of the Writers League
> had leaflets distributed on Stalin Allee
> where one could read that the people
> had forfeited the confidence of the government
> and could regain it only through redoubled efforts.
> Wouldn't it be simpler under these circumstances
> for the government to dissolve the people
> and elect another one?

No more bitter and fitting epitaph could be written to the dream of a "better Germany," which Brecht and his contemporaries had come to the GDR to realize. Thus, by 1953, the infusion into the GDR of a Weimar liberal spirit had virtually come to a dead end. That the presence of this spirit in the early days of the GDR was more ornamental than anything else is not really the issue here. Rather, it is that its demise—in large part a logical consequence—broke a link of political continuity. It is one of the reasons why, unlike in the other East European countries, political dissent in the GDR today shows relatively less fallback on the more liberal national traditions.

There are other reasons as well, all of them connected with the aberration of Nazism and the circumstances under which the GDR was created to become a separate society. From its inception, the GDR has always lived in a state of ideological quarantine, designed to make fellow-Germans in the West appear as hostile foreigners. Official ideology has even produced a version of the Berlin Wall in the curious concept of *Abgrenzung* (literally delimitation): let us be separate, let us live as if there were nothing German outside the GDR borders.

And while self-styled ideological purity may be the only remaining pillar of the GDR's doubtful legitimacy as a German state, it has been reinforced by what author Guenter Grass has called *das Systemdenken der Deutschen* (the Germans' tendency toward systemic thinking). This tendency toward an all-encompassing perfectionism and either-or propositions has given East Germany's official ideology an aggressive self-righteousness unequalled elsewhere in Eastern Europe; it would be surprising if it does not frequently grate on the Soviet guardians of true Marxist-Leninist orthodoxy.

But dissident thought in the GDR is not wholly unaffected by the environment it rebels against. The gap between the strident perfectionism of official theory and the totally different reality that produces and inflames dissident thought is in itself an invitation to another *Systemdenken* and utopia.

The GDR, a splinter of a nation founded as if to begin Year Zero in German history, is indeed a unique political environment in relation to the rest of Eastern Europe.

The grand old man of East German political dissent is unquestionably Robert Havemann. Born in 1910, Havemann joined the German Communist Party in 1932 and the anti-Nazi resistance during the war. He was caught and condemned to death for high treason in 1943; at one point, he was a jail cell neighbor of Erich Honecker. But because of Havemann's scientific expertise in physical chemistry, his sentence was commuted to hard labor. Liberated at war's end by the Soviets, he wound up in West Berlin and was appointed by the American forces to head what later became the Max Planck Institute. But the Americans removed him from this position in 1948—Havemann believes they suspected him of being a Soviet spy.

He thereupon moved to the GDR and, as party member and respected scientist, was in good graces with the regime. But his personal beliefs increasingly clashed with official policy, and by the early 1960s, when virtually all critical voices in the GDR fell silent, Havemann was the sole exception. In university and public lectures, he called for greater freedom and discussion and attacked the Stalinist features of the GDR regime. He repeatedly incurred the wrath of the GDR authorities by publishing his views in West Germany, often in social-democratic journals. Refusing to recant, Havemann was ultimately expelled from the party and forced into retirement. Yet he has remained defiant and, despite police surveillance and harassment, managed to send statements of his personal views to the West. Among the most recent was a taped interview broadcast by the Berlin RIAS network in October, 1978. In the statement, Havemann recalled the events of June 17, 1953, when in his view the East German party should have stood by the workers rather than given way to the Soviet military. Condemning the life style of the

GDR leaders, who live behind high walls and barbed wire and travel in armored limousines, Havemann said:

> This kind of actual socialism is not viable; it cannot sustain itself, especially in competition with an actual capitalism. Socialism without democracy, without democratic control over all power functions, without a democratic decision process in establishing production plans, in setting goals of social labor and creative social work, is unthinkable. It is no socialism when the overwhelming majority of people are totally at the mercy of the decisions of a tiny group. Socialism is the road toward a goal. This goal is by its nature phantastic and great and utopian.

In a new book of Havemann's writings, published in October, 1978,* the effects of his own long isolation, enforced by the GDR regime, becomes increasingly visible. Still calling himself "a German Communist," he envisions a social order in which there would be no privileged stratum, no poverty, no constraints on individual freedom, and everyone would have access to humanity's cultural treasures: "I believe that if a world without armament and without the mindless waste of capitalism is conceivable, such a Communism has long been feasible for all."† According to recent reports, Havemann is planning to design a convincing Communist utopia as an alternative not only to capitalism but also to "actual socialism."

While Havemann's statements and writings have always been those of an individual merely stating his personal beliefs, his views and his courage in speaking out cannot have failed to influence other dissidents in the GDR. He was outspoken in supporting the Dubcek reform course in Czechoslovakia in 1968 (his two sons were jailed for a protest against the Warsaw Pact invasion), and the essay, perhaps, most representative of his thinking was written in regard to the Czechoslovak events. Originally published on 10 October 1969 in the Hamburg liberal weekly, *Die Zeit,* and reprinted in a 1977 collection of Havemann's writings,** it is included here.

Ein Deutscher Kommunist. Rueckblicke und Perspektiven aus der Isolation (A German Communist: Reflections and Perspectives of an Isolated Life) (Reinbeck: Rowohlt Verlag, 1978).
†*Der Spiegel,* 2 October 1978.
**Robert Havemann, *Berliner Schriften (Berlin Writings)* Andreas W. Mytze (Berlin: Verlag Europaeische Ideen, 1977).

* * *

However much Havemann's lonely courage might have inspired others in the GDR to express their dissent, his *ouvriériste* version of a Communist future has apparently had few followers among the younger critics of the regime. If this impression is correct, one may wonder why a thoughtful man whose socialist and antifascist credentials are beyond reproach should be unable to bridge the generation gap, unlike what prevails elsewhere in Eastern Europe. Once again the history of the GDR may be a factor, but there is also the East German regime's remarkably successful suppression of any public debate on reforms (as well as conducting its internal struggles entirely in camera). Unlike in most other East European countries, in East Germany it is very hard to judge the extent to which the ideas of individual critics are shared by the population at large. There is virtually no *samizdat* being circulated in the GDR, perhaps owing not so much to the efficiency of the GDR police as to the fact that banned manuscripts can be and are easily published in the FRG, from where the texts are broadcast to the GDR population. But it would be rash to infer from this atomization a political apathy on the part of the East German population.

In any event, the literary scene has long been a problem child for the GDR authorities, who have meanwhile adopted a policy of wholesale expulsion of inconvenient authors. Often times, young GDR writers committed to Marxist socialism have irked the authorities by deriding the official emphasis on the presumed material accomplishments of the GDR. In the view of these critics, the GDR has reverted to capitalist yardsticks and obscured the "fundamental" difference between East and West German societies. Others write merciless portrayals of the alienated GDR worker, the very same worker alleged to be the real master of the productive process. These and similar literary themes have been common elsewhere in Eastern Europe, where as a rule they become part of the broader current calling for political reform. If this process is under way in the GDR, it is not easily discernible to the outside observer. Open political, especially Marxist or socialist, dissent, still seems a matter of individuals and their personal beliefs.

Apart from Havemann, the two prominent names in the GDR's Marxist dissent are those of Wolfgang Harich and Rudolf Bahro. Unlike Havemann, both derive their entire political experience from the GDR; in fact, they are products of the SED apparatus. No less utopian than Havemann (or the late Ernst Bloch), they do not espouse any comparable version of an open socialist society; despite major differences between them, both seem to have in mind what would be essentially an authoritarian welfare state.

Harich, who joined the SED in 1946 when in his mid-twenties, rose rapidly to become professor of Marxist philosophy and editor of a major theoretical journal. And his fall was equally rapid in 1956, when he was arrested for "organizing a conspiratory antistate group" and sentenced to ten years in prison.

At that time, his inspiration was the Twentieth Congress of the Soviet Communist Party, at which Khrushchev denounced Stalin's crimes. In the belief that the anti-Stalin trend in the USSR gave a green light to Ulbricht's opponents in the GDR to oust him, in July 1956 Harich drew up "sixteen theses" on the German road to socialism. He demanded a doctrinal and organizational transformation of the SED to eliminate party dictatorship over the state (but pointed out that the reformed SED "should remain in control"). Pleading for a creative discussion of Marxist theory, Harich suggested that it encompass the ideas of Trotsky, Bukharin, Rosa Luxemburg (whose criticism of Lenin's Blanquist principles of party organization he expressly supported), and also Kautsky and some social-democratic theorists. His platform also called on the SED to "adopt aspects of the Yugoslav experience and those characteristic elements of theoretical discussions in Poland and China." For good measure, Harich expressed admiration for Karl Liebknecht's moral fortitude in breaking party discipline.

This would have been enough to raise the hackles of every apparatchik from East Berlin to Vladivostok. However, Harich's misreading of what was politically possible at the time went even further. Having previously established contact with some West German social democrats, Harich in effect proposed to scuttle Moscow's German policy and substitute his own proposals for a German reunification in socialism. Reformation of the East German party was to be a stage leading to reunification, in the process of which the GDR could even adopt a parliamentary coalition government with the FRG. Worse still, he concluded that Soviet Communism, shaped by Russia's backwardness and absence of democratic tradition, was not and could not be a model for Europe; exported to Eastern Europe after the war, in Harich's view it played a reactionary role. Consequently, he viewed resistance to Soviet hegemony (and the "sacred caste of generals") as an expression of the popular revolutionary struggle against the Stalinist party apparatus.

It says something of Harich that he took his theses to the SED authorities and to the Soviet ambassador in East Berlin. Failing their acceptance, he took them to the West German magazine, *Der Spiegel,* attempting to convince its editors of his plan's "historical inevitability." The outcome was not difficult to predict, except perhaps by Harich himself.

When released from prison in 1964, Harich was "resocialized," according to some of his critics. Employed in a minor editorial position, he was permitted to publish in 1968. But his main work since then, *Communism Without Growth,* * has appeared only in West Germany.

The book indicates Harich has abandoned the more liberal views he advocated in 1956. As he put it in an interview in 1975, "Pluralism, a call for more freedom or the like, is clearly not a concern of mine." The following year, he supported the expulsion of balladeer Wolf Biermann, perhaps the closest of East German dissidents to Robert Havemann. Biermann's comment on Harich, understandably emotional ("he wants total-world Stalinism"), is nevertheless not far off the mark.

Harich, ever the utopian, has his own recipe for solving the problems of ecology: a world proletarian revolution that would facilitate an immediate transition to communism. In his view, this means "rationing everything now" on a socialist basis; "and, with rationed distribution, would we not then find ourselves in a communism à la Babeuf?"—a revealing reference indeed. Harich's communism of rationing is a "home of ecological reason with strict social justice." People will have to be dictated and reeducated, disabused of "prosperity striving, the fetish of growth, the illusions of consumerism."

But, according to Harich, the East has been ahead in this effort: its authoritarian (Stalinist?) structures have already enforced much of the sacrifice that is now necessary for the West. Ecological pressure is now becoming the means of forcing the West into communism. Harich's vision of the future is a puritan society submissive to

---

**Kommunismus ohne Wachstum* (Reinbeck: Rowohlt Verlag, 1975).

ecological (planning) authority: the future is more discipline, more sacrifice, and more regimentation.

It is fair to assume that this utopia of an ascetic police state is unlikely to attract a wide popular following. In any event, it was not published in the GDR, where the regime remains obsessed with economic growth, in the hope that improved living standards would at least defuse political discontent. So Harich has in effect removed himself from any possible following and practical influence in the GDR. His is perhaps the extreme case of *Systemdenken* and the virtual inability to combine critical reasoning with practical politics.

But if the SED apparatus ever congratulated itself on "resocializing" Harich, it was unprepared for the new and much more formidable challenge to arise in the person of Rudolf Bahro. He is in some ways the most unlikely and most unexpected kind of a dissident; again, probably without parallel elsewhere in Eastern Europe. No party apparatchik can dismiss Bahro as a mere *intelligenzler* (as he can sneer at Professor Havemann, singer Biermann, or any literary figure). Bahro, a lifelong apparatchik himself, knows what he is talking about, and his critique hits all the harder coming, as it does, from within the very heart of the system.

Bahro, born in 1935, is wholly a product of the GDR. He studied philosophy and served the party as an agitator in factories and as an editor of party youth journals. But the crucial years of Eastern Europe—1956 and 1968—had an impact on him too. In 1956, student Bahro was dissatisfied with the official explanation of the Hungarian events and later got involved in minor controversies over magazine articles, but by 1967 he was settled as an administrator of an East Berlin rubber factory. It was here that Bahro gained insight into "actual socialism" as it is practiced in the world of production, on the factory floor. With the Warsaw Pact invasion of Czechoslovakia in 1968—an event which Bahro says ultimately determined his position—the skeptic came to challenge the entire system.

Working in the apparatus by day, Bahro spent years studying and writing in his spare time; his colleagues and the party had no inkling of his off-hour plans or activities. In five years, by 1976, Bahro had completed a manuscript, and the following years he arranged for its publication in West Germany.* With meticulous preparation, and

---

*Rudolf Bahro, *Die Alternative. Zur Kritik des real existierenden Sozialismus* (Cologne-Frankfurt: Europaeische Verlagsanstalt, 1977).

clearly expecting to be arrested on publication of his book, Bahro organized a veritable publicity blitz. He taped interviews with both West German TV networks and the RAIS radio in West Berlin to be broadcast on publication day—the East German police obliged by arresting him within hours of the broadcasts. Bahro also prepared his own summary of the book in the form of six lectures (included here).

Emerging from lifelong obscurity, Bahro nonetheless compared himself with Marx, in the sense that he subjected "actual socialism" to the kind of critique Marx applied to capitalism. But the Marxist provenance of Bahro's thought is unquestionable: he can hardly be dismissed as a revisionist bourgeois critic (and the East German regime did not even try). As a West German reviewer put it, Bahro is "erudite, authentic, angry, and, on top of it all, so original in his utopian thinking."

And a Marxist utopia is precisely what Bahro has in mind. Unlike Czechoslovak or Polish reform communists, he does not propose to modify "actual socialism" by attaching to it liberal or market features. He gives no consideration to aspects of "bourgeois" pluralist society; when he refers to freedom of opinion, he recognizes it solely within the framework of the party. Nor does Bahro call for observance of human rights as an end in itself; rather, he calls for a "cultural revolution" (to follow the communist revolution) when society would become reconstituted on the basis of communes integrated by a party that forswears any dictatorial role. Equality is more important to him than freedom. In a less extreme fashion than Harich, Bahro nevertheless envisions a system in which material allocation is totally controlled and money ultimately eliminated.*

Bahro's finding that the root of the problem lies in combining state authority with economic power, and that, as a result, communist bureaucracies develop special interests—which they pursue brazenly and with impunity—is not original. Bahro's related concept of the worker's "subalternity," for example, echoes Milovan

---

*In an interview with the *Koelner Stadtanzeiger*, 12 May 1978, Wolfgang Harich expressed agreement with Bahro's approach to material allocation and elimination of money. A society as designed by Bahro would be workable and desirable in Harich's view, as long as political apparatchiks remain in power. "A political apparatchik, however obtuse, is still closer to me than the cleverest degreed engineer or the smartest manager; and I have nothing against them being somewhat curbed in our system by the politburocracy so disliked by Bahro."

Djilas in *The New Class*. As Djilas noted, in both capitalism and socialism the worker is forced to sell his labor as his only asset, but in a bureaucratic communist state acting as sole employer he has to do so under terms and conditions he is unable to influence. Or, as some Hungarian dissidents have put it, the worker remains a worker whether under capitalism or under socialism, only more so under the latter.

However, Bahro's utopian economic solution, which emphasizes levelling as well as a degree of puritanical asceticism, is unique among the dissidents. The West German news magazine, *Der Spiegel*, 30 October 1978, carried the text of what was described as a letter by Bahro to a fellow inmate in prison. In it, Bahro tried to summarize his views on where the ultimate emancipation of mankind lies. If authentic, the letter reveals Bahro at his most utopian (prison can concentrate man's mind wonderfully, as it apparently did in Harich's case): the axis of the whole problem, according to Bahro, lies "not just in the overturn of capitalist production relations but the entire industrial civilization created since 1789." This civilization has not brought any happiness to man and sacrificed the individual to "growth"—a concept outlined, though without such Rousseau-like language, in the discussion on the new despotism of industrialization in *The Alternative*.

In *The Alternative*, it is difficult to discern whom Bahro is addressing—dissident Marxist intellectuals, oppositionists in the SED apparatus, or just workers and the general population (who may have some difficulty with the nature of Bahro's utopia and his nearly religious Marxist faith). In actual fact, his proposed solutions have little to attract anyone, but his incisive and merciless dissection of the system is sure to have a wide impact. The GDR regime's clumsy handling of Bahro may well have extended the reach of his ideas. Arrested within hours of first publicizing his thought in the West, he was absurdly charged with "intelligence activities"; indeed, he did spy on the apparatus of which he was a part. In June 1978, Bahro was sentenced to eight years in prison for "betraying secrets to circles hostile to the GDR, deliberately fabricating false reports, gross distortions, and untruthful allegations"—perhaps the best possible advertising Bahro could have wished for himself. In what may have been the most realistic comment on his impact, Bahro observed prior to his arrest: "Es denkt in der DDR," which may be loosely translated as, "There is some thinking going on in the

GDR," and which recalls Leszek Kolakowski's observation in Poland in 1956 that "thinking has a colossal future."

*   *   *

Just how many are prepared to follow him on the road to a new communist utopia is an open question. Bahro himself has recognized that another version of Marxism may not be what the proletariat in the GDR, or elsewhere in the East, is hankering for.

Just as these issues were being mulled over by observers of the German scene, *Der Spiegel* came up with a new document. Carried in two installments on 2 and 9 January 1978 by the Hamburg news magazine, the "Manifesto of the First Organized Opposition in the GDR" added fuel to the debate started by Bahro. From the outset, the authenticity of the document (dated "Berlin, October 1977") was doubted. The East German authorities, not surprisingly, declared it to be a forgery by the West German intelligence agencies. Official West German reaction was evidently dictated by concern over what publication of this document, with its anti-Soviet and German nationalist overtones, might do to Bonn's efforts to improve relations with the GDR and the Soviet Union. Some of the official speculations suggested that it was a deliberate effort by the GDR's Stalinists, or its security apparatus, to disturb bilateral relations; Herbert Wehner, a leader of the West German social-democrat party, described it as a deliberate provocation by whoever was responsible for it.

Among the East German dissidents, the judgment was on the whole more positive. Robert Havemann saw the document as genuine insofar as invention was unnecessary to describe the popular mood in the GDR. Wolfgang Harich faulted it on not reflecting the language of genuine Communists and suggested that the expelled balladeer, Wolf Biermann, might be the author. Biermann disclaimed authorship ("Do I write such bad German?") but published, in the respected political weekly, *Die Zeit,* 27 January 1978, a letter to the "comrades" in the GDR both welcoming and criticizing the document. What he welcomed in it was the idea of a left-wing East-West entente and articulation of what had been his own experience in the GDR. His criticism was directed at the document's lack of respect for Marx, its "Chinese-style" anti-Sovietism and "hysterical" language; he also deplored the comparison between Nazism and Stalinism. He concluded his open letter by saying, "I'll eat a broomstick if there are more of you than twenty."

Der Spiegel, for its part, has maintained that the document is genuine and a product of middle and upper level SED functionaries. It has refused to give their names, but, under the circumstances, this is understandable.

When the dust settled, the considered judgment of the majority of experts was that the claim of an existing "organized group" in opposition to the GDR regime may be exaggerated, but the document itself, as *Die Zeit* put it, is probably genuine. (It may be recalled in this context that some Czechoslovak and Polish dissident texts, ultimately turning out to be the work of an individual or small coterie, nevertheless articulated much broader sentiment and exercised a major influence in the reform process.)

The main problem with the "manifesto" is its language. It indicates that no real Marxist or even economist had a hand in its drafting. It has been suggested that the authors may be former social democrats, brought into the SED by forced merger, who have a pronounced dislike of the regime's political style, its self-praise and sycophancy before the Soviets. The use of words such as *Hiwi* (non-German volunteer helpers of the Nazi occupation in the East) and *Quisling* (after Vidkun Quisling, the Norwegian politician who administered Norway for the Nazis during World War II—stands for traitor), which are no longer current with the younger generation, and references to the conspiratorial practices of the Nazi regime seem to give some substance to this supposition. (Unlike the former social democrats, inveterate Communists, being old practitioners, don't get upset over conspiratorial methods.)

On the other hand, the text's "Chinese" language was thought by some to imply participation of younger oppositionists. But the document reveals little real knowledge of Chinese theories or policies. References to the Soviet Union's "red imperialism" and the "red popes in Moscow" or arguments against detente may sound "Chinese," but they may simply reflect the kind of language common among GDR citizens in private discussions.

Thus, the authenticity of the "manifesto" and what status its alleged authors hold remains unclear. But the text may well reflect discussions inspired by the Bahro affair and a reaction to his thesis which, because of Bahro's Marxist commitment and his utopianism, may not be acceptable to the broader population. The "manifesto" is strongly resentful of the country's subservience to the Soviet Union and emphasizes German unity. That these themes would be raised in any unofficial discussion by GDR citizens may well be taken for granted.

Even if the organizational claim is almost surely exaggerated, the language uneven and often uninformed, and the authorship a mystery, the "manifesto" is certain to have political consequences in East Germany. The document appears to be the work of several hands, the result of an argument rather than an actual, definite movement; its language of resentment seems in any event to represent a wider undercurrent of critical discontent. The GDR authorities reacted furiously to the document's publication, indicating, perhaps, that a more "popular" version of an opposition platform was at least as unwelcome as the meticulous Marxism of Bahro's critique.

Included here are excerpts from the "Manifesto" compiled by "the First Organized Opposition in the GDR."

Karl Reyman

THE SOCIALISM OF TOMORROW

ROBERT HAVEMANN

It is both difficult and hazardous to draw comparisons between historical epochs. It is impossible to compare our epoch with any past one. Ours is unique.

From the earliest aircraft to the moon landing; from the first steam engine to the nuclear power plant; from the manual calculator to the electronic computer; from Edison's phonograph and Bell's telephone to direct telecast of a moon landing; from the first grenade to an intercontinental rocket with a hydrogen warhead—all this within barely a hundred years.

In the medieval craft guilds it was strictly forbidden for master craftsmen to gain personal advantage from using any new technique, new materials, or new tools in their work. In India, in the huge city of New Delhi, I saw an old man in his shop treading a large wheel that operated, by means of long belts, a variety of small lathes and drills. When I asked why a small electric motor was not used, the reply was: but then our products would not be "pure" handicraft. Once such notions were swept away and it became permissible to gain unlimited personal advantage from producing better and more cheaply than the competition, the era of technological progress and modern capitalism was ushered in.

Capitalism lives on technological progress and generates it. Marx prophesied that the capitalist production relations—that is, the private acquisition of products made by society—will increasingly lead to shackling the development of productive forces. The ever-sharpening contradiction between labor and capital would finally lead to a revolutionary upheaval of society, to a socialist revolution, as a result of which the development of productive forces would be freed from their shackles and would undergo a new dynamic upsurge for the benefit of humanity as a whole.

Thus far, Marx's prophecy has not materialized. Capitalism is least endangered by revolutionary forces precisely in those countries where technological progress has advanced the most. Rather, the first victorious socialist revolution took place in a very backward country, in tsarist Russia, having been made possible primarily by Russia's military defeat in World War I. But in Germany, the socialist revolution failed, however much it was assisted by the chaos of defeat. Only in the aftermath of World War II could the revolution be expanded successfully. With the Red Army victory over Hitler's Wehrmacht, the revolution spread to the East European countries, the only exceptions being Finland, Austria, and Greece. The collapse of Hitler's Germany also led to the establishment of the first socialist German state, the German Democratic Republic. Perhaps the most momentous socialist revolution after World War II, however, took place in the huge country of China, where the Chinese Communists arose, largely, on their own and took power aided only by the collapse of Japan. Finally, Fidel Castro's revolution in Cuba, a victory of communism without a Communist party, without any external aid, in a small country right on the front door steps of the United States, on which it, as a single-crop producer of sugar, totally depended economically—therefore a country with an economy deformed, to a large extent, by colonial exploitation, which is typical for most Latin American states.

Lenin explained the victory of the socialist revolution in a backward country by his theory of the weakest link. The capitalist chain first broke, not where it was the strongest, but in backward Russia. But the hope of the Russian revolutionaries that once the chain is broken the entire capitalist system would fall into the abyss has not materialized. Trotsky flatly denied the possibility of building socialism in a single country, especially one so politically and economically backward as Russia. In his view, the revolution could not be allowed to stop, it had to be permanent.

So Marx was wrong. They all were wrong, Lenin and Trotsky as well. The capitalist chain withstood the break in its weakest links. Socialist revolution is typical not of the advanced but of the backward countries. The building of socialism in one country is possible: the Soviet Union today is one of the world's two superpowers, capitalist America being the other. Yet one man was right, the man who has left the deepest imprint on the face of the Soviet Union: Stalin.

After Lenin's death Stalin ended the New Economic Policy and began systematically to build up the economy by means of five-year plans. He rigorously enforced the collectivization of farming, and he gave priority to developing heavy industries to strengthen the country militarily and prepare it for war with Hitler's Germany. In order to gain time, he concluded a pact with Hitler hoping that Hitler would destroy himself in a war with the Western powers. In the end, Stalin, with the help of Russian winter, defeated Hitler and chased the fascist occupiers and land robbers to the devil. Stalin managed to assure the Soviet Union's survival through the difficult and dangerous decades of capitalist encirclement and ultimately, during World War II, even to win capitalist allies in his struggle against Hitler's Germany, his most dangerous capitalist enemy.

The deadly external threat to the Soviet Union, which existed in varying degrees of acuteness from 1917 to 1950 when a nuclear stand-off with the United States was achieved, of necessity led to a feeling of great internal insecurity. At no time during this long period could the regime allow even the slightest political turmoil in the country. It was virtually inevitable that this situation lead to a system of brutal repression. Murder is almost always committed out of fear. And this was particularly true for the mass murder of millions in Stalin's camps. The terrible aspect of fear, however justified it may be, is that it causes blindness. The fear in a Stalinist regime remains terrible in its blindness to this very day.

The essential aspect of Stalinist socialism, however, is not police terror, an unrestrained secret police, or suppression of all critical—not to mention oppositional—political and ideological opinion. In principle what is much more important is the economic structure. This is the foundation upon which the Stalinist superstructure grows and thrives. In economic terms, the socialist revolution is only half completed in Stalinist socialism: it is not the producers, the workers, and farmers who are the owners replacing capitalists and landowners; rather, it is the state. The masses do not at all exercise a dictatorship of the proletariat. This would be a dictatorship by the majority over an historically bankrupt minority. But instead of the popular masses, it is a minority of functionaries who exercise the dictatorship and who regard themselves as representatives of the popular masses. So we have the emergence of all the characteristics of a dictatorship by a minority. The question is: could the October Revolution not have stopped halfway? Were the workers already able at that time to take over the factories with all the powers of decision vested in their former owners? What then would have been the role of the state in the economic field?

There is little doubt that such a completion of the revolution in October 1917, and even for a long time thereafter, was a virtual impossibility. Trotsky was right after all: the building of socialism in a single country, which was threatened from both outside and inside and saddled with an extremely backward economy, was not possible. This reaffirms Marx's fundamental thesis on the economic prerequisites for a socialist revolution. Because the economic prerequisites were entirely lacking in the Russia of that time, the revolutionary movement was still able to win but could not achieve its goals. There was only one thing it could do: wage a desperate struggle to preserve the revolutionary power against the counterrevolution. For this reason Lenin introduced a ban on Party factionalism—after he had himself made masterly use of factional techniques. This ban, as well as all other restrictions on intraparty and state democracy, were at that time considered provisional measures, applicable only for a temporary period of internal and external danger. But they outlasted their time and became the foundation of political Stalinism.

In the Stalinist state the entire economy is directed as a unit by the state. It is unimportant to what limited extent individual factory managements or leaders of factory groupings may have freedom of decision making. All important matters are decided by the state and the (party) Central Committee. In principle this system resembles a giant monopoly corporation. Any effect of economic competition is effectively screened out, even in the foreign trade area. The prices at which the state trading authorities sell goods in the country or abroad are without any economic significance for the producers. Before economic reforms were introduced over the past few years, the decisive yardstick for the factories was solely the qualitative and quantitative fulfillment of the plan. It was a hazardous undertaking, at best, to calculate production costs in units of money. Most prices were wholly unrealistic. Although construction costs in the GDR probably are not below those in the Federal Republic, rents in the FRG are about three or four times higher. Similarly, the prices for electricity, gas, water, transportation, postal service, and telephone are substantially lower in the GDR. However, prices for cigarettes, coffee, wine, and many industrial products such as TV sets, refrigerators, washing machines, bicycles, and cars are twice or three times over those in West Germany. Profits obtained from one group of goods pay for price subsidies in another group. But the overall calculation always adds up—it must add up since the state has the complete freedom of setting prices. However, in the tangle of unrealistic prices, any yardstick for calculating effective economic costs of production is lost. Without knowing the true production costs it is absolutely impossible to carry on reasonable economic planning. The danger lies in the economy becoming organized in such a way that it functions smoothly but only at a fraction of what would be attainable with the available labor and resources.

From the point of view of Marxist economic theory, we see here the consequences of ignoring the law of value. This law is applicable to socialist economies as well. Many years ago in Czechoslovakia the disproportion between meat and bread prices was so great that it was cheaper to obtain meat by feeding cheap bread to one's own pig or rabbit. The law of value requires that the value of a product and its price—leaving aside temporary market variations—should in the long run remain in balance. Value is an abstract entity. It is determined by the socially necessary input of labor required for the production of a commodity. Price is a concrete entity. In a market economy it is negotiated daily by means of supply and demand in the commodity market. If the demand rises, so does price. If the price rises, the additional profit stimulates production, as a result of which the supply rises and deflates the price again. The market is a cybernetic regulator of the economy. According to Stalin, in a socialist economy the market must not exercise any feedback effect on production. But a market that has no such feedback is no market at all—it is merely an imperfectly and unjustly functioning place where rationed goods are being distributed. As long as the output of goods is insufficient to satisfy demand, it is possible to make do with such a market substitute. But as soon as goods offered in a socialist state are priced beyond the range of the buyers, the state must either lower prices or restrict production. It does both, even though most reluctantly.

The shortage economy, indeed for the most part the virtual war economy of the Stalinist period, has led a series of wholly untenable fixed ideas in the heads of party economists. Because a genuine market where prices are negotiated according to supply and demand allows for capitalist profit, it is regarded as evil business where buyers are cheated and exploitation reaches its zenith. That according to Marx exploitation takes place in the sphere of production, that the market itself exploits at most only the sales personnel, and that in the capitalist market there occurs a relatively insignificant redistribution of the surplus value created in production (due only to the retention of capital in the form of stocked goods and facilities), seems to have been forgotten. Indeed, there is virtually no surplus value created in the market. The market is a most serviceable method for automatic regulation of the production processes and provides for the optimum satisfaction of buyers' desires. Naturally, it is a fact that in capitalism the market serves the interests of capital. Why, under socialist conditions, should it not serve the interests of the whole community equally well or better?

An absolutely free market delineated in the liberal theory, of course, does not exist and has never existed anywhere. At all times the market is subject to manipulation. In capitalism this is by the big corporations and trusts, and lately also to a growing extent by the state. The socialist state, too, will manipulate the market, with a variety of conceivable motives: in the interest of the country's defense, of economic independence, and finally to promote its own withering away, to the extent that this process is under way. As the state withers away, the market too will disappear. The market will become superfluous as social consumption proceeds to replace individual consumption. In communism, at last, there will be no market.

Many of the ideas I have only sketched out here have been under discussion for years by a variety of Marxist theorists in socialist countries—Oskar Lange in Poland, Liberman in the Soviet Union, Fritz Behrens in the GDR, and Ota Sik in Czechoslovakia. Initial experiments in economic reform have already been undertaken. In the GDR an attempt was made to gradually reduce the extreme violations of the law of value by a reform of industrial pricing. But recently the ideas of these reformers have again been brought into disrepute. They are criticized as representing modern revisionism.

The source of the difficulty is simply that economic questions are also political questions, that they are questions of power. Stalinist economy cannot be reformed in economic terms without also reforming it in political terms—that is, without overcoming Stalinism as a political system. Economic democracy, meaning the people's mastery over the economy, requires the implementation of political democracy, a transition toward democratic socialism. The socialist revolution can be completed politically and socially only when this has occurred, and not before.

Czechoslovakia's Communists took this decisive step toward completing the socialist revolution in January 1968. After long years of the repression and crime of the Stalinist Novotny regime, which disrupted the country's economy and shackled its science, arts, and culture, a group of reformers headed by Alexander Dubcek emerged victorious in the Central Committee. It was a revolution from above, a victory of the better Communists over the Stalinists. For the first time they combined not only in their words but also in their actions socialism with freedom. The result was the broadest mass support ever enjoyed by a Communist party, above all among industrial workers and students.

The eight months from January through August 1968 were a time of great hopes. What was happening in Czechoslovakia was the long-awaited realization of an old and almost no longer believed dream. Socialism and democracy were to be brought into harmony. The fascinating ramifications of the Czechoslovak developments radiated farther from month to month. In May there were heavy revolutionary struggles in France that almost led to an overthrow. But the movement petered out, for lack of a clear and determined leadership. In Czechoslovakia the process advanced inexorably— until that fateful, black day in the history of the communist movement when troops of five Warsaw Pact states marched in and occupied the country that had embarked on the road to a humane socialism.

Since that time, dark clouds have again shadowed socialism's future. Alexander Dubcek, first arrested, later reinstated but ultimately deposed, was replaced by the pliant Husak, who had himself spent ten years in Novotny's prisons. The only encouraging aspect of this time was the mass protest against the invasion by Communist parties world-wide; there were also protests inside the five states, but these were harshly suppressed. The Soviet party leadership has attempted to justify the invasion as an act of assistance in defense against a threatening counter-revolution. A heated debate is going on in the communist movement in regard to this so-called Brezhnev Doctrine. And it is emphatically rejected by many Communist parties especially in Western Europe—among them the largest, in France and Italy—but also in the East by the Romanian and Yugoslav parties. It was not only the reformers' victory in Prague but also their suppression which has caused turmoil and movement in world communism!

The repercussions of historical events of such magnitude cannot be undone. On the contrary, one can see here a replay of the old theme in Greek tragedy: people bring upon themselves the very fate they had been trying to escape. But this inexorable and imminent tragedy will not only be of Stalinism, which must be eliminated for the simple reason that it no longer corresponds to current reality. The anxious questions that nowadays concern all communists is how, and under what convulsions, will this colossus fall, and how long will the agonizing spectacle of its death throes last.

One of the fundamental discoveries of Marxism is that all historical processes are subject to objective laws. This does not mean that historical processes are strictly predetermined, even in their larger outline. The laws of history determine only what is possible under conditions existing at a given moment. And there are always several, indeed numerous, possible alternative courses of development. Which of these will materialize depends on people. This is the meaning of Marx's formulation: the people themselves make their history. For this reason, too, we cannot simply fold our hands in our laps and wait until Stalinism has breathed its last. Its defeat is possible today—as demonstrated by the Czechoslovak events—but if we don't raise our hands against it, its life can be much prolonged.

It was, indeed, no accident that Soviet socialism has degenerated into Stalinism. It was not just the consequence of errors, or party power struggles. Under the historically given political, military, and economic conditions, Stalinism was simply one of the possibilities, the forebodings of which, by the way, evidently troubled Lenin a great deal. There was an extremely high probability that this variant of postrevolutionary development would materialize. Now, in hindsight, it makes little sense to debate what the chances were of other variants, such as Trotsky's, which may have been merely another variation of Stalinism. The more important question is why Stalinism became possible. Reduced to a single sentence, it may be put as follows: it became possible because the capitalist production relations in tsarist Russia had just begun to propel the development of productive forces, and because the socialist production relations forced by the revolution upon this backward economy were wholly inadequate to the level of development of these productive forces, thus hindering rather than fostering them. As a result, there emerged a bureaucratic state socialism without democratic controls. As noted earlier, another decisive factor was the constant external threat to the Soviet Union. If one considers the history of the last fifty years since the Revolution, and what this first socialist country has achieved in the face of the terrible famines and the destruction of industrial equipment during World War II, one can only have the highest regard for its successes. All the handicaps and anachronistic contradictions with which the revolution had to contend following its victory, and also all the external threats, are now a matter of the past. An indigenous emergence of Stalinism in the USSR would be no longer possible under the present economic conditions. The more so it is today in the Soviet Union a possibility, or rather a task on history's agenda, to overcome this deformation and eliminate its last remnants.

The transition to democratic socialism in a modern, highly industrialized state such as the USSR today means simply an adjustment of the superstructure to the base. This overthrow of the superstructure is a decisive phase of the socialist revolution. The first phase, the seizure of power and removal of the bourgeoisie from power, of necessity takes on the forms of a dictatorship of the proletariat. Only in economically and politically backward countries is there the danger of becoming stuck in this phase. The faster it is possible to overcome the economic backwardness, the sooner will the revolution be able to enter its second, decisive phase. In its dictatorship phase, the revolution destroys the privileges of the previously ruling class—in capitalism it is the privileges based on private ownership that reduce freedom and democracy largely to an illusion. In the second phase, in which the dictatorship is abandoned following the end of the split in society between antagonistic classes, freedom of the individual and democracy of the state are established for the first time in history as true foundations of society. In the first phase it is the foundation of revolutionary power which is established, but only in the second phase, in which the revolution achieves its consummation, is this power ultimately secured.

The time interval between these two phases, that is, the duration of the first phase, could in the highly industrialized states be so short that both phases would merge into one. But even if the first phase should linger, the overall development constitutes a single revolutionary process. This makes it seem as if the transition to the second phase were strictly a revolution from above. The only example of this happening in actual fact is the Czechoslovak upheaval in 1968 and its evolution. The transition was carried out by the party, not against it. But it could be accomplished only because it was, at the same time, sustained by a movement of the popular masses. The more the Stalinist superstructure runs into a contradiction with the socialist base, the greater the growth of tensions between the state and the popular masses. These tensions nurture the revolutionary forces with whose assistance it becomes possible to put the second phase into effect. But if in this critical phase the party fails in its role and turns against the popular masses, then the revolutionary force degenerates. The result is mostly leaderless and uncoordinated counter-revolutionary rebellions, the suppression of which leads to lasting deep disappointment and discouragement. Examples of this tragic process are the rebellions in the GDR and Hungary.

With the transition to democratic socialism, the revolution is indeed completed, but only now begins the long phase of the solution of its tasks. At last all the creative forces are freed. Culture, literature, and science flourish and unfold a spectrum of limitless variety and individuality. This is the time when the popular masses can mature and free themselves of the hollow ideals and barbarian wants inculcated during the preceding epoch.

There are three socialist countries whose evolution seems less easy to judge from the standpoint I have outlined here. They are China, Yugoslavia, and Cuba.

China is a country Europeans find hard to fathom. In 1951, two years after the establishment of the People's Republic of China, I spent several weeks there. As with every European, I came full of silly prejudice. But the Chinese managed to dispel this prejudice in their wonderful gentle way, almost unnoticeably with an indescribable naturalness, displayed only by a people of high culture. The Chinese culture has advanced much further from barbarism than European culture. There may be many reasons for this, but, in my view, one of them is that nowhere else in the world is there a comparable number of peoples who over thousands of years have formed a single great cultural unity, a unity which, despite all differences of language and living conditions, is held together by a rather unusual means: the Chinese script. For us Europeans the Chinese culture has accomplished a strange synthesis—strange to us still very much barbarians—between individuality and collectivity. For the Chinese, the "I" is encompassed, almost submerged, in the "We." The "I" is not in the forefront there, blocking any outside view, as it does with us. But this relegation of "I" expresses neither subordination nor hypocrisy, as we might perceive it from our perspective. The Chinese "I" is much stronger than ours, because it is at peace. I believe that the admirable characteristics of the Chinese —diligence, perseverance, and courage—are closely intertwined with this basic structure of their spirit.

In China, no capitalism and no bourgeoisie had ever developed indigenously. Only under the influence of the European colonial powers did a capitalist trading and industrial establishment and a class closely collaborating with the colonial powers—now termed the national bourgeoisie—arise in the coastal cities, and there was never a slaveholding society in China, as there was in Egypt and ancient Rome. Chinese feudalism developed directly from an original gentry system and attained an incomparable level of development.

Chinese Communism represents the second attempt to translate European ideas into Chinese. The first was the Tai Ping peasant rebellion in the middle of the last century, when huge popular masses under the flag of Christendom overthrew the emperor and the feudal masters, abolished money, and tried to set up a sort of Christian communism. The power of the Tai Ping collapsed in a few years, in contrast to the permanence of Chinese Communism.

Chinese Communism cannot be compared with European Communism, at least in regard to its forms and inner laws. The deep estrangement that has developed between the Russian and Chinese Communists is a great misfortune for the further development of socialist revolution world-wide. To no small extent it is due to both sides simply not understanding each other. Understanding in this context means both acknowledging the great difference between them, the right—indeed, the necessity—to respect and comprehend this difference.

The Chinese nation of 700 million will free industrial labor from its huge peasant reserve pool to the extent it succeeds in raising farm productivity. It appears that in this respect much has already been accomplished. When industrialization finally comes to China on a grand scale, China will inevitably move up to the top among the world's industrial nations. I am convinced that China, too, will then introduce a democratic socialism, still a very Chinese one but hardly a bad socialism. Then, too, the time will come for all flowers to bloom. It seems that the Chinese revolution will proceed in more numerous phases and stages. The Cultural Revolution, which has smashed the already ossified bureaucratic power apparatus, will surely not usher in its final phase.

Yugoslav socialism represents a transitional form. Its superstructure is no longer Stalinist, especially since Rankovic was ousted, but it is not yet fully democratic. This corresponds to the still inadequate development level of the economic base. In Yugoslavia, production relations are much more socialist than in any other European socialist state. But the development of the productive forces still has a long way to go. Still, it appears that Yugoslav industrialization will reach a high level within a few years, a level which will call for a free unfolding of democracy.

The Cuban revolution owes its victory to the barbarism of the Batista regime, which was sustained by the US, and to the cleverness, courage, and perseverance of its revolutionary leaders: Fidel Castro, Chè Guevara, and their comrades. The old Communist Party of Cuba had no part in this. Like all Latin American states, Cuba certainly was a backward country, but hardly an "underdeveloped" one. The economy of these countries is not underdeveloped but rather wrongly developed, due to colonial or semi-colonial oppression and exploitation. It is deformed. The first task of the revolution is to overcome this deformation, starting in agriculture by putting an end to the sugar monoculture and rapidly increasing productivity. Small Cuba can quickly become a rich country. Only then will it become a revolutionary dagger in the back of US capitalism. But then, too, it will continue to be threatened by US capitalism. I believe that Cuba's role as trailblazer and initiator of revolution in the Latin American countries will be manifested in giving the Cuban revolution a special and incomparable development.

Where should one look for socialism? Still in the future. This is true of the GDR as well. But one cannot discuss the GDR without considering revolution in the whole of Germany. In recent years the Federal Republic has experienced a mighty surge of revolutionary forces. The movement did not spring from the established parties, whether the banned KPD (Communist party) or the left wing of the Social Democrats. It formed in opposition to the entire establishment, to all these parties seen as part of the establishment regardless of how revolutionary their posture may be. Essentially, the movement began in Berkeley in the US. The university's students organized a sit-in to protest the US war in Vietnam. This war, and its cynically open reporting in the press and on television, exposed the entire political leadership of the state, with all their unctuous speeches, as hypocrites and liars. All of the big words mouthed by these bosses—freedom, justice, democracy, equal rights, human dignity, love—became a shameless lie. From this frustration it was only one step to deciding for a revolutionary struggle against the whole system, against capitalism. This protest movement, which became increasingly more radical, subsequently spread to Europe and other continents. But initially it managed to rally only students. Among workers the movement found little echo, and Communists viewed it with great distrust. Herbert Marcuse gave the movement a tailor-made theory, asserting that a working class, as Marx understood it, no longer exists, that whatever remains of this class has long joined the establishment and—in a late-capitalist consumer society sated with cars, refrigerators, and washing machines—has lost its revolutionary spirit. The great revolutionary strike movement in France in May, 1968, during which students and workers joined together in the fight and gave a deadly scare to the French bourgeoisie, has refuted this theory. From the French experience the movement deduced that it must win a mass base among workers if its revolutionary struggle is to advance beyond the protest stage. But this is painstaking work, requiring patience and substantive knowledge. It requires, in particular, that sectarianism, which strongly permeates the intellectual groups, must be overcome.

For the moment, the GDR, with its political contradictions, the Berlin Wall, its shackled arts and literature, and its petty-bourgeois puritanism, continues to present a heavy obstacle to the young revolutionary movement. This movement must put a distance between itself and the GDR, but, on the other hand, it still must recognize that in this part of Germany capitalism and fascism have been swept away once and for all. When will this unhappy situation change? It will change, and radically so, only when Dubcek's spark will ignite throughout Eastern Europe and the USSR.

Then it will be possible to say: The future of socialism has begun

translated by Karl Reyman

INTRODUCTORY LECTURE TO THE ALTERNATIVE

RUDOLF BAHRO

I would like to start by discussing my book's point of departure and purpose. Its original title was "A Contribution to the Critique of Actual Socialism"—perhaps somewhat old-fashioned. Now this is simply the subtitle. It is deliberately reminiscent of Marx's celebrated analysis of social formations, particularly the 1859 preliminary study for *Capital* which he called "A Contribution to the Critique of Political Economy." For a period of some ten years, I have devoted practically the whole of my free time to analyzing this actual socialism as a social formation of its own type. The result so far may not yet have the same degree of completeness that Marx was to achieve in his critique of bourgeois society. Yet the text must now reach the public—and naturally enough not just outside Eastern Europe, but even in the German Democratic Republic itself, difficult as it is to distribute it here. Moreover, I had decided right from the start that it should appear under my own name. A direct challenge, and this is the aim of my book, is incompatible with fear, not simply in the moral sense, but politically too.

A RADICAL COMMUNIST ALTERNATIVE

The revolutionary process since 1917 has led to a quite different social order than its pioneers anticipated. This is familiar enough to all who live under this new order. If our conditions are officially depicted in terms of the traditional Marxist categories, this has long since been conscious hypocrisy, the deliberate production of false consciousness. My critique of actual socialism is directed at founding a radical communist alternative, i.e., one that gets down to the

---

The following was intended by Bahro as a course of lectures to outline the main themes of his book, *The Alternative*.

economic roots, to the politburocratic dictatorship which keeps our society's labor, and its whole social life, in chains. I put forward programmatic proposals for the new League of Communists that I am convinced must be built up on all fronts to prepare and lead the breakthrough from "actual" socialism to genuine socialism. As I see it, there is no other perspective than a socialist or communist one. And since this kind of alternative does not bear simply on some particulars, but rather involves the revolutionizing of the whole social framework, in fact the dissolution of a social formation, it must at least be outlined in its full complexity, even if it cannot yet be completely detailed.

The socialism which Marx and Engels foresaw, and which Lenin and his comrades undoubtedly hoped for also in Russia, will come. It must be the goal of our struggle, as it is more than ever the sole alternative to a global catastrophe for civilization. But nowhere in the world have there yet been more than the first attempts in this direction, for instance in Yugoslavia. In the other East European countries there is not even this. What Marx understood by socialism and communism is not very familiar to present-day communists, even to those who genuinely are such. But it is evident enough that Soviet and East European society is incompatible with the goals set by Marxism. Socialism as it actually exists, irrespective of its many achievements, is characterized by: the persistence of wage-labor, commodity production and money; the rationalization of the traditional division of labor; a cultivation of social inequalities that extends far beyond the range of money incomes; official corporations for the ordering and tutelage of the population; liquidation of the freedoms conquered by the masses in the bourgeois era, instead of the preservation and realization of these freedoms (only consider the all-embracing censorship, and the pronounced formality and factual unreality of so-called socialist democracy). It is also characterized by: a staff of functionaries, a standing army and police, which are all responsible only to those above them; the duplication of the unwieldy state machine into a state and a party apparatus; its isolation within national frontiers. Let us confine ourselves for the time being to this list. Its elements are familiar enough. What is not so well known is their internal and historically conditioned interconnection. But more on that later.

In the more developed countries, in particular, a system with features such as these brings the masses too little real progress towards freedom. What it provides above all is a different dependence from the old dependence on capital. Relations of alienation and subalternity have only acquired an added layer; they persist at a new level. And in as much as positive achievements of the preceding epochs have been lost *en route,* this new dependence is in many respects more oppressive than the old. This social order has no prospect of winning people to it, in its present political constitution. Given the total concentration of social power, the insignificance of the individual comes still more visibly and universally to the fore here than it does in the play of accidents and probabilities on the kaleidoscopic surface of the capitalist reproduction process.

The colossus that we know as "party and government," which of course includes the trade unions, etc., "represents" the free association aspired to by the classical exponents of socialism in the same way as the state represented society in all earlier civilizations. We have the kind of state machine Marx and Engels sought to smash by proletarian revolution, and which was not to be allowed to reemerge in any form or on any pretext. This is irrefutably clear from their own writings, particularly those on the Paris Commune. The state, in their eyes—and these are the original expressions—is a parasitic excrescence, a monster, a boa constrictor which entoils the living society, a supernaturalist abortion, a horrid machinery of class domination. All of this and more. Already in *The German Ideology* of 1845-6, Marx had written that "the proletarians, if they are to assert themselves as individuals ... must overthrow the state."* In his writings on the Commune, Marx anticipated something else that we can see all around us today. "Every minor solitary interest engendered by the relations of social groups [is] separated from society itself ... and opposed to it in the form of state interest, administered by state priests with exactly determined hierarchical functions."† Marx and Engels certainly did not imagine a socialism like this. In Yugoslavia, in particular, where the League of Communists has not reconciled itself to this phenomenon, the expression "étatism" (from the French *état*—state) has been used as a shorthand term for the principle of bureaucratic-centralist dictatorship.

---

*Collected Works (English edition), Volume 5, p. 80.
†First Draft of *The Civil War in France,"* in *The First International and After* (Pelican Marx Library, 1974), p. 247.

DEFINING THE POSTCAPITALIST SOCIETIES

In seeking to call the prevailing social relations by their proper name, therefore, I could not use the concept of socialism. On the other hand, the concept of étatism seemed too narrow, though it does correctly point to one particular aspect. I hesitated for a long while on the label. Yet the system's own self-description as "actual socialism," reluctantly reproduced here, at least admits indirectly that there is a difference between the socialist tradition as ostensibly still maintained, and the actuality of the new society. So in the end I accepted this formula, and even abandoned the apostrophes, with the intention of elaborating this difference all the more unmistakably.

This is in no way a charge of departure from some kind of sacred principles. The only purpose of polemic here is to dismantle false appearances. I strongly believe that it is high time for revolutionary Marxists to abandon all theories of deformation, and call a halt to the old anger about the distortion and "betrayal" of socialism, understandable as this at one time was. If the historical drama is reduced to a problem of poor realization, then one is proceeding from unreal assumptions and theory is led astray. Certainly, we can confront the practice of actual socialism with the classical theory, and must do so, in order to preserve—in the face of this practice— the substance of the socialist idea. But this practice must be explained on the basis of its own laws. For it is very far from arbitrarily produced, or "permitted" by some weakness. It has completely different foundations to those originally conceived. And so it does not require justification, apology, or embellishment, but rather truthful description and analysis.

I would like briefly to characterize the basic position by which I have been guided on this question. Incontestably, the revolution has generally brought the peoples involved considerable progress, both materially and in terms of mass culture. In many cases it has protected or reestablished their national existence and character against the dissolving and destructive influence of capitalist industrialism. We can say with certainty that this process as now taking place in Asia and Africa, where it is far more appropriate, corresponds to a basic historical necessity. But communists must know that what they are participating in there does not have a socialist or communist perspective; not a perspective of general emancipation. The new order may call itself proto-socialist, i.e., socialism in embryo, the preparation for socialism, but in just the same sense, if not with the same emphases, late capitalism too has been seen as proto-socialist, as socialism in embryo, the preparation for socialism. And in so far as communists in such a society exert their influence in favor of the established power, and do not struggle to overcome the existing conditions, they must be aware that they are taking part in another rule of man over man, another system of oppression and exploitation—yes, exploitation. The functionary of actual socialism —the boss, the *nachalnik*, and moreover not just in the shape of the high politburocratic dignitary, but even the normal party, state and economic functionary—represents, often against his will, the most recent type of this gentleman. I have myself played and experienced this role for long enough.

The established apparatus identifies its rule, seemingly accredited by history, with the Marxist idea, the idea of communism. In this way, it simply makes all the old socialist aspirations a joke for the masses. From the Elbe to the Amur, it daily feeds the desire for the restoration of at least some of the old conditions. It is characteristic of the rapid ideological decay in the East European countries since the invasion of Czechoslovakia in August 1968 that the greater part of the opposition elements now find themselves thrown back to purely liberal-democratic demands, to a campaign for human rights —a position, in other words, that is not just the broadest but also the flattest, the most unconstructive, so far as its content goes. The violations that are justifiably attacked can disappear only with the political superstructure that has need of them. It remains, of course, a disgrace into which the regime has led our whole society, that the most prominent section of the domestic opposition seeks aid and succor from the president of the United States. Human rights and political democracy—yes, indeed! But what is lacking in the East European countries, and not least in the Soviet Union itself, is the organized and long-term struggle for a different overall policy. It is this struggle above all for which we must prepare, first and foremost by a broad educational movement to spread understanding of the context in which present relations arose, and of their inner logic, as a precondition to overcoming them.

At the moment, we generally lack the kind of understanding for the overall historical movement which Marx and Engels worked for in their day. One major cause of this consists in the failure to master the experience of the Russian revolution and its consequences. It is this disturbing loss of perspective, and not simply the threat of suppression, that explains the spread of pessimistic and defeatist moods even among those who are potential candidates for a revolutionary communist opposition. Communists must bear in mind that they have inherited the most developed theory and method of social knowledge, which has already been worked out and tested. It still remains the appropriate instrument for discovering the alternative point of departure in the present reality itself.

FOR A CULTURAL REVOLUTION

Socialism once meant the promise to create a new and higher civilization, to solve the basic problems of mankind in such a way that the individual would be at the same time both satisfied and liberated. When the movement first took shape it spoke of general human liberation, and not just of this moderate welfare, devoid of prospects, in which we vainly seek to outbid late capitalism. Up to now, however, it seems that communists have only come to power in order to continue the old civilization at an accelerated tempo. In the most comprehensive sense of the term—not just a political sense, but a cultural one—the countries of actual socialism are compulsively, as it were, "following the capitalist road." Preeminently reactive in its approach, what passes for socialist construction is insufficiently distinctive—in its capacity as a noncapitalist road—so far as the mode of human life, the existential problems of individuals, are concerned.

In competing for a higher level of commodity output and productivity, we bend all our efforts to making our own those evils which we once intended to avoid at all costs. It is never permissible to point out publicly that the growth dynamic typical of capitalism, which determines our economic and social planning, is in the process of becoming economically, politically and psychologically untenable, within a relatively brief historical period. People's thoughts are systematically provincialized and thrown one-sidedly back on private needs, and this at a time when the mobilization of reason and understanding is extremely urgent. The environmental and resource problems of today are the result of not more than 200 years of industrial progress undertaken by a small fraction of humanity. When made universal, and extended into the future, this model is a sure route to catastrophe. The tempo at which the world is changing should be a cause for dismay rather than enthusiasm, so long as the overall process still runs its course spontaneously, in patterns that no one intended. And the economic process in the countries of actual socialism forms part of this flow, deliberately so in detail, blindly so on the large scale.

The communist alternative, therefore, must not be restricted to an appeal to immediate needs, nor to the understandable resentments to which the phenomenal forms of our political conditions give rise. The dissolution of the politburocratic dictatorship has a much deeper necessity. The ruling political interests prevent the population of our countries from progressively taking a stand on the problems that are raised by the present world situation. Individually, many people suspect that the idea of progress must be conceived quite differently from how it customarily has been. But their alienated social conditions, which have led to mechanically and irrationally functioning institutions, prevent them from living according to their better understanding, which in turn means they are quite unable to develop this understanding to the full.

My draft outline is directed not at a sect of crypto-communists, but at all those, irrespective of their official position and former official appearance, who hope for an emancipation in our countries from the modern slavery to material things and to the state. The communist perspective, and this is how one must envisage also the new league of communists, is not a party monopoly, not even the monopoly of some kind of closed political school defined by a particular world outlook. On the contrary. As can readily be seen, the dynamic of social development is gradually shifting from material expansion to the development of human subjectivity; in other words, from the great needs to have and display, it is shifting to a life for deeper human knowledge, feeling and being. From this arises the possibility for a grand alliance of all those forces and tendencies that would like to lead men out of their imprisonment by material compulsions they themselves have created.

The new political and social revolution now necessarily affects the deepest layers of our civilization. What I have in mind here is a cultural revolution in the broadest sense of the term, a revolution —if essentially nonviolent—in the entire subjective form of mass life. This must, of course, come about as much by the conscious will of individuals as by their unconscious feelings. Its aim is really to create the social framework for the free development of each person, which according to the *Communist Manifesto* is the precondition for the free development of all. Communism cannot advance in any other way than by proving itself in relation to man, to his visible and perceptible climb towards freedom, and this means, above everything external, also inward freedom. Here history faces us with an inescapable demand. Our civilization has reached a limit of extension at which the inner freedom of the individual appears as the very condition for survival. This inner freedom is the precondition for a collective renunciation, based on understanding, of a continued material expansion which is both disastrous and subjectively purposeless. General emancipation is becoming an absolute historical necessity.

NONCAPITALIST INDUSTRIALIZATION

Proclaiming the freedom of the individual as an absolute necessity, the condition for survival, might easily suggest retreat to an old-style utopia, the latest construction of an ideal society likely to produce this free man. Such a short cut must be avoided. The alternative can only be based on a critique that is focused on uncovering and understanding the present barriers to emancipation, the causes of unfreedom. This understanding can only be obtained from history. The first question is how this actual socialism has come about. For Marx, and thus originally also for Lenin, communism was to proceed from the abolition of capitalist private property in its most developed form. It was to come into being by the positive appropriation of the social wealth produced under the rule of capital. And the revolution required for this was to be the simultaneous act of the most advanced nations.

Did the Russian revolution fit into this perspective? Was the old Russian Empire, which was to merge into the Soviet Union, a capitalist country at all, even an undeveloped one? In 1881, Marx and

Engels still did not see it as even feudal.* In their view it was semi-Asiatic, and this was no geographical characteristic, but a precise concept of political economy. For Russia, therefore, the abolition of capitalist private property could not have a great positive significance, since there was little capitalist private property there, and economic life was affected by it only at certain points. The tragedy of the Russian socialist vanguard was that they found a different task to fulfill in practice from that which the influence of their West European models had suggested to them. The October Revolution was to introduce a completely different process from the socialist revolution anticipated in Western Europe.

The path that Russia pioneered in 1917, under the added burden of the World War, was evidently induced far more by the external contradictions of world imperialism than by capitalism's "normal" internal contradictions. Since modern capitalism disrupted the traditional way of life of all peoples who had a different social organization, with its technical and economic expansion and with the by-products of its civilization, it compelled them to attempt to reform their social and economic life in new ways. Where their strength was sufficient, and the world-political conjuncture permitted, they won back their autonomy from capitalism by this means. This is the phenomenon of the noncapitalist road to industrial society, which I investigate in the first part of my book. It is not by chance that this road has been pursued with particular success where the vanguard has organized itself according to the principles that Stalin canonized as Marxism-Leninism.

The East European countries in general, and Czechoslovakia and the GDR in particular, are of course not characteristic of this noncapitalist road, though they have traveled it since 1945. Actual socialism is the arrangement under which countries with a precapitalist formation work independently to produce the preconditions of socialism, and it is the pressure of the industrial productive forces created by capitalism that gives this process its decisive impulse. In Asia and Africa, as well as in those countries of Latin America where there is still a significant Indian sub-proletariat, it was preeminently what Marx called the Asiatic mode of production that capitalist colonization met with. It is clear enough, then, that

---

*Bahro is apparently referring here to Marx's "Drafts for a Letter to Vera Zasulich."

the new organization cannot be a transition period between capitalism and communism, even though in the ideal case it actually does bypass capitalism. Its place in history is determined by the way that, just like capitalism, it brings the productive forces to the threshold of socialist restructuring, but in a completely different manner so far as the social formation is concerned.

This is the reason why all criticism that seeks to equate the economic essence of actual socialism with state capitalism, by virtue of certain analogies, completely misfires. Undoubtedly, state centralization plays a decisive role in our society, and it is evident enough that the conditions of production do not thereby become the property of the people. Nationalization, and not socialization, is in fact the decisive feature. But this no more points to state capitalism than did the granaries of the Pharaohs. The reason for mentioning ancient Egypt here is that the phenomenon of the noncapitalist road has both its historical and its logical roots there, where class society began by and large as an economic despotism.

Historically, the state as a corporate apparatus is the original expropriator of society. Today it is the final instance that keeps society from its property, even after private ownership has gone. This tendency, by the way, is displayed also in late capitalism. For the political organization of the noncapitalist countries, it means the transition from a stagnant agricultural despotism to a dynamic despotism of industrialization. At the head of the apparatus-state it created, Lenin's Bolshevik party in Russia was to a large extent the extraordinary representative of the expelled capitalist exploiting class (without, however, taking the place of this class), which had not been deeply rooted enough in the economic life of a gigantic peasant country that was still primarily semi-Asiatic.

To call the new social order and its superstructure socialist or communist is a monstrous misconception. It was from its very beginnings not a system of real freedom and equality, nor could it have been. It regularly and inevitably reproduces precisely those barriers that block the way to the free development of self-conscious subjectivity and individual autonomy. It precisely embodies all the structural conditions of individual subalternity. This is its regular dilemma, for subalternity, in other words the mentality and behavior of dependent "little people" alienated from the overall totality, cannot be overcome within this structure, but rather only by its dissolution.

THE PROBLEM OF SUBALTERNITY

The entire second part of my book pursues the question of on what general basis the rule of man over man persists in our society, and how our socio-economic structure concretely functions so as to give rise to this oppressive socio-psychological effect. The problem of subalternity is the cornerstone of my alternative conception. For as regards the practical political perspective of the barriers to be attacked, the movement of general emancipation today has precisely the task of liquidating those conditions that produce subaltern individuals, a species of thinking ants, instead of free people.

The concept of subalternity refers to an objective structure that produces this mentality on a massive scale, and which moreover also possesses the power of organizing inwardly free men as subalterns in a formal sense and treating them as such. First of all, a subaltern is simply someone placed under someone else in rank, who cannot act independently or make independent decisions beyond a certain sphere of competence defined from above. He is the foundation stone of every hierarchy. If, however, this role defines the total social behavior of those subjected to it, if their entire life process runs its course principally under the sign of some subordinate partial functions for an uncontrollable totality, then this subalternity is no longer simply a property of the subordinate function, but becomes a property of the individual charged with its execution. It now dominates subjective behavior, automatically bringing with it incapacity to be responsible for the more general context. All class society, every relationship of domination, produces subalternity. But no other class society since the Asiatic mode of production has fundamentally subalternized the great mass of its free members in such a thoroughgoing way as actual socialism. It is subalternity as a system, and—as Andreas Hegedüs already established several years ago—accordingly also a system of organized irresponsibility.

To what can this fact be attributed? To clarify this, I analyze in detail: 1. the hierarchical organization of labor in noncapitalist industrial society, which reproduces the despotism of the factory on an overall social scale, and extends its rules to all branches of social activity; 2. its social structure and the mechanism of stratification, which is bound up with the subordination of men according to various functional levels of labor, and in a hierarchy of competence as regards management; 3. the pronounced powerlessness of the immediate producers, to whom the concept of a working class is no longer applicable; and 4. the inhibitions on the motive forces of society that the system produces.

Since imaginative literature can yield sociological information where official social science dissembles or keeps quiet, I have amplified on the subjective effects proceeding from this situation with a digression on Soviet literature of the 1960s. Many books bear witness to the unproductive character of government regimentation, in the context of the present-day level of development of the productive forces. They denounce the restrictions on initiative and the decay of individuality caused by the all-embracing authoritarianism. And they disclose, which is also very important, the patriarchal bedrock of the most up-to-date relations of domination.

The factors listed above, however, are simply the most visible and superficial causes of the subaltern phenomenon. We may indeed recognize this for what it is. But can it be changed? By all immediate appearances, for example, the hierarchical organization of labor is objectively conditioned, in its turn, by the laws of processing and assembling information, without which there would be no management and regulation of our highly complex society. According to appearances, social differentiation largely reflects, beyond the traditional class division, the differentiation of work functions itself, and so on. At this level of analysis, therefore, demands bearing on the overcoming of subalternity can still easily be rejected as unrealistic. Many people, even those who see themselves as Marxists, fall into the old ideological fallacy of seeing the subordination and inferiority of individuals as the cause of the prevailing relations of domination, instead of their consequence.

If we are to find the source of an alternative, we must pursue the analysis at a deeper level. We must search for the general relation of production that gives actual socialism its character as a social formation, and appears as a common denominator in the various factors giving rise to subalternity. This underlying relation of production is the organization of the entire society on the basis of the traditional division of labor. On this basis, in other words, the general organization of the state can only take such a form that we find, to put it more precisely, relations of the traditional division of labor and of the state in actual socialism. The "and" here is not a coupling of disparate factors, but is intended to draw the two determinations together into one: relations of the traditional division of labor and of the state.

THE DIVISION OF LABOR

In this conception, I emphasize the "traditional division of labor." By this division of labor, like Marx, I do not mean specialization as such, i.e., concentration on these activities or the other, but rather the already mentioned subordination of individuals and their entire life process to specialized partial functions. It is only this subordination that makes individuals so rarely appear as social beings, and so often merely as saleswomen, chauffeurs, schoolteachers, engineers, politicians, generals, etc. The dilemma of the traditional division of labor even begins with distinctions at the same level of activity, between fitter and bricklayer, physicist and economist, in as much as their reduction to mere compartmentalized spheres of competence, while it does not give rise to a power relationship between them, can still give rise to a particular unifying instance over them. What is decisive for social inequality, however, is the vertical division of labor by functions requiring varying levels of ability and knowledge, accordingly by varying levels of education, and not least by a hierarchical pyramid of managerial powers.

As psychology has clearly shown, distinctions of human ability persistently depend on the activities pursued. Someone who always has to perform work that does not develop his powers of judgment, his capacities for abstraction, will thereby to a large extent be precluded from helping to decide on more general affairs. In actual socialism, democracy is understood to mean that people should participate in work, planning and government according to their competence. The cleaning woman is competent with the dishcloth, and the politburo member in preparing war and peace.

By excluding people in a varying degree, but sometimes definitively and decisively, from comprehensive functions and the formation of the general will, this traditional division of labor creates the home base of subalternity. Subaltern behavior arises from social and political impotence. The historical root still showing its effects today, for all its modifications, is the antithesis between predominantly manual or executive work, and predominantly mental work

—work of planning and command. "Those who work with their hands carry others; those who work with their heads are carried by others," so the Chinese philosopher Mencius taught more than 2000 years ago. The vertical division of labor spills over into the state without needing any further intermediate term.

In the ancient economic despotism, the state function is almost identical with the management of large-scale cooperation and society's overall life. Marx writes in *Capital* of the ancient Egyptian priestly caste as the managers of agriculture. We know that the oriental state bureaucracy and theocracy, with or without a great king at the head, had private ownership neither of land nor of workers. "Only" as a corporation, i.e., as an administrative and ideological state apparatus, did it have power of disposal over the surplus in goods and labor-power. The general type of this relationship of domination is the same as in actual socialism, and what is involved here is not a superficial analogy, but rather a substantial affinity in the basic structure of the relations of production.

This may seem astonishing at first, given the great distance in time and history, and the striking difference in the technical basis. But I would recall Marx's well-known idea that modern communism would be a kind of return to primitive communism at a higher level. In this perspective, the earliest and latest class societies fit logically together, in a general sense, in their quality as transition periods, at the dawn of class society in the one case and at its demise in the other. We should also bear in mind that Marx explained the development of modes of production also—and not least—with a geotectonic model, the depositing of successive strata. The primitive community is the primary formation. Above it are deposited secondary and tertiary social formations. In this sense, the relations of the traditional division of labor and the state are a secondary formation. They represent the oldest, most fundamental and most general relation of production of class society. This persists as the original and basic support for all oppression, all exploitation, all alienation of individuals from the totality, from the decline of the primitive community through to our own day. It is only on top of this stratum that the specifically developed class societies of the tertiary formation are erected, with the dominance of private property in the means of production: i.e., slavery, feudalism, and capitalism.

A CRUCIAL MISCONCEPTION

The early socialists failed to draw the ultimate theoretical conclusions from the visible sickness of the capitalist formation, given their hope that with its dissolution all emancipation could be achieved at once. They were certainly always aware that without abolishing the traditional division of labor and the state there could be no social justice, no real freedom, no equality, no brotherhood. Yet no special problem seemed to arise here, since this process was to be accomplished simultaneously with the abolition of capitalist private property itself. It has become evident in the meantime that it is only the tertiary formation that is removed with private property, while the common basis of all relations of domination is still an epoch-making problem. The economic nucleus of all class rule, with its consequences for the position of man in society, always remains the same: society's own surplus product, in the beginning directly its own surplus labor, is withdrawn from its control and disposal and concentrated against it as a means of power in the hands of others. The specific nature of actual socialism as a social formation is precisely its reduction to this general essence of all class society.

The relations of private property gradually drove the state function to the margin of the economic process. The classical bourgeois state in particular was—as the young Marx called it—simply a "political state," in other words merely an additional shield for the relations of production, in the last analysis economically superfluous. In actual socialism, on the other hand, the state wins back its original all-pervading character in an expanded sense. What we have here is the socialization of the reproduction process and its performance function in the alienated form of universal nationalization. The noncapitalist apparatus-state is at once administrative superstructure and political expression of the traditional division of labor. It appears as the absolute taskmaster of society. It functions, as Marx in his time characterized the universal bank of the Saint-Simonians, as a "papacy of production." This order of things inevitably suggests to us the words of Mephistopheles as the fundamental watchword of subalternity: "Believe the likes of me: the single whole/was fashioned for a god alone."*

---

*Goethe's *Faust,* Part One, lines 1780–81.

REVOLUTIONARY POTENTIAL AND THE PARTY

The analysis of actual socialism as a social formation leads to the necessity of a new social and political revolution, a cultural revolution against the rule of the traditional division of labor and the state. The task, however, is to discover in the present social relations themselves the source of the movement that will abolish the existing conditions. Where then are the forces that will undertake this? Do they exist at all? It is true that up to now they have not appeared in any very striking form. The great exception was the year 1968 in Czechoslovakia, and I shall come back to this. For the moment I would simply like to recognize one fact. At that time, not only was the potential shown to exist, but the factor that generally blocks this potential was also visible. It became visible precisely by disappearing for a few months. This factor was the rule of a party which originally made its appearance with a program of general emancipation, but which represents today the center of all oppression in our society. This party, with its apparatus, occupies the very place that rightly belongs to a vanguard for the interests of emancipation. And the moment the Czech Communist Party showed even the attempt to resume the original emancipatory function of a communist party, all pointers of social hope immediately began to cluster together and orient themselves towards it.

We can already see in this, at an empirical level, how closely the problem of the revolutionary potential in actual socialism is linked with the problem of the party. These two problems still pertain to the analysis of the present relations of production. They even bear on the decisive, dynamic aspect of these relations with the perspective of change. To start with, the two problems should be given more precise names. First, there is the massive production of surplus consciousness by the general process of reproduction under actual socialism. Secondly, there is the leading role of the party as a sociological reality. The two are both constitutive factors of our relations of production. The first factor has scarcely been recognized up till now as a fact of political economy; the second is only rarely classified theoretically as consistently as it is practiced in political domination. These two factors, to anticipate somewhat here, are presently acting against one another. This is the dilemma in which actual socialism is stagnating after a preliminary period of accumulation, in which little surplus consciousness was as yet produced.

If, in the search for the subject of change, we direct attention to this surplus consciousness, if we see in this the potential, the reservoir, from which that subject will be recruited, then we are departing from an old theoretical custom which is easily if wrongly equated with historical materialism itself. The general rule would be to immediately look for a particular class or social stratum disposed to play the corresponding historical role. The intelligentsia, for example, might be suggested. This would certainly have a rational kernel, but it would still involve an erroneous point of departure. The social structure in late class society, class society in the process of dissolution, can only be described in these categories in a backward perspective.

What has become particularly unserviceable is the concept of the working class. On the far side of capitalism, this concept serves only to conceal the real power and give it a pseudo-legitimation. There can be no question of the rule of the working class, and certainly not for the future. Nor does the apparatus rule as a kind of representative of the working class, it rules over the working class. The workers have as much say in the state that is given their name as common soldiers do in a regular army. Yet it is not the contradiction between the people and the functionaries, or more accurately between the masses and the apparatus, which we can establish by analysis, that gives us our basis of hope. What is involved here is only the contradiction in which actual socialism moves just as normally as classical bourgeois society does in the contradiction of wage-labor and capital. Certainly there are crises and peaks of intensity, but they generally give rise to partially regenerative compromises, as in Poland in 1970, when Edward Gierek used the following formula in addressing the workers: "You work well, and we will govern well." In this way, we only get a new cycle of the dilemma already established. The contradiction between the masses and the apparatus, by its very nature, does not lead us out of the existing system.

AN INADEQUATE MODEL

When this is considered more closely, the reason is that this contradiction conceives the overall social situation in too narrow and one-sided a way, i.e., from the perspective of the apparatus. In relation to the apparatus, and as defined from its point of view, the masses represent above all the mass of subalternity, which is the result and reverse side of the concentration of all officially recognized knowledge and all power of decision in the bureaucratic hierarchy. One side of the main contradiction driving our political development forward, the domination of the apparatus, is adequately and completely represented in this antithesis. The concept of the apparatus, as the pole to be attacked, is precise enough for strategic purposes. To break its domination—which however is not the same thing as its abolition—is the historical task. But "the masses" will not be the subject that accomplishes this task—unless the concept of the masses is extended in the same way that Marx in his time extended the concept of the proletariat, when he ascribed to it a world-historical mission. I think it is clear today that this was a mystification, even if not a groundless or infertile one. It reflected the role of the revolutionary intelligentsia, which was supposed to convey "consciousness" into what, taken by itself, was still just a subaltern class, and thus take the leadership of this class. In this very way, as it happens, the rule of the postcapitalist or noncapitalist apparatus was already prefigured in the prerevolutionary workers' organizations.

The inadequacy of the model of apparatus and masses (the masses taken in their actuality, i.e., without a mission) consists above all in that it is situated entirely in the realm of "alienated" consciousness, consciousness absorbed by necessary labor and its regulation, and leaves surplus consciousness simply out of account. This is, however, to introduce into the theory the standpoint of the apparatus itself, which has no use for this surplus, but rather fears it. What I call absorbed consciousness is that expenditure of psychosocial energy which is spent on the one hand in the hierarchy of managerial functions, on the other hand in the routine activities of the reproduction process. Thus we have a confrontation between 1. the bureaucratic knowledge organized for command over the labor process and the process of life in general, which is politically expressed in the interests of the apparatus, in the arrogant exercise of power that is provocative right from the start; and 2. the abstract, alienated labor in production, services and management which is expressed in subaltern reactions and modes of behavior, in poor performance and kowtowing, in lack of interest and indifference to public affairs. In short, these are two sides of one and the same coin; and as long as these forces persist at the level of this model, there is a constellation which is ultimately unfruitful. The bureaucratic apparatus and the subaltern masses are each as good as the other.

SURPLUS CONSCIOUSNESS

But it is precisely what is left out in this confrontation, surplus consciousness, that is the decisive potential for social change. Surplus consciousness is the growing quantity of free psychosocial energy which is no longer tied up in necessary labor and hierarchical knowledge. To a certain extent, there has always been this energy. It is precisely a human characteristic never to be completely consumed in the restricted conditions imposed by the necessary and official framework of society at the time. Formerly, it was the religions, in particular, that drew their impulse from this transcendence of human essential powers. As long as society produced only a small amount of skill, only a small elite, the apparatus absorbed the greater part of the mental energy and capacity released from immediate production. The form of the ancient economic despotism was decisively connected also with the size, in fact the small size, of the disposable elite, its skill and the laws of its reproduction. At that time, this level of skill was produced simply in the measure required by the simple reproduction of the relations of dominance of the time. In material production, there was scarcely any need for intellectual work!

Today, we are faced with a thoroughgoing intellectualization of the subjective forces of production. Even though the apparatus is a burden on the rate of development, society produces such a quantity of general ability, human skill in the abstract, that this cannot possibly be directly employed by the apparatus. This is why we see such unflinching attempts by this apparatus, partly to disperse the unspent surplus consciousness in unproductive occupations, partly to paralyze it with terror, and above all to divert it into substitute satisfactions. This latter is, incidentally, the real political purpose of our much prized "unity of economic and social policy."

In actual socialism, this surplus consciousness gains additional disruptive force by coming up against barriers that are erected specifically against it, against the preventive jealousy of the bureaucratic power monopoly which cannot be tamed. It comes systematically to challenge the real quality of the bureaucracy, its potential as a productive force, its competence in social knowledge and decision-making. The apparatus acts in the terms of reference of its usurpation, i.e., that it already represents all meaningful consciousness in itself. What would things come to, if someone else in society had greater and better knowledge than the politburocracy? At the very least, everyone must subordinate his insights and wait modestly and patiently to see whether his proposals are "viable," i.e., can be assimilated by the machinery or not. Everything has to be adapted to the final purpose of bureaucratic stability. The arts and sciences must be above all else organs for preserving this power. Everything which oversteps the official universe, and particularly that which constitutes the essence of surplus consciousness, is either blocked or driven back into the sphere of isolated private affairs, each separate from the other.

Alienated labor and the pressure of the apparatus firstly determine that a certain quantity of surplus consciousness must use its free time to strive for suitable substitute satisfactions, and these are provided as fully as possible. Circumstances limit and impede the growth, development and self-confidence of innumerable people, from earliest youth. They are then compelled to seek compensation in consumption, in passive amusement, and in attitudes governed by prestige and power. This is what the compensatory interests depend on. This concept is very important for me; I shall come back again to how the cultural revolution will react on it. Yet the specific nature, the most inner tendency of surplus consciousness is expressed not in the interests of compensation, but in those of emancipation. These are oriented to the growth of man as a personality, to the differentiation and self-realization of individuality in all dimensions of social activity. They demand above all the potentially all-round appropriation of culture which, while it certainly has to do with things that one can consume, is fundamentally aimed at something else: at the powers of human nature that are realized in other individuals, in objects, modes of behavior, relationships, even in institutions. The highest goal of this appropriation is liberation from all confinement, and above all from subalternity of thinking, feeling, and behavior; it is the raising of the individual to the level of the general life of society. As Goethe put it, "Whatever is the lot of humankind, I want to taste within my deepest self."* In their conscious form, the emancipatory interests are revolutionary, and their political program then becomes the struggle for the conditions of general emancipation.

WHERE THE CULTURAL REVOLUTION WILL BE FOUGHT

In order to discover the potential for the impending transformation, I have proceeded by way of a structural analysis of social consciousness, which I take in its capacity as a thoroughly material and socio-economic reality. The apparatus, the state itself, is of course an "ideological superstructure," and is in its substance an alienated consciousness with the function of domination. The entire mental life of society is the battlefield of the coming cultural revolution—and this mental life does not run counter to material existence, but precisely by way of the reproduction process and its goals, its center of gravity being information and decision. What is at stake is a new constitution for the whole of social life, and a new order for the work of science and its institutional framework.

It follows from this that a revolutionary strategy must find its bearings in the context of a quite specific balance of forces in social consciousness, one could even say a balance of forces in the recruitment of skill of all kinds, of the subjective productive forces. It must find its bearings in the structure of the transformation and expenditure of society's mental energy. With this in view, I have distinguished the four fractions of social consciousness briefly mentioned above, two in absorbed consciousness, two in surplus consciousness. In absorbed consciousness, as we saw, the interests of the bureaucratic apparatus and the subaltern reactions of the masses stand in opposition, while in surplus consciousness the compensatory interests of individuals confront their emancipatory interests. These four factors, which arise regularly and inevitably from the responses men make to the contradictions of the mode of production under actual socialism, constitute the political field of forces typical of our social relations.

---

*Faust, in *Faust,* Part One, lines 1770–71.

The problem here is not, or is only exceptionally, to reduce particular individuals to particular fractions of consciousness as thus defined. In general, we can proceed from the assumption that each individual participates to a greater or lesser extent in all four fractions. The question is simply which orientation of interests momemtarily prevails in their structure of motivations and hence in their behavior. This is how people's minds are divided. There are, however, some people who are so bureaucratized through and through, even subjectively, and so identified with the apparatus, that they can simply be reduced to their official role. This minority is the apparatus party in the narrow sense, the party of politburocratic reaction against whom the attack must be focused.

This attack can only be carried forward by the emancipatory interests. Between these two poles there is an ideological battle for influence on the mass of psychosocial potential bound up in necessary labor and compensatory satisfactions. As long as the apparatus is dominant, the emancipatory interests, which are then also sociologically atomized so to speak, see themselves confronted with a behavioral tendency of all other fractions of consciousness—which under these circumstances is predominantly subaltern: i.e., the apparatus subordinates all other consciousness by the exercise of political power. But in the cultural revolution whose preconditions are maturing, the dominant apparatus is on the contrary isolated, and individuals acquire even in their necessary labor and in their free activities or enjoyments an integral behavior, i.e., one oriented to an intelligent insertion into the totality.

The emancipatory interests provide the substance that must be brought together and organized to create the subject of the impending transformation. From a purely empirical standpoint, this subject consists of the energetic and creative elements in all strata and areas of society, of all people in whose individuality the emancipatory interests predominate, or at least play a major part—one influencing their behavior. It is the task of a genuine communist party in actual socialism to form this force, to give it the convergent political organization which it needs, if it is to struggle against the rule of the apparatus and maintain its identity against all influences of merely subaltern and compensatory behavior.

The ruling parties in actual socialism quite evidently do not offer the basis for this. Their "leading role" has a quite other content, one that is repressive through and through. They have completely sold out to the interests of the apparatus. Still more, they expressly form its militant summit. They are the jealous watchdogs of the state authority. Thus they leave the space open for a new league of communists, one which offers solidaristic support for emancipatory needs, and provides a moral and political authority higher than any apparatus. The communist movement must be created anew, a movement which again inscribes human liberation clearly on its banner and transforms human life on this basis.

THE BUREAUCRATIZED PARTY

Why is a new league of communists needed in the countries of actual socialism? To answer this question, one must first find out what the leading role of the parties now ruling actually consists in, and how we have reached the point where the ruling parties stand in direct opposition to the interests of emancipation. The heart of the matter is their own bureaucratization, which makes them incapable of distancing themselves from the state machine, from "étatism." Never before has there existed a form of domination whose authoritative representatives described themselves as "bureau members" and "secretaries," as they do in our countries—in those precise terms. These designations alone would allow us to deduce that the living body of the party had been overpowered by its bureaucracy. In the "growing role of the state," as it is described, the party apparatus celebrates above all the condition for its own neverending reproduction. It is precisely the given form of existence of the party itself (not so much that of the state) which makes the deification of the state a necessity. In the structures of the party, right up to the Central Committee apparatus (which is in reality only the totality of functions of the politburo spread out more widely), one finds a reduplication in compressed form of all branches and levels of the state and other bureaucracy—just as all branches of social life, without exception, have already been duplicated in the apparatus of government and official "social organizations."

To explain the party apparatus, one must recall the origins of our situation. The Leninist conception of the mechanism of proletarian dictatorship had reckoned on the activity of the masses. The so-called "transmission" of the energies of the party was supposed to proceed not in a primarily repressive fashion, via the state, but in an educational way, through the trade unions and other social organizations. The trade unions, in particular, were supposed to be not only schools for socialism, but at the same time instruments of struggle against the bureaucratic degeneration of state power. However, they became neither the one nor the other. Their role has suffered from a dystrophy so serious as to be already dangerous to the state machine itself, as has been demonstrated again and again by the situation in Poland since 1970. Even in Lenin's lifetime, the real transmission took place through the state apparatus. And now, in view of the absence of powerful correctives from below, there naturally arises the question of how the party is to control the state machine, so that it does not degenerate and become corrupt in the automatic course of bureaucratic routine. The solution is now said to consist in the construction of a further bureaucracy, placed over the state apparatus as a party apparatus. At the summit of this there stands, in the shape of the politburo, an institution that is *de facto* self-recruiting. Who is to be accepted as a fresh member of this leadership is decided by those who are already in there, and not even by all of them. These "Communists" go so far as to provide their own order of precedence for internal seating arrangements, according to levels of rank within the politburo.

The dictatorship of the politburo is a fateful exaggeration of the bureaucratic principle, because the party apparatus which obeys it is, so to speak, an ecclesiastical hierarchy and a supra-state rolled into one. The whole structure is quasi-theocratic. For the essence of political power here—to say nothing of the hypertrophy of executive and police organs—is spiritual power, with its constant tendency towards an inquisition, so that the party itself is the actual political police. The party apparatus as the nucleus of state power signifies the secularization of the theocratic state. Never, since the collapse of the theocracies of antiquity, have the secular and spiritual authorities been concentrated in this way in a single hand. This institutional identity between the authority of the state, the power to make economic decisions, and the claim to an ideological monopoly, as well as the consequent lack of any control over the politburo and its apparatus, which reaches right down to the base, is the main politico-economic problem in socialism as it actually exists. That is the Gordian knot which has first to be cut.

The apparatus is blind towards any reaction by society to its own burdensome existence. This blindness goes far beyond the individual blinkers worn by the most important people in it. The present-day party organization is a structure that actively produces false consciousness on a mass scale, not only for society but also for its own use. It ought to be a social structure allowing development of the social process of knowledge. It ought to be a system in which all the thinking elements of the people can take part. Instead of this, the ideology put out by the apparatus inserts itself between social thought and reality, like a tinted and distorting lens with numerous blind spots. The masses, who cannot be informed of how this lens grew and was constructed, how it is adjusted and turned, can only abandon any attempt to utilize the instrument. And they do too: they "switch off" even before the official prayer-mills have churned out the first phrase.

But the tragedy here is this, that they must then give up any hope of differentiated knowledge at all, because the society does not possess an alternative structure for this. Worse still: thanks to the total control exercised by the apparatus over the means of mass communication and the educational system, the theory which is best suited to penetrate the jungle of bureaucratic centralism and its holy of holies the politburo—namely revolutionary Marxism—is still so effectively usurped by the party bureaucracy that the masses' ever-present distrust strikes at it as well. Whatever the variant in which it presents itself, the people suspect it has been deliberately created to justify the present domination of the party. Inquisitorially all-powerful, the party is at the same time increasingly, and quite literally, despised for something previous epochs called spiritual powerlessness. And naturally, wherever the West's techniques of communication are adequate, its ideological mass production pours into the extremely rarefied vacuum that has arisen in this way.

WHY A NEW PARTY IS NECESSARY

Thus the establishment of a monopoly of all political, economic, and intellectual power of decision has led to an insuperable contradiction between the social task of the party and its politico-organizational form of existence. Its internal constitution and its leading role as a suprastate apparatus form today the decisive obstacles in the way of a development towards the further emancipation of humanity within our system. The party is destroying the ideas in whose name it stepped onto the stage. It is destroying the continuity of the communist movement in the individuals who should be the repositories of that continuity. Already by its mere physical existence, without commiting any more specific perfidy, the present party apparatus is the grave-digger of the party idea and any individual party convictions. Precisely those people who are communists by conviction and character are made superfluous as party members. Furthermore, if the apparatus does not succeed in making them into bureaucrats, in integrating them into itself, they can only disturb the normal, completely externalized "life of the party," and endanger its stability, so that it is logical to hold the machinery in a state of readiness for action against them. In such a party, the communists are organized against themselves and against the people. No further analysis is needed to show that in the developed countries of actual socialism this type of party is historically superfluous, and must therefore be liquidated. Upon its ruins, a new organization, with a fundamentally different function, must be set up, an organization best called a league of communists.

When I say in this way "the Communist party is dead; long live the Communist party," I am not referring to some kind of metaphysical necessity whereby the party must exist always and under all circumstances. It is rather that the party has an entirely concrete task as an instrument of social change, and in a quite specific situation. I also have my reasons for speaking of a single-party, for counterposing a single new party to the old one.

I have shown that, so long as the old division of labor has not been overcome, down to its last roots in the individuals themselves, there will necessarily exist a contradiction between the emancipatory needs of human beings and the apparatus they require for the regulation of their conditions of existence. For as long as this situation prevails, this apparatus will be a state, essentially a repressive machine. The historic necessity for a communist party in protosocialist society is founded on nothing other than the existence of this contradiction. The party's most basic theme, then, is the relation between society and the state, the perspective of the reentry of the state into society.

In my view, the tendency towards a single, united party which can be observed in all variants of the noncapitalist path is connected with the peculiar nature of this social structure—and specifically with its dominant problem, this relation between society and the state. If the whole social organization is once generally brought to realization as a state system, there is simply no necessary starting-point left for a multiplicity of parties. This starting-point can then only be the narrow and restricted sphere of particular interests, in distinction from and opposition to the general interest—no matter how alienated the form taken initially by the latter. Particular interests must attain their full rights—and prior to this, of course, gain unrestricted articulation—in another way than through political parties. One example among others would be through sovereign trade unions.

Nevertheless, the unity (the oneness) of the party, prescribed in this as it were ideal-typical manner by noncapitalist relations, can only be understood as a dialectical process. If the party forgets after the revolution that it is the superstructure of an as yet unchanged or scarcely changed society, in which it now sits as a superstructure which is unconditionally to be comprehended and transcended, as the provisional, larval form of the new order—if it forgets this, then it cannot remain united, but must be split.

If, on the other hand, it succeeds in organizing itself in such a way as to be able to initiate and lead a series of opportune and successive readaptations of the institutions, then let the dialectic of unity-division-unity remain latent, let the continuity of the single party be maintained (although there should never be a complete continuity in its leading personnel). But it must be clear that one political structure is genuinely being replaced by another, as a lever to assist a further economic transformation, rather than that petty reforms and "structural alterations" are being made to one or another isolated institution. The society cannot wait too long for this decision. Because for there to be an advance towards general emancipation, under conditions where the whole of society is organized, there must exist a party. And for this very reason, the existing party must be burst asunder and split as soon as it falls short in face of its main task, which is to dismantle the old division of labor, and with it its prerequisite: the state, the étatist-bureaucratic syndrome.

The oppositional grouping, which must already form spontaneously under such conditions, does not endeavor to become a second party alongside the old one—or, more precisely, to remain a party. It can in fact, both subjectively and objectively, have no other intention that the restoration of unity on the basis of a renewed program and a renewed internal constitution. The split is a transitory moment of the historical process. It is directed not against the idea of the party, but against its apparatus; against the party's entanglement with the state, of which the party apparatus is an embodiment. Society should once again have a leadership which is not fixed in the apparatus. The leaders must live in society and participate in its day-to-day work.

TASKS OF THE NEW PARTY

In the first phase of actual socialism, the party revolutionized society with the aid of the state, of the apparatus, and in this it was up to a certain point successful. Now it is a matter of making a fresh alignment between the state and the apparatus, on the one hand, and society on the other; basing this on the superabundance of new consciousness stored up in society. If the absence of control from below of the bureaucracy is the reason why the party has so far played the role of a suprastate apparatus, there is only one solution to the problem: the party itself must establish, as the very center of its policy, control of the bureaucracy—of the state machine—by the forces of society. It must shape these forces in such a way that they massively confront the apparatus as autonomous powers, and are able to force it towards progressive compromises. This requires the organization of communism as a mass movement. In principle, this signifies a division of social power: the establishment of a progressive dialectic between the state and the forces of society. The communists must themselves bring the contradiction into the government apparatus. The result will be a situation of regulated dual power, in which the étatist side of the equation gradually loses its predominance. Stick fast with étatism or go forward to the cultural revolution—those are the two alternatives.

In order to maintain and prove itself in this situation, the party must achieve ideological hegemony, something it will never again attain if it remains constituted as at present. To do this, it must organize itself not as an apparatus superior to the state, but as the collective intellectual through which is mediated the whole society's awareness of the problems of its development. The concept of the collective intellectual is a legacy from Antonio Gramsci. Gramsci's starting-point was the way the ideological authority of the party depends directly on the quality of its intellectual production; on the power of comprehension and mobilization possessed by the model in which it reflects social reality and prescribes the direction of change.

Accordingly, the league of communists must be organized differently from the way the party has so far been organized. The organizational structure must fit in with the character of the league's chief activity. Successful work in the field of knowledge requires that all participants have access to the totality of significant information; it requires a "horizontal," nonhierarchical coordination of investigations on the basis of the self-activity of the interested persons; it requires the admission of hypotheses which burst through the customary conceptual framework; and finally, it requires the free discussion of different interpretations, without evaluation by any official authorities empowered to confirm or invalidate them. If the organization of communists is to serve in this way to socialize political understanding and decision making, the first condition to be met is a party structure open to all the authentic forces of a tendentially nonantagonistic society. Any kind of exclusive sectarianism, any trading over the secrets of power behind closed and padded doors will prevent the utilization of all the living, productive elements of work and culture.

If the task of liquidating subalternity is correctly posed, people within the party must unconditionally rid themselves of any glorification of so-called proletarian discipline—something which Lenin took over from Kautsky because it was suitable for Russian reality. What Lenin emphasized in his time was the capacity for military organization, and the readiness of the working masses to obey commands and subordinate themselves to the superior foresight and intellectual power of a political general staff. Lenin obliterated the contrast between factory discipline and party discipline, which was being elaborated at that very time by Rosa Luxemburg. It goes without saying that at present too an effective organization requires an apparatus and discipline, not only in the administration but also in the party. But in their organization, communists must invert the relation of forces between, on the one hand, the level of discussion and decision about the values, goals, ways and means of policy and, on the other hand, the sphere of the apparatus for implementing policy. The process by which the state machine is turned into an instrument of service and administration can only be set in motion if it starts within the party; if the domination of the secretaries and secretariats over the party is broken. Communists must free their policies from any determining influence whatsoever on the part of a party apparatus, and establish their collective sovereignty over the apparatus. It must be possible for every Communist to step out of his role as a disciplined member if need be, and make a decision on conscientious grounds.

Bringing all this together, one can say that the party must wager its old institutional existence against its spiritual renewal. I want to compress into a number of antitheses what should characterize a league of communists today. It would have to be: 1. not a working-class party in the old—and far too narrow—sense, but a combination of all those people, from all strata and groups in society, whose consciousness is dominated by emancipatory needs and interests; 2. not a mass party of the sort where a self-appointed élite leadership of authoritarian intellectuals manipulates those labeled "members," but a union of individuals who are like-minded, i.e., interested in solving the same problems and all regarded as equally competent; 3. not a sectarian corporation of "those who know best," closed off from society, but a revolutionary community open towards society and which anyone striving in the same direction can join; 4. not a supra-state organization which guides and controls the actual apparatus of the state and administration from outside and from above, but the ideal inspirer of an integrated activity of all groups at the base, which gives people the capacity to control all decision making processes from within; 5. not an obedient army carrying out bureaucratic decisions about maintaining and extending the status quo, but what Gramsci called a collective intellectual, creating and exercising majority consensus for change, in democratic communication with all interests in society. The main function of this league of communists will consist in so introducing society into the cultural revolution that it passes through a planned —and yet not imposed—practical change; a change, therefore, which is brought about by overwhelmingly positive needs.

THE ECONOMIC ALTERNATIVE

If we may conclude from what has been said so far that there exists a broad emancipatory interest in actual socialist society; and if we find it conceivable to organize this interest politically in the shape of a new league of communists; then the question of an economic strategy of general emancipation, and an action program for the cultural revolution, becomes our central concern. More than a political revolution is required to dam up the sources of subalternity and alienation. What is required is a radical economic alternative. This economic alternative must reckon with the fact that the existing relations have struck deep roots in the habits and attitudes of the masses. That means above all that it must be conceptually armed to confront the compensatory needs of the masses, so that they are prevented from blocking the transition into the emancipatory process.

Marxism does not utter laments about the indolence and submissiveness of human beings; about their apparent—or even on occasion their actual—unwillingness to be free. It advocates an active, Promethean solidarity with those who are most oppressed; and a concentration of forces on raising up less-developed, disadvantaged, and underprivileged strata and groups. For one thing is clear: if conditions for the ripening of free individuality—and these are realities of the economic and political process which can be stated quite precisely—are not created for everyone, all emancipation must remain incomplete and hence once again become untrue. This means, therefore, something in the nature of a two-stage program. Before we turn to our conception of the goal, i.e., the question of how a society must be organized to ensure the free development of each of its members, we must concentrate in practical political terms on the prerequisites for moving in that direction, and develop the whole strategy as an outline of the path to be followed. So the first problem is as follows: how can one neutralize the compensatory interests which bind human beings to the existing form of civilization?

The solution naturally depends on one's conception of the goal. The two stages of the cultural revolution cannot simply run their course mechanically, one after the other. It is necessary to set a course towards a totally new type of economic reproduction; not only, as we have already stated, because of the environmental and resource crisis, but also in order to relax the tension which leads to the drive for substitute satisfactions. Competition in growth exaggerates inequalities in the material living standard of human beings and peoples, and thereby also their need for compensations. The more is produced, the more must be striven for, possessed and consumed, and the more psychological energy is tied up in abstract labor and compensatory enjoyments, which means it is subtracted from the emancipatory forces. Material insatiability costs us the freedom for higher development, subjects us to regulations which rest on compulsion, and gives society a stepmotherly character. If the explosion of material needs cannot be brought to a halt, communism will become not only economically but also psychologically impossible. When Marx said that communism presupposed an abundance of goods, he meant in the first instance an abundance of the actual means of subsistence, the necessities of life. In the industrialized countries, the driving dialectic of production and needs has shifted its emphasis to the field of the means of enjoyment and development. The compensatory desire and compulsion to possess, to use, to consume, has forced the continuation of a fight for production, in which we shall still be too poor for communism in a hundred years. But the infernal cycle of capitalist growth-dynamics must be broken.

For practical economic policy, the first problem posed is the initial impulse for such a breakthrough. What can be done to blunt the edge of the massive need for compensations? This need must be satisfied as far as possible, but also as cheaply as possible. There is a series of immediate measures, a number of "abolitions" in the first place, whose common denominator is their appeal to the yearning for social justice. These negative measures thereby point beyond themselves to further action. First, bureaucratic corruption from above must be liquidated in all its open and concealed, sanctified and nonsanctified forms without exception. Included in this would be such steps as an upper limitation of the scale of incomes; the removal of all special arrangements made to care for the material, social, medicinal, cultural, and other requirements of the apparatus of functionaries; and the reduction of expenses for official visits and security. Included too would be an end to the petty-bourgeois pomp of orders and decorations, and the elimination of all extra payments connected with these.

Secondly, work norms and piece wages should be abolished. Because of its unjustness in principle towards the victims, the situation in which some workers are seen as "superefficient" stimulates attitudes of protest and self-defense; it causes maneuvers which disturb, for example, the optimal functioning of machinery and technology; it is costly in terms of quality and material; it causes workers to solidarize against more efficient colleagues; it increases the amount of illness; it prevents an exact measurement of individual capacity, and so on. The entire sum of psychic energy which is invested in—or diverted by—the conflict of interests bound up with work norms and piece wages is lost to the development of the productive forces; it works actively and passively against this development.

What is needed, in the third place, is periodic, planned participation of all the directing and intellectual personnel of society in the simple labor of material production—as also in other areas. For this purpose, a mode of regular and relatively lasting attachment to given work-collectives must be created; and it must be possible to apply this flexibly, so that the choice of this second place of work does not take place without the active participation of the individual—albeit within a helpful institutional framework. From this, an impulse will go out (which could otherwise hardly be achieved) from all those who, on the basis of the old—and still extant—division of labor, performed largely directive and creative activities, towards unceasing confrontation with the causes and consequences of social inequality in the distribution of labor and education in our society, and without any self-satisfied idealization of their own position in it.

Finally, a rigorous correction of the wage structure is needed, to be prepared through a somewhat longer-term discussion at the base. The establishment of a just wage, which is at present distorted by innumerable disproportions, must at the same time be conceived as an advance towards the equalization of incomes. For later on, the cultural revolution will put a question-mark over both the general validity of the efficiency principle for the distribution of income, and the application of so-called material incentives as the most important regulator of efficiency. A leveling-out of the quality of consumption throughout society would be the condition for getting beyond the principle of quantity, beyond compensatory consumption.

A TRANSFORMED STRUCTURE OF NEEDS

Thus the aim of the conception of cultural revolution, in its first stage, is that the greatest possible amount of psychic energy should be drawn off from the complex of compensatory modes of behavior;

and that this energy should then be applied towards a radical reconstruction of the structure of needs. The center of gravity of the conflict between social interests will then be displaced to the conditions for the appropriation of culture. This will then "of itself" bring about an altered structure of material consumption. The reduction of compensatory needs to a subordinate position can only succeed if impulses positively thrust towards much more far-reaching perspectives. The communist goal of production is a free and rich individuality, as a real fact which determines in its entirety the way in which society is connected together. It is measured in the first place by that quality of individual knowing, feeling and acting, which is required at a given cultural level in order to set oneself in an active relation to the social whole. As the laws of social life have the whole *ensemble* as their subject, individuals do not attain their full development if their circumstances forbid access to this level. In the second place, this free and rich individuality is also bound up with the all-round nature of the individual's activities and relations. We therefore have to realize the conditions for emancipation from the vertical division of labor altogether, and from as many as possible of the restrictions of the horizontal division of labor.

In order to reshape the objective conditions for the development of human subjectivity in this sense, the cultural revolution must above all set in motion a redistribution of labor, according to the principle that everyone will have an equal share in activities at the different levels of functioning, and that the equal social validity of the individuals carrying on all the necessary labor will be anchored in the only possible way: no one will any longer be confined to the function of a specific, restricted or subordinate activity. All monopolization of activities favorable to self-development must cease, if we are to overcome its counterpart, the preprogramed underdevelopment of other individuals—and thereby bring to an end the last form of exploitation.

There follows from this the necessity of unrestricted access by the whole population, at the highest "university" level, to a general education comprising society and the arts, nature, and technology. This is the alternative to a differentiation of strata according to levels of education and socially incompetent specialisms of every kind. Specialization should be ascribed a subordinate and subsequent significance. In opposition to the whole thousand-year tradition of the patriarchal achievement-society, the cultural revolution must shape the situation of children and the process of socialization so that the overwhelming majority of the rising generation can maintain and heighten an appropriate capacity and motivational readiness for development. Such a process of education naturally demands a general practice within which it can be brought to fruition. It demands above all the recovery of a communal life on the basis of autonomous group activities, of different types according to individuals; for only around these can self-fulfilled human relations crystallize. The isolation and particularization of human beings in the solitary cells of the modern world of work-time, school-time, family time, and free time becomes the deepest source of social unhappiness and social incapacity.

The decisive political requirement is the socialization—and at the same time democratization—of the general processes of knowledge and decision; it is that they should take place outside and above any kind of hierarchical apparatus. Without a political practice of complete freedom to participate in communication with others about social values, goals and paths, there no longer exists any progress towards human emancipation. Only when this freedom is presupposed can a realizable economic strategy for cultural revolution be worked out. For the reprograming of the whole economy, the whole of the relation between production and need, as well as the informational regulation of the process of reproduction, would inevitably lead to wasteful social conflicts if there was no success in bringing about the constantly renewed assent of the majority.

If a society is industrialized to such a degree that it can provide for its members a relatively reliable satisfaction of elementary needs at the cultural level it has attained, economic planning must gradually—but definitely—be redirected to give priority to the all-around development of human beings and the expansion of their positive possibilities for happiness. Both the growth of production and the growth of the productivity of labor will in practice lose their aureole as inescapable economic necessities. This will not mean, inversely, that zero growth is in its turn made into a law; but that the criterion of quantity is altogether deprived of its paramount position. The social framework should no longer be based on the presuppositions of scarcity and poverty, which have since become incorrect. This means that we must finally stop allowing late capitalism to prescribe for us what wealth is; what—and for what purposes—we must produce; and what criteria of effectiveness must determine our production.

THE OVERTHROW OF OBJECTIFIED LABOR

In the realm of necessity too, a socialist society will offer a general area where there is room for independent activity, for the self-realization and growth of the personality. That means, economically speaking, that it will end the rule of objectified labor over living labor. There should be no more living, learning, consuming, relaxing, enjoying oneself, merely to restore labor-power for the next cycle of production. Planning must start not with a balance-sheet of labor-time, but with one of social time as a whole; with a budget of people's time for the totality of expressions of their life. It must provide a framework of conditions furthering development for all individual time-plans. One of the most important conditions to aim at is a reserve of labor-power in relation to the plan: an excess capacity of living labor in relation to the available machinery must be provided for in advance. A socialist right to work would have quite another purpose than full employment with alienated labor, up to and including preplanned overtime. The most important demand today is for a shortening of psychologically unproductive labor-time, which is not identical with the shortening of labor-time altogether.

The organization of labor must be adapted to the needs of education policy, and not primarily the converse. It is a matter of giving a further active impulse to the production of surplus consciousness, which has already set itself in motion spontaneously. The deliberate aim should be to create a surplus of education, which the scientifico-technical factory system and its superstructure will no longer be able to assimilate in its present social constitution. Thus the attack on the old division of labor will become unavoidable.

Hand in hand with the construction of a differently directed motivational structure will go a harmonizing of economic activity, made possible by measures such as: 1. a shift of priorities from the exploitation of nature by production to its incorporation in the natural cycle, from expanded to simple reproduction, from the raising of labor-productivity to the improvement of the conditions and atmosphere of labor; 2. the development of a technique and a technology appropriate to nature and to man, and the reestablishment of a due proportion between large-scale (industrial) and small-scale (artisanal) production. The retention of the ruling habits of production would inevitably bring to a head not only the ecological, but also the psychological crisis, which has its expression in the paralysis of labor-motivation.

What shape will be taken by the social organization of the whole of labor and life when the old division of labor has been broken down? In order that human beings may be capable of appropriating to themselves the general framework of their lives, of actually exerting influence on the social synthesis, one must give up the type of centralist superorganization which is hostile from the outset to individuality and initiative. The social framework is bound to escape the grip of individuals when it is organized in such a way that the only people who can act are specialized branch directors, coordinated exclusively and compulsorily at the summit, who issue instructions from on high and forbid the appropriate horizontal cooperation and communication at the base. If a rich individuality is really to be the goal of production, a form of economic regulation must be found to secure concrete individual initiative and genuine communality.

The solution lies in bringing out the federative principle, which is inherent in the well-known idea of free association, and which also characterized for example Marx's option for the commune system of organization. The fundamental units of associated labor and social life must be relatively autonomous sovereign combinations on a territorial basis, which will form microcosms of society. A communal organization of this type could also be the framework within which the isolating separation of the spheres of education, living and work might be dismantled, without allowing the reincarnation of old limitations, restrictions of locality, and exclusiveness. In particular, they would also offer room for forms of communal living, which are in my view the economic foundation for the emancipation of women and a condition for firmly securing to the children a full capacity for education and motivation for learning—for protecting children against the danger of neurosis inherent in the nuclear family.

The organization of society according to the commune principle signifies placing hierarchic regulation in a subordinate position (this is not to be equated with its abolition). It means coordination instead of subordination of human beings to their different activities. And it means the linking together of these different interfunctional associations into units which, though complex, are still observable as a whole, owing to their territorial structure. These units will comprise all aspects of the life-process, and no decisions will be taken over their heads. The communes, which are naturally specialized at certain points within the framework of the planned social division of labor, associate to form the national society. And finally, the idea of association between nations—rather than the frightful idea of a hyper-bureaucratic world government—is already penetrating into modern international law. The mediation to each respectively higher unit could be accomplished by delegates elected from the base. Control of particular interests which overstep the mark could be achieved by establishing full publicity for the flow of information, and by guaranteeing a genuine right and duty on the part of the individual to expose institutional manipulations, in place of the bureaucratic assemblies customary at present.

This then, in a very compressed form, is how one may conceive the social order in which the conditions of real freedom coincide with those of real equality and fraternity. Communism is not only necessary, it is possible. Whether it becomes actual is a question to be decided in the struggle to establish its conditions.

POLITICAL PERSPECTIVES

In conclusion, I must speak of political perspectives. How can a communist opposition hope to realize its goals? I first ask this question, of course, on behalf of that minority of existentially engaged human beings who have not attached their hopes to momentary, political conjunctures—even changes in the behavior of the secret police—and who do not speculate on certain success. In 1922 a book of essays by Karl Liebknecht was published in Munich, in which the author reacts among other things to the slogan that "politics is the art of the possible." Let me cite the following passage: "The extreme limit of the possible can only be attained by grasping for the impossible. The realized possibility is the resultant of the impossibilities which have been striven for. Willing what is objectively impossible does not, therefore, signify senseless fantasy-spinning and self-delusion, but practical politics in the deepest sense. To demonstrate the impossibility of realizing a political goal is not to show its senselessness. All it shows, at most, is the critic's lack of insight into society's laws of motion, particularly the laws that govern the formation of the social will. What is the true and the strongest policy? It is the art of the impossible." The impossible here means the sum of everything that "will not work" when taken by itself, but only in the context of a total transformation of a kind that well-adapted, healthy common sense does not usually risk thinking about.

The communist alternative aims at a transformation down to the deepest levels of the culture. It has no time for the naive illusion that the opposition only needs to get power into its hands for history thereafter to proceed along different lines. Unlike a *coup d'état*, the cultural revolution cannot take society by surprise. The opposition does not strive directly for power, but rather places its confidence in a long-term growth of its influence—which depends on the possibility for public and unhindered discussion about its program and an organization and propaganda of its own. A phase of open conflict between it and the official scribes and pharisees is unavoidable. The masses cannot attain reason under the tutelage of the politburo. People's so-called immaturity is more and more a product of the domination of the apparatus, even if it was originally one of the causes of the latter. The program of cultural revolution is directed, as a kind of modern inversion of ideology, against the habits and customs of the masses, which tend towards spontaneous adaptation to capitalist civilization. Probably a similar reaction will take place, after the first antibureaucratic impetus is spent, to that alleged to have occurred after the Sermon on the Mount in the New Testament, when the people got into a fury over such teachings. We must reckon with this obstinate resistance, which is determined by the way bureaucracy and subalternity complement each other. The purpose of a patient policy directed at neutralizing compensatory interests is precisely to snap this connection.

There are many people within the party intelligentsia and the circles around it who still their consciences by proving that "there is nothing one can do," while they rhetorically bemoan the absence of credible alternatives. In Aitmatow's story, "Departure from Gülsary," the hero says to his oldest friend: "At some point you ceased to be a communist." However, anyone who is genuinely discouraged in his convictions by this impossibility should remember the words said in praise of the dialectic: "The certain is not certain, it does not remain as it is." One only has to risk asking oneself some radical questions. How long will there be unquestioning acceptance of the sterile "economic competition" in extracting the maximum —in productivity tailored to capital—for which we are sacrificing everything else? Or again: why must individuals be stimulated to work mainly by financial incentives, and why must they be restrictively controlled? And again: is it really impossible to get beyond diplomatic participation in the so-called balance of terror? What are the interests that prevent us from putting the Western military-industrial complex under pressure by a practical escalation in disarmament? And another question: will the bureaucratic apparatus which rules the Soviet Union not increasingly prove to be a prominent part of world reaction, when its function of backing movements for national liberation ceases to exist after the present final phase of the struggle in South Africa? And then again: where could troops be found to act against a Soviet Dubcek? All these political questions should be thought through anew.

Let us just take the situation with respect to military policy. Every genuine disarmament initiative presupposes today that the progressive forces in both blocs put the power complexes under coordinated pressure, and make an end of the habit of picturing the other side as the enemy. Social changes, in both the capitalist and the noncapitalist countries of Europe, are the precondition for shattering the reactionary universe of the arms planners and disarmament diplomats, and for setting in motion an escalation of reciprocal disarmament. Naturally, the armed forces must at first remain capable of functioning without restriction, during a shift of political power. This was shown to be perfectly possible in Czechoslovakia in 1968. But the next step must be a political offensive to break out of the witches' cauldron of supermilitarism, in which mankind's struggle for liberation is expiring.

The relation of forces between the interests of emancipation and those of the apparatus appears much more one-sided politically than it is socio-economically. The reason is simply this, that the tendency towards a subordinate attitude has in its very essence been thoroughly institutionalized; whereas in their human interests individuals are kept in a condition of preventive atomization, as well as being prevented by the police from developing a corresponding political articulation and organization. A communist opposition may, therefore, at first sight appear to lack prospects. But the irony of history wills it that apparatuses which previously could deal with all kinds of communist heresy are helpless as never before in face of the new and apparently quite unqualified challenge from civil-rights movements.

In reality, this is an entirely new and favorable situation for communist oppositions. We must, of course, free ourselves from the old orthodox-Marxist sectarianism. We cannot learn the path to follow from that opposition which lost the fight against the rise of Stalinism. Every revolutionary communist since 1917 has had Trotskyist feelings at a certain stage in the move away from domination by the apparatus. But this position really does lack historical prospects. We do not want to reestablish old norms, but to create new ones. We are no longer forced to rely on inner-party constellations. Instead, we must consciously base ourselves on the broad social forces which, at once naively and cleverly, hold constitutional texts and United Nations resolutions under the noses of the political police. We do not have to identify ourselves with the direction taken by, for example, Sakharov; and a Solzhenitsyn stands directly at the opposite pole to us. But it is not our main concern to make this dissociation, while we positively seek recruits to our own standpoint. The removal of the dictatorship of the politburo is the first commandment!

THE NEW COMMUNIST OPPOSITION

Today in the Soviet Union itself there is already a new communist opposition, even if a weak and scattered one, represented to some extent by people like the Medvedev brothers. One has existed for the past fifteen years in Hungary, working on strictly scientific lines, and enjoying if not semi- then quarter-legality. One continues to exist unswervingly in Czechoslovakia, where it has only withdrawn tactically to constitutional questions in order to take up from that position the fight for its own legality, which is in fact its most immediate aim. One is growing in Poland, where it is aiming to establish links with the workers and where it has recently attained a considerable degree of broad support and organization. And one is forming anew in the GDR as well. Today, there exists in all the East European countries a considerable Marxist potential. More and more communists are beginning to work consciously on two levels (and no longer just to think on two levels—psychologically, too, this is a quite different quality). The apparatus can no longer find in these circles a Judas for every twelve disciples, and hardly manages it for twelve times twelve. The ideological impotence of the old forces since 1968 is a matter of notoriety. They control a church in which no one believes any more. And they are no longer capable of engaging in discussion. The proclamations they continue to make are hopelessly threadbare, and measured against the minimal Marxist requirements of the intellectual standing of a leadership they are beneath criticism. Only the defensive mechanisms continue to function. Productive reactions are no longer to be met with. The apparatus remains for the moment in power, but solely on the basis of police repression and latent military intervention.

The year 1968 was and remains an important turning point. For once, in the sixty years since the Russian October Revolution, the forces which are pressing towards a fresh organization of noncapitalist industrial society came fully into the light of history. At the latest by 1968 in Czechoslovakia it became apparent that there exists in actual socialism in general a progressive bloc of interests opposed to the domination of the apparatus. It became clear, moreover, that the majority of active party members was waiting to set off in a new direction. Finally, what was proved in Prague and Bratislava was nothing less than the capacity of our social order to exist without the dictatorship of a politburo. The catchword of "counter-revolution" put forward by Reaction always meant, in the first place, the consistent reform policy itself. It was—and it remains—the greatest political crime committed by the Soviet leadership since the Second World War, that it deprived the peoples of Eastern Europe, including its own people, and the whole of progressive humanity, of the irreplaceable experiences gained by the ripening of the Czechoslovak experiment. German Communists are still faced with the task of making clear in formal terms to the population of Czechoslovakia that they dissociate themselves from their party's cooperation in this act of international bureaucratic reaction.

The Czechoslovak experiences remain encouraging, nonetheless, especially when one goes beyond the national framework in evaluating them. They indicate to the opposition that it must strive for the long-term goal of political hegemony in the framework of the entire

Soviet bloc. It is not national differences and animosities which are decisive. What is decisive is the fundamental contradiction between the social interests of all the peoples of Eastern Europe and the interests of their political bureaucracies. Just like the peoples of the Soviet Union, the peoples of Poland, Hungary, and so on need a new political order.

THE IMPACT OF EUROCOMMUNISM

In recent years, the strategic position of the apparatuses has deteriorated still more. They cannot deal with the consequences of the Helsinki Conference, in which they had to agree to participate in order to secure economic cooperation with the West. And the danger which became apparent at the Berlin conference of the European Communist parties is still greater, because the issue here is stability at the very center of the apparatus's domination. The truth is that so-called Eurocommunism introduces the spirit of a split into the East European parties, and into the personnel of their apparatuses—right up to Politburo level.

As everyone knows, the form of political superstructure under which the anticapitalist transformations were carried through in Eastern Europe after 1945 was imposed from above on the peoples of that region. Neither in its substance, nor in its form, nor in the point of time at which it occurred, was it the consequence of an indigenous national development. The export of the Soviet model originally had a progressive significance, despite everything. It was the anticapitalist solution which was practically possible. The historical situation did not provide for a better solution in Eastern Europe. But now the role of the post-Stalinist apparatus in the Soviet Union, in its domination over Eastern Europe, consists in preventing the peoples from advancing to the form of socialism appropriate to them. They are thereby driven in the long run into the arms of a political restoration. The increasing nationalism—and concretely that means "anti-Sovietism"—in the Eastern European countries has a progressive function to the extent that it is directed against the fetters imposed by the hegemony of the Soviet apparatus on their internal development. The essence of the problem of sovereignty, its salient point, is for the Eastern European peoples the need to make their own socialist progress as far as possible independent of the differently articulated and far too slowly changing internal situation in the Soviet Union. For they now need not only—like the Soviet Union—a readaptation of the superstructure to much more developed productive forces, but also and at the same time the restoration of national continuity in respect of the kind of social institutions they possess.

As soon as there exists in practice a Western European path to socialism, the political process in Eastern Europe will steer a stronger course not only towards a more independent foreign policy, but also, and above all, towards the as yet suppressed reform of institutions. A reaction against the existing situation is unavoidable. The continuity of the noncapitalist path and the stability of peace in Europe require that communists should be ready in good time to give this turn a constructive and gradual form. The Eastern European peoples certainly want political institutions in the spirit of the views of Berlinguer. Marchais, Carrillo, and others at the Berlin Conference. If the Soviet superstructure should be incapable of adapting itself to the process of democratic transition to socialism in Italy, Spain, and France, the Soviet Union would most probably lose its Western periphery—lose it completely, for it is not possible in any case to retain it with its present-day status of reduced sovereignty. From the angle of the properly considered future interests of the Soviet Union, which the opposition there will make its own point of view, the issue is precisely the preventive relief of the Eastern European countries from their burdens, and the strengthening of their function as reliable partners in economic cooperation and voluntary integration. A servile "proletarian internationalism" such as could be heard from the tribunes of the most recent SED party congresses, because of the anti-Soviet mood it provokes, is much more dangerous to the long-term interests of the alliance than is a temporarily somewhat overcompensatory national communism such as exists in Rumania. The Soviet Union could give the Eastern European peoples an opportunity to get to know the real advantages of the alliance, in particular its extremely far-reaching economic perspectives.

For the opposition which is in process of formation, what matters now is the construction of a counter-position which is adequate to the specific conditions of actual socialism, as many-sided as possible, and strategically decisive—so as to compel the bureaucracy to adopt a perspective of open intellectual and political combat. Now the apparatus has had to recognize that different parties can have different standpoints on absolutely decisive problems, it will next be confronted with a demand that it recognize the same thing in the inner life of its parties and countries. The apparatus would like a kind of Peace of Augsburg to prevail: *cuius regio, eius religio* as they said in those days. This course of warding off new ideas and setting up boundaries against them must be actively thwarted. Away with the mentality of nonintervention in ideological matters!

THE WAY FORWARD

The apparatus still has a certain amount of success with its well-tried tactic of making the articulation of any kind of fundamental criticism within one's own society impossible, and at the same time presenting its expression outside the area of jurisdiction as proof of its alien character. The opposition is given the choice of either keeping silent—and this means being absent politically—or "serving the enemy." As may easily be seen, we are dealing here with something the dictatorship itself has offered, because its urgent need is to externalize the internal contradictions and to turn them into something alien. This is the ultimate ideological insurance of the politburo's tutelage over society. Let us have done with this, and ruthlessly draw a dividing-line between our loyalty to the noncapitalist base and loyalty to its outdated superstructure. It is extraordinarily important to use all the possibilities of communication within our own country, and if possible to create our own network for that purpose. But we should not be scared to use the techniques of the other power bloc in our political struggle. Whose sealed wagon was it which brought Lenin from Switzerland to Russia, and who gave the green light for that journey? What was decisive there was what the "German spy," as slanderers called him, drew from his pocket in Petrograd—the famous April Theses, the strategic guidelines for the path to October.

As the years have gone by, the internal, subjective conditions for a more effective formation of oppositional elements have also improved. The first generation not formed by the Second World War is now entering the age of political maturity. There is clearly an increased readiness to take risks with social stability and urge to show a true face to the surrounding world. Those who felt oppositionally inclined right up to the time when the central organ of the party could devote an obituary to their loyal services were not really of the opposition, which is why they held their posts so long. What is still lacking is the initiative to form groups; to join together for a conscious, purposeful struggle. The prevailing situation directly prescribes the proper path. Since we must regard ourselves—in so far as we belong to the party—as statutarily expelled immediately we unite on a platform of our own, we must fall back in the question of organization onto civil rights in general. The constitutional texts promise freedom of assembly and—given that public places are entirely out of the question from the outset—inviolability of domicile. The time is ripe to bring together people who want to involve themselves, without being too conspiratorial, in fact rather with the knowledge and under the protection of a certain interested section of the public. This will certainly at first be a matter of predominantly theoretico-ideological and propagandistic activities, and not of a mass movement. A start must be made.

The prospect of a shift of power within the party, which has many historical experiences speaking in its favor, can no longer be pursued solely in the manner of a long, silent and tortuous march through the institutions. The kernel of the new association can only lie outside the existing structure. Quite apart from the expulsions to be expected, the objective *locus* of a new, changed consciousness is not to be found within the charmed circle of official party expertise, or in what the apparatus sees as feasible. We must accustom the apparatus to looking an open opposition in the face. It will doubtless have recourse to more than one method of repression; but circumstances will not allow it to resort to the most extreme methods. As soon as it comes up against the decision of even a small group of people to give up family life, wealth, and popularity rather than abandon the goals it places above these goods, the whole machinery of the apparatus's resistance must fail lamentably. For example, the "organs" will not be able to continue for too long to deport communists who are unambiguously regarded by the revolutionary and progressive forces in the rest of the world as people completely rooted in the situation of actual socialism, and conscious of their responsibilities. Measures of repression will only speed up the process, and not just because they bring international solidarity onto the scene. In the longer term, we shall achieve legality for ourselves and a public presence as a communist opposition.

There are a number of signs that the locomotive of history would like to get moving to the next station. When this will happen is not independent of subjective decisions. It rather depends on the critical mass constituted by a set of individual impulses. Today, in all Eastern European countries, there are large numbers of people who —in spite of the certain prospect of years of unpleasantness arising therefrom—put in applications for permission to emigrate. This shows that it is time the communist minority began to come into the open, in order to achieve a thorough change in the way life is lived here, in the countries of actual socialism.

Translated by David Fernbach and Ben Fowkes

MANIFESTO
BDKD

We hereby address the public of Germany and announce that we, the humanistically and democratically thinking communists in the GDR, have illegally organized a League of Democratic Communists of Germany (BDKD), since present conditions do not as yet offer us an opportunity to associate legally.

It is our expectation that sympathetic comrades in the FRG and West Berlin will organize legally to establish the unity of communist-democratic forces in Germany.

We have begun to form an understanding of the theory and practice of democratic communism. But our mimeographed materials cannot be distributed without endangering our comrades. This is why we deliberately turn to a liberal FRG magazine, known for its critical attitude toward both East and West, for the dissemination of our thought. At the same time we are asking all communist, socialist, social democratic, and liberal journalists in the FRG to assist us.

It is our objective to work in the whole of Germany toward a democratic-communist order in which all human rights are fully implemented, in accordance with the Marxist dictum that it is necessary to eliminate all oppressing, degrading, and enslaving conditions. We do not know when, if at all, this will be achieved.

We do not believe in Marx as the Divine Father,* nor in Engels as Jesus, or even Lenin as the Holy Ghost, nor do we believe in a fatalistic inevitability of history, but we give due respect to the more long-standing classical interpreters of Marxism-Leninism, from Morus to Campanella, through the French, English, and German utopians, the Enlightenment, the classical period, Bebel, Rosa Lux-

---

The following are excerpts. Substantial portions have been omitted dealing chiefly with detailed, personal accounts of corruption among the present GDR leadership.

*In the original: "Wir glauben nicht an Gottvater Marx ..."

emburg and Liebknecht (both of whom, in their philosophical credoes banned in the GDR, clearly espouse a pluralistic communism), and up to Bloch, Harich, Havemann, and Bahro.

In this regard, one can always discern a general line of thought: a rational, rather than an orthodox, analysis of the social processes and the communist's commitment to social justice, the struggle against asocial parasitism and for a militant humanism.

If Marx, Engels, and Lenin were alive today, they would view with abhorrence the dogmatic, primitive idolatry into which their legacy has been transformed. And they would once again become emigres in the West, joining the Eurocommunists. If Marx and Engels were to draw up their "Manifesto" today, they would probably begin it by saying, "A specter is haunting Eastern Europe—the specter of West European communism."

We are proposing some theses on the main theoretical and practical problems of advancing BDKD policy in Germany. They are intended to clarify our own understanding and, after discussion, are to be refined into a program and a statute. In this process the conspiratorial rules learned in the Nazi era must be observed and polished.

I. *War and Peace*

1. We are against clouding issues by reference to "universal inevitability." Truth is always concrete. The soul of Marxism is concrete analysis of concrete situations.

2. The uneven development of state capitalism has led to a situation in which two imperialist superpowers exist—the United States and the Soviet Union. In the interest of safeguarding peace one can only hope that an international, pluralistically balanced distribution of forces will be attained.

3. The danger of war emanates from both imperialist centers. The brutal use of napalm by the Soviet Union against border troops of the People's Republic of China and continuing tension along the Sino-Soviet border are evidence that the Soviet Union's claim as a guarantor of peace is mere demagogy. As the superpowers continue arming, the danger of a war-like clash mounts. Disarmament must be enforced.

4. Interdependence has become global in the Western imperialist system, in the economy as well as in politics and culture. This is why there is no longer a threat of war among the industrialized capitalist countries.

5. The Soviet arms build-up on land, sea, and in the air, the fanning of military conflicts in the African-Arab area by supplying arms, personnel, and instructors, the growing militarization of public life in the Eastern bloc are a threat to world peace. The Soviet Union must be bound by treaty—for instance, at the MBFR (Mutual Balance Force Reduction) talks in Vienna—to a balanced disarmament and withdrawal of its troops from Eastern Europe. An end to the colonial system is something that must be applied to the red imperialism as well.

6. Overseas NATO troops must be withdrawn from Western Europe. The FRG should withdraw from NATO, the GDR from the Warsaw Pact, and all of Germany should be completely disarmed. The United Nations Security Council can guarantee Germany's neutrality; the funds thus released in Germany should be placed, down to the last pfennig, at UN disposal for the benefit of the fourth world.*

7. Final peace treaties must be concluded with Germany in accordance with Lenin's wise admonition, "peace without tribute and without annexation." Russia possesses vast territories. Why does she have to behave like a land robber? We appreciate the attitude of our Japanese comrades in regard to the Kurile Islands. They have right on their side. In Asia and Europe alike, the Soviet attitude is that of great-power chauvinism.

8. It was due to its economic and technological backwardness that the Soviet Union has opted for a policy of detente. And it is doing all it can to achieve military superiority by cooperative agreements, scientific-technological cooperation, and the like. But it would do even more of this in a cold war atmosphere. Hence there is no alternative to detente. It is detente alone that opens up the prospect of a peaceful, fundamental reform in the Soviet power sphere, of a transition from the Asiatic mode of production of bureaucratic state capitalism to a socialist national economy and society.

II. *Reformed Communism and Soviet Orthodoxy*

1. According to Marx, what concerns man must occupy his mind. We would add, his mind must be exposed to the right things. In Western Europe, human rights became historically established in

---

*Fourth world, a peculiar German invention, meaning countries so poor that they cannot expect to become "developing."

conformity with the invention and dissemination of printed materials, books, leaflets, and newspapers. In present-day Eastern Europe, establishment of human rights is drawing sustenance from the world-wide communication system, through the mass media in general and television in particular. This accounts for the remarkable fear the red popes in the Kremlin have of the media and for their attempt to ban satellite broadcasts in the United Nations. But the question is whether Marxism is preserved by slavish faith or, rather, in accordance with its first principle, by the resolution following from a clash of opinions?

2. Moscow's politburocratic orthodoxy has objectively become reactionary. In the interest of preserving its own power, it hinders the world communist movement in searching for new discoveries and theories and embarking on new courses of action. It pursues a great-power policy without regard for the international workers movement or the so-called fraternal countries. In league with reactionary feudal states, it dictates an oil price policy that spells inflation for workers under capitalism and socialism alike, maintains tension around West Berlin, sends Cuban mercenaries to developing countries, and the like. All this amounts to the opposite of a progressive policy.

3. Russia never experienced a reformation or enlightenment, or a liberal regime. And it shows. A theocratic society, imbuing the party with pre-Christian myths, Great Russian nationalism, a tradition of anti-Semitic, antidemocratic, and antinational thought, rhetoric, and action, can only earn contempt in Western Europe. We insist on the right to our own German national road to socialism, a right Moscow has always conceded to us in word but has always blocked politically.

4. Stalinism was not an anomaly. It is a system. With state monopolist conditions, and their struggle to expand their power, Stalinism and fascism are twin brothers. We recall what concentration camp inmate Kurt Schumacher said of Stalinists: they are Nazis painted red. By setting German Communists against the "social fascists" of the SPD [Social-Democratic Party], Stalin facilitated Hitler's rise to power and thus his attack on the USSR. In 1947–8, he again set the SED against "social democratism" (Communist term for Socialists who repudiate Communism) and consequently strengthened the cold warriors, neo-Nazis, and revanchists in the FRG.

5. This is why we share the Chinese comrades' view of the Soviet leadership as neofascist in nature. It was the Soviets who gave Hitler the idea of concentration camps. And they continue to practice anti-Semitism. The tsar provided for his political prisoners and let them live in exile—as did Lenin and Stalin in a Siberian farmhouse. It was left for the Stalinist politburo to create the nightmare of labor camps, prison colonies, and insane asylums for critics. The barbarism of the system took more lives among comrades in the Soviet Union and in many subjugated East European states after 1945 than did Nazism and the war. It is more than symbolic that Lenin's last surviving fellow-fighter [Ernest Kolman, philosopher] left the USSR in 1977.

6. The Soviet Union's working class is being exploited by a parasitic bureaucratic class that appropriates much of the country's wealth. There has been a general social insurance scheme for labor and white collar workers only since 1956, and the kolkhoz peasant, who is tied to the land and lives virtually in a state of serfdom, has become entitled to a small pension only since 1966. There is no normal freedom of movement in the Soviet Union. The standard of living is much lower than in the industrialized capitalist countries. Where are the social and, above all, the political achievements? It is true that unemployment has been eliminated. The state pays for hordes of parasites who have sham jobs in the apparatus of oppression. Otherwise, there would be the same unemployment which in the Western version of state monopolism is caused by rationalization and automation. But where, in particular, is the humane, democratic feature of this presumed socialism? Completely uncontrolled in the Russian feudal society of our days, the rulers are more powerful than the absolute princely rulers of earlier millennia. They don't even share power with the church.

7. No epochal scientific-technological invention has originated in the Soviet Union since the October Revolution. And the country, which in tsarist times exported large quantities of agricultural products, is now dependent on US imports of wheat. The charlatanism of such people as Lysenko, who managed to destroy frost-resistant grain varieties in Russia, demonstrates the truly pernicious influence Marxism-Leninism has had on science. Its antiquated religious norms stifle creative thought and action. Whether in regard to the relativity theory, cybernetics, or the synthetic fibers of electronics, the Soviets continue to lag behind new Western advances.

8. The Soviets now claim that they have caught up with the United States in the production of steel and cement. At the same time they say that productive capacities in the US are underused. Yet, in an emergency, the US could outproduce the Soviets by fifty percent. The tonnage ideology of the Soviets completely disregards the material, structural, and efficiency factors that have transformed modern Western economies. As in the past, Soviet production is primitive and wasteful—of which it is even proud. And it is the CMEA* states who are paying, through intensive rigging of the market in the Soviet's favor. The Soviets offer volume instead of long overdue quality.

9. Contradictions between productive forces and production conditions in the Soviet Union press for a solution. Social, racial, national, and religious oppression are shameful for a party calling itself Communist and pretending to represent the society as a whole. We state clearly that our sympathies are with all the peoples of the Soviet Union, but we disown the totally corrupted ruling class. Nor do we want to have any truck with its provincial governors in the GDR, who rule mainly for personal gain at the expense of the GDR workers.

10. We advocate a totally reformed communism theoretically and then ideologically, which according to Lenin should represent the best achievement of mankind. We are, therefore, against a single party dictatorship, which is dictatorship of a clique of secretaries and politburo members; we are against the dictatorship of the proletariat, which is a dictatorship of the bureaucracy over the proletariat and against the entire people.

We are for party pluralism, because freedom, as Rosa Luxemburg said, always means freedom for those who think differently; for an independent parliament elected by the voters; for an independent Supreme Court where every citizen can have redress for abuse of power. Even in Prussia a miller could win a case against the king.

We are for eliminating "democratic centralism" in the party, state, and society, because it is contrary to democracy; we are for a trusting cooperation among democratic communists, socialists, and social democrats in Germany, Europe, and the world.

We are in favor of ending the fateful division in the international workers' movement, which has been triggered, and to an extent

---

**Council of Mutual Economic Assistance,* a communist version of the European Common Market for the USSR and its client states.

enforced, by those acting on the Russians' instruction. We consider Lenin's concept of party, democracy, and state to be useless. Perhaps it was correct for the Soviet Union. But we must consider historical facts and experience relevant to us. We are for a legally and constitutionally secure press, freedom of organization and religion as well as freedom of assembly. Public servants must not be bound to the despotic ambitions of a narrow-minded party secretary but to law and the community. We favor eliminating Marxism-Leninism as a state religion. Science, the arts, literature, and intellectual life in general must not be subject to regimentation. The human spirit must not be subordinated to an inhuman bureaucracy, but the inhuman bureaucracy must be subordinated to a human spirit!

III. *German Policy*

1. The Soviets have so far ultimately failed to realize German partition. The SED leadership's German policy has also been a failure. No theoretical concept can eliminate border tension [between the two Germanies]. No pseudo-theoretical hair splitting about the nation can dispel the fact that there is a national problem. So a trouble spot continues to threaten world peace in spite of all the detente talk. All power struggles in the SED politburo . . . are connected with the national problem. The Soviet Union's own historical experience, as well as the examples of Vietnam and Korea, have proven the theoretical conclusions of Soviet scientists who maintain that the national component will outlast the social component. The theory and practice of the SED politburo under Honecker stand in direct contrast to the theory and practice of communist parties in Vietnam and Korea. Democratic communists in Germany can achieve political influence only if they adopt and pursue Marx's first demand of the 1848 revolution. "All of Germany will be declared a single, indivisible republic."

2. Processes under way today permit new approaches to German policy. We advocate a more militant national policy aimed at the reunification of Germany in which social democrats, socialists, and democratic communists will prevail over conservative forces. This will be a decisive contribution to the European solution by which German peace will ultimately be assured. Germany can and must be a bridge between East and West, a peace-stabilizing factor. What is called for is the removal of all foreign troops as a consequence of detente; withdrawal from military pacts; peace treaties between the two German states; neutrality guaranteed by the UN Security Coun-

cil; complete disarmament; transfer of monies saved on armaments to the fourth world; association between the European Economic Community and CMEA; legalization of all FRG and GDR parties throughout all of Germany; free and secret national assembly elections; establishment of a national assembly to draft a constitution; a gradual standardization of legal norms in all social spheres.

IV. *On the International Situation of the GDR*

Why is it that the gap between the GDR and the FRG in labor productivity, according to Lenin the decisive criterion for the superiority of a social system, is increasing in the major branches of the economy?

Why do the waves of exit applications and attempted escapes, even under the risk of life and limb, not abate?

Why is it that 94 percent of all GDR citizens, meaning also the majority of functionaries, engage nightly in an intellectual escape by tuning in [the two West German TV networks]? Because the political-ideological terror is unbearable, and the escape into another world is a necessity for survival!

The East German worker is capable of being just as smart, ingenious, and skillful as his West German colleague. But does he want to be? Does he possess the ambition to drive labor productivity higher? Does he have the incentive to earn more money honestly, by a genuine increase in performance? Or would he not better use his energy, tools, and materials from the factory for a private job after hours? Anyone working in industry or agriculture, in the health services or transport, in commerce or as a minor state employee, sees the point: those who do not work live the best. Should they not be emulated?

The GDR allegedly suffers from a labor shortage, but what skilled personnel is available is often underutilized due to an inadequate supply of materials, energy, to inadaquate transport capacity, or something else. The plan is fulfilled on the brigade level by a stroke of the pencil: performance is faked so that the amount in the pay envelope matches.

Corruption, abuse of official power, scandalous parasitism, and nepotism are everywhere. Yet, according to statute, comrades guilty of such behavior should have long been expelled from the party.

Take a close look at them. They create a climate of political-ideological schizophrenia for the GDR citizen. Publicly and verbally he supports this strange socialism, but privately and in his heart he dreams of the West, and every day practices an intellectual, and on occasion a real, escape from the republic.

This clique at the top harms the socialist idea in Germany and Europe more than all the so-called enemy propaganda [attributed to the West]. They conduct themselves according to the old quack recipe: quantity helps, and, as a result, their political patients are overdosed. Such conditions explain why the party in the GDR in 1953, in Poland and Hungary in 1956, and in Czechoslovakia in 1968 collapsed overnight.

The schizophrenia described above is also alive among communists forced to execute orders contrary to their better judgment, or sacrifice their political, material, and economic existence under the undemocratic centralism. They have no way of defending themselves. . . . Wherever they may lodge a complaint, they will hear only the voice of the number one on the responsible management level, of the respective special secretary and his duty apparatchik.

We have been thrown back beyond the reactionary feudal system. We live in pretsarist conditions. This kills every initiative, any sense of responsibility, and it paves the way for slovenliness, disorder, waste, theft, and a strangulation of the social process. This is the reason why the GDR is going around in circles politically, economically, and nationally: there is nothing new in the East. . . .

Let's assume that the politburocrats have read at least the first chapter of Marx's principal work, *Capital.* They ought to know then what the law of value is. Consequently, it would make sense that they use the economic mechanism and begin real planning with real prices. But they are too proud of maintaining completely unreal prices, so-called stable ones, which in reality are increasing every year with the exception of basic foodstuffs. This is rather harmful to agriculture, which also must be subsidized, and the industrial worker must make up the subsidy.

It is hard to fathom the logic behind why prices must remain stable when costs are constantly changing; hence, also the logic behind the nonsensical industrial and consumer prices; subsidies; compensation payments in the private sphere; prices varying, for equal values, between normal shops, special shops, "Exquisit" shops, "Delikat" shops, or in housing construction, rents; and so on and so forth.

Leading economic experts have clearly established that value and its expression in money as a price are impossible to determine in this chaotic situation. So every real calculation of effectiveness is out, together with the much-vaunted efficiency principle, the theoretical basis of so-called actual socialism!

We are spending hundreds of millions of dollars for raw materials because it is not financially rewarding for craftsmen, in the repair services, for instance, to save copper spools, brass rings, or the like. We are not even in a position to exploit secondary raw materials collected by children, which lie for weeks in schoolyards to spoil. We import, for foreign currency, expensive furniture for the bosses, while our timber reserves are not being economically used.

A panacea for all this was suddenly discovered out of the blue: rationalization, economy improved quality, improved efficiency. But economizing punishes the productive rather than the unproductive sectors. It is possible also to economize oneself to death. Bonus-rewarded economy in materials, raw materials, and energy have resulted in a sudden deterioration in the quality of our products.

The honor of the German skilled worker has been eroded by talk of his "sloppy Russian workmanship." Every knowledgeable salesman warns you against buying consumer goods produced in the last weeks of the year.

Comrades! propagate our critique, popularize the ideas of European and Japanese reform communists, demand the publication of the basic documents issued by the fraternal West European and Japanese parties, unmask by any means the contemptible practices of the self-appointed party bureaucrats for life! Expose the SED's moral decay, demonstrate how shamelessly the careerists, cynics, and well-adapted functionaries are permanently at war with the most elementary rules of human decency!

Propagate and organize! The world-wide tendency in the international workers movement aims at the decay of Muscovite theory and practice. A creative, undogmatic, democratic-humanitarian reform communism is developing. The times of a Communist feudal system are giving way to a renaissance and enlightenment, which can again win the confidence of Germany's workers. Only in this way will we be able to bring responsible influence to bear on the problems of our German people's future.

Berlin, October 1977
BDKD, Central Coordinating Group

translated by Karl Reyman